JUDGES
& METHOD

JUDGES
& METHOD

NEW APPROACHES IN
BIBLICAL STUDIES

SECOND EDITION

EDITED BY
GALE A. YEE

FORTRESS PRESS
MINNEAPOLIS

JUDGES AND METHOD
New Approaches in Biblical Studies. 2d Edition
Copyright © 2007 Fortress Press, an imprint of Augsburg Fortress. All rights
reserved. Except for brief quotations in critical articles or reviews, no part of this
book may be reproduced in any manner without prior written permission from
the publisher. Visit http://www.augsburgfortress.org/copyrights/ or write to Per-
missions, Augsburg Fortress, Box 1209, Minneapolis, MN 55440.

Cover design: Douglas Schmitz
Book design: HK Scriptorium

Cover art: *After the slaying by Ehud of Eglon, King of Moab, the Moabites are sub-
dued (Judg 3:20-30). Deborah the Prophetess encourages Barak to attack Sisera,
Captain of the Army of Jabin, King of Canaan (Judg 4:8-16).* Illustrated manuscript.
France (probably Paris), ca. 1250 CE. MS. M.638, f.12. © copyright the Pierpont
Morgan Library / Art Resource, NY.

Library of Congress Cataloging-in-Publication Data

Judges and method : new approaches in biblical studies / edited by Gale A. Yee. —
2nd ed.
    p. cm.
Includes indexes.
ISBN-13: 978-0-8006-3858-0 (alk. paper)
ISBN-10: 0-8006-3858-1 (alk. paper)
    1. Bible. O.T. Judges—Criticism, interpretation, etc. 2. Bible—Hermeneutics.
I. Yee, Gale A., 1949-
BS1305.52.J83 2007
222'.3206'01—dc22

                                                    2007016007

Manufactured in the U.S.A.   AF-1-2745
    5 6 7 8 9 10

CONTENTS

CONTRIBUTORS

RICHARD G. BOWMAN is Professor of Religion and Chair of the Humanities Division at Augustana College, Sioux Falls, South Dakota. He received his doctorate from Union Theological Seminary in Virginia and is the author of "The Complexity of Character and the Ethics of Complexity: The Case of King David," in *Character in Scripture*, ed. William P. Brown (Eerdmans, 2002) and the coauthor of "Samson and the Son of God or Dead Heroes and Dead Goats: Ethical Readings of Narrative Violence in Judges and Matthew," *Semeia* 77 (Scholars Press, 1997).

J. CHERYL EXUM is Professor of Biblical Studies at the University of Sheffield, England. She is the Executive Editor of *Biblical Interpretation* and a Director of Sheffield Phoenix Press. She is the author of *Tragedy and Biblical Narrative: Arrows of the Almighty* (Cambridge University Press, 1992); *Fragmented Women: Feminist (Sub)versions of Biblical Narratives* (Sheffield Academic Press and Trinity Press International, 1993); *Plotted, Shot, and Painted: Cultural Representations of Biblical Women* (Sheffield Academic Press, 1996); and *Song of Songs: A Commentary* (Westminster John Knox, 2005).

DANNA NOLAN FEWELL is Professor of Hebrew Bible at Drew University, Madison, New Jersey. Her published works include *The Children of Israel: Reading the Bible for the Sake of Our Children* (Abingdon, 2003), *Circle of Sovereignty: Plotting Politics in the Book of Daniel* (Abingdon, 1991); with David M. Gunn: *Compromising Redemption: Relating Characters in the Book of Ruth* (Westminster/John Knox, 1990); *Narrative in the Hebrew Bible* (Oxford University Press, 1993); *Gender, Power, and Promise: The Subject of the Bible's First Story* (Abingdon, 1993). She is the editor of *Reading between Texts: Intertextuality and the Hebrew Bible* (Westminster/John Knox, 1992) and coeditor with Gary Phillips of *Bible and Ethics of Reading* (*Semeia* 77; Society of Biblical Literature, 1997).

DAVID M. GUNN is the A. A. Bradford Professor of Religion at Texas Christian University in Fort Worth, Texas. He has written books on the biblical David and Saul, coauthored with Danna Nolan Fewell books on

Ruth, Genesis–Kings and Hebrew narrative, and edited many volumes of literary and feminist biblical criticism. His reception-history commentary on Judges appeared in 2005 (Blackwell Bible Commentaries) and he is now writing a companion volume on 1 and 2 Samuel.

DAVID JOBLING recently retired as Professor of Hebrew Scriptures at St. Andrew's College, Saskatoon. A former President of the Canadian Society of Biblical Studies, he is the author of *The Sense of Biblical Narrative, vol.1* (JSOT Press, 1978), *The Sense of Biblical Narrative, vol. 2* (JSOT Press, 1986), *1 Samuel* in the Berit Olam series, and coeditor of *The Bible and the Politics of Exegesis: Essays in Honor of Norman K. Gottwald* (Pilgrim, 1991). As a member of the Bible and Culture Collective, he cowrote and coedited *The Postmodern Bible* (new ed., Yale University Press, 1997) and *The Postmodern Bible Reader* (Blackwell, 2001). For some years he was General Editor of the journal *Semeia*.

URIAH Y. KIM is Professor of Hebrew Bible at Hartford Seminary, Hartford, Connecticut. He received his doctorate from Graduate Theological Union in Berkeley and is the author of *Decolonizing Josiah: Toward a Postcolonial Reading of the Deuteronomistic History* (Sheffield Phoenix Press, 2005).

NAOMI STEINBERG is Associate Professor of Religious Studies at DePaul University, Chicago, Illinois. She is the author of *Kinship and Marriage in Genesis: A Household Economics Perspective* (Fortress Press, 1993) and writes frequently about issues related to family life in ancient Israel.

KEN STONE is Professor of Bible, Culture and Hermeneutics at Chicago Theological Seminary. He is the author of *Sex, Honor and Power in the Deuteronomistic History* (Sheffield Academic Press, 1996) and *Practicing Safer Texts: Food, Sex and Bible in Queer Perspective* (T & T Clark, 2005), and editor of *Queer Commentary and the Hebrew Bible* (Sheffield Academic Press/Pilgrim Press, 2001).

GALE A. YEE is Professor of Biblical Studies (Hebrew Bible) at Episcopal Divinity School in Cambridge, Massachusetts. She is author of *Composition and Tradition in the Book of Hosea: A Redaction Critical Investigation* (Scholars Press, 1987), *Jewish Feasts and the Gospel of John* (Zacchaeus Studies; Michael Glazier, 1989), "The Book of Hosea," in *The New Interpreter's Bible* (Abingdon, 1996), and *Poor Banished Children of Eve: Woman as Evil in the Hebrew Bible* (Fortress Press, 2003). She is currently the General Editor of Semeia Studies.

PREFACE TO THE SECOND EDITION

The 1995 edition of *Judges and Method* has enjoyed considerable success in Bible classes in seminaries, colleges, and universities in the United States and abroad. Several new and exciting methods have come on the scene since its publication, however, prompting this second edition.

The essays of the 1995 edition have been revised or updated. Three new essays appear in this second edition: "Post-colonial Criticism," by Uriah Y. Kim, "Gender Criticism," by Ken Stone, and "Cultural Criticism," by David M. Gunn. As usual, the difficult process of choosing which new methods to incorporate into this edition reminds us that the task of biblical interpretation is ongoing. Two approaches that are quite significant for today's world, minority criticism and global criticism, are not represented in distinct essays in this volume; instead, the contributors wish through the essays that follow to underscore the importance of integrating issues of race and globalism with discussions of gender, class, colonial history, and culture in analyses of the biblical text.[1]

We would like to thank the Episcopal Divinity School, University of St. Thomas, Augustana College, and the Perkins School of Theology for their financial support and release time needed to realize this project. We are grateful to Elizabeth Struthers Malbon, chair of the Society of Biblical Literature section on Biblical Criticism and Literary Criticism, for inviting us to present our work from the first edition in one of her sessions at the 1993 annual meeting in Washington, D.C. Finally, we wish to thank the editors of Fortress Press—Neil Elliott and Michael West, and former editors Charles B. Puskas, Marshall D. Johnson, and Cynthia L. Thompson—for all their help in the completion of this project.

This book is dedicated to the students we teach and who teach us.

1

INTRODUCTION

Why Judges?

GALE A. YEE

This book introduces the student and interested teacher to a variety of the newer methods of biblical interpretation being used by scholars. It includes revised or updated essays on the approaches discussed in the 1995 edition of *Judges and Method*: narrative, social-scientific, feminist, structuralist, deconstructive, and ideological criticism. In addition, the present volume brings new essays on postcolonial, gender, and cultural criticism into the ongoing exegetical conversation. It not only presents the theory behind each method, the kinds of questions it asks, the presuppositions undergirding it, and its central characteristics, but also applies the method to the book of Judges.

There are several reasons for choosing the book of Judges as a testing ground for these methods. Its narratives are not as recognizable to students as those in the books of Genesis or Exodus. The stories of Adam and Eve or Moses and the Ten Commandments are more widely circulated than the deeds of the left-handed Ehud, the warrior-woman Deborah, the assassin Jael, or the indecisive Gideon. Less familiar as well is the tribal period of Israelite history that the book relates. One thus learns a new text in addition to new approaches to this text. Moreover, the book of Judges contains some of the most absorbing and terrifying stories in the Hebrew Bible. The book is about murder, death, betrayal, and war. In contrast to other sections of the Hebrew Bible, it includes a number of stories involving women, the violence they inflict, and (much more often) the violence they endure.

JUDGES: THE (WO)MEN

Based on the Latin *Judices,* the English title of the book, Judges, can be misleading. In present-day usage, the word *judge* carries a juridical denotation. One automatically thinks of magistrates dressed in black, sitting in mahogany-paneled courtrooms settling legal cases. In the biblical book, only Deborah functions as a judge in this forensic sense of the term. According to Judges 4:4, the Israelites came to her for judgement (*mishpat*). Nevertheless, we do not know how "official" Deborah's status was, and she certainly did not have a formal courtroom. The text describes her as sitting under a palm tree (Judg 4:5).

The designation "judge" translates the Hebrew participle *shophet,* which is derived from the verb *shapat. Shapat* has a broad range of meaning that is difficult to render into English: to decide (or judge), to govern, to vindicate, and to deliver. Indeed, most biblical "judges" rescued their people from the hands of their enemies. They functioned as military leaders during times of crisis. Moreover, many governed the land during the rest of their lifetimes.[1] However, except for the general, introductory description of the Judges in 2:16-18, not one person in the rest of the book is actually called a *shophet.* So, why "Judges"?

Another difficulty with the English title "Judges" from the perspective of the newer approaches discussed here is that it privileges men, their politics, and their wars as the foci of the book. Even though women like Deborah and Jael did participate and lead in the arena of war, when references to the Judges recur in the biblical tradition, the spotlight is on the men.[2] Ben Sirach's admiration for the judges is set within his triumphalistic hymn "singing the praises of famous *men*" (Sir 44:1; 46:11-12, emphasis added). Samuel, the last judge of Israel, reminds the people that "the Lord sent Jerubbaal and Barak, and Jephthah, and Samson, and rescued you out of the hand of your enemies on every side" (1 Sam 12:11).

In its roll call of faith-filled individuals in Israelite history, Hebrews 11:32 highlights Gideon, Barak, Samson, and Jephthah. The selection of these four individuals is itself surprising. They are hardly the paragons of faith the book of Hebrews would have us believe. Gideon (Jerubbaal) continually tested God (Judg 6:15, 17, 36-40). Barak was reluctant to fulfill God's oracle unless Deborah (a woman!) accompanied him into battle (Judg 4:8). Samson betrayed his Nazirite vow for a woman. His exploits were conducted more on the personal than on the military battlefield (Judg 15:4-8, 15-17; 16:4-31). Jephthah's own victory in combat came at the price of his daughter's life, taken to fulfill a rashly uttered vow (Judg 11:34-40). Although not a judge, Abimelech is said to have ruled Israel for three years (Judg 9:22). A usurper and tyrant, Abimelech achieved his rule through the slaughter of his fifty brothers (Judg 9:5). Fatally wounded by a woman, he orders his armor bearer to slay him, lest it be remarked that "a woman killed him" (Judg 9:53-54).

All pretenses at heroism and glorious victory are abandoned in the last five chapters of Judges. This section culminates in the most atrocious events in the book. Cultic and social chaos reigns. A wife is betrayed, gang-raped, and dismembered. A tribe is almost extinguished in a fierce civil war, and six hundred women are seized and raped to restock this tribe. The explanation given is that "in those days there was no king in Israel; every man did what was right in his own eyes" (Judg 21:25, RSV).

Although ostensibly about the military and political adventures of male heroes, the Book of Judges is studded from beginning to end with the stories of women, which flicker in and out. Reading the book from their points of view unfolds a "countercoherence" that clashes with the apparently male emphasis on public politics, wars, and mighty deeds.[3] The narratives of women qualify any designation of "hero" for these male leaders by foregrounding their cowardice, betrayal, and brutality in their relations with women. Through these women's stories, the personal in the book becomes political; the private becomes public.

JUDGES: THE BOOK

In light of the countercoherence of women's lives in the book of Judges, one cannot simply outline the book, as is customary, according to the stories of these male leaders. Although the narrative frame is oriented toward the male, women's stories appear at the book's most important junctures. In the outline below, their stories appear in **boldface** to underscore this interweaving.

Judges is structured in three parts. The first section summarizes the conquest and settlement of the promised land, revealing that not all the Canaanites are eliminated by the Israelite tribes. These Canaanites seduce the tribes into worshipping their fertility gods. God sends foreign oppressors to punish the tribes for their covenantal infidelity. In their suffering the tribes cry out to God, who empowers the judges to deliver them from their enemies. The second section—the body of the book—details the escapades of these judges. As the book progresses, the leadership and character of these judges deteriorate, so that by the end religious and social anarchy is rampant. The conclusion highlights the absence of a king (and the order he is thought to bring) by relating violent stories about the lawlessness of the period. These final chapters prepare for the establishment of the monarchy in the next biblical book, 1 Samuel.

OUTLINE OF THE BOOK OF JUDGES

I. Introduction: The Conquest and Settlement of the Land (1:1—3:6)

    A. *The Military Problem:* The qualified success of the Israelite tribes in Canaanite territory (1:1-36)

        1. The three southern tribes: Judah, Simeon, Benjamin (1:1-21)

The future judge Othniel takes Achsah as wife (1:11-15).

        2. The six northern tribes: Manasseh, Ephraim, Zebulun, Asher, Naphthali, Dan (1:22-36)

    B. *The Religious Problem:* The tribes break their covenant with YHWH and worship the gods of "the inhabitants of this land" (2:1—3:6)

        1. The angel of YHWH prophesies that these gods will be a "snare" to the tribes (2:1-5)

        2. The apostasy of the new generation and God's punishment (2:6-15)

        3. YHWH raises up Judges to deliver Israel from foreign oppressors (2:16-21)

        4. YHWH allows the indigenous peoples of the land to test the Israelites (2:22—3:6)

The Israelites intermarry with these indigenous peoples and worship their gods (3:6).

II. The Lives of the Judges (3:7—16:31)

    A. *Othniel of Judah* (3:7-11)

In contrast to those who intermarried with indigenous women, Othniel, who married the ideal Israelite wife, Achsah, is presented as the ideal judge.

    B. *Ehud of Benjamin* (3:12-30)

    C. *Shamgar* (3:31)

    D. *Deborah and Barak* (4:1—5:31)

Deborah urges Barak to defeat Sisera. Jael kills Sisera instead (4:1-24). Deborah sings of Sisera's execution by Jael and the imminent disgrace of his mother (5:1-31).

    E. *Gideon of Manasseh* (6:1—8:35)

Gideon has many wives, with whom he has seventy sons. He also has a secondary wife who bears him a son named Abimelech (8:29-31).

Deut 28 is paralled of what happens when you disobey God

    F. *Abimelech of Shechem* (9:1-57)

Abimelech slays his seventy brothers, the sons of his father's primary wives. Jotham, the youngest of these sons, escapes and predicts Abimelech's death (9:1-21).

During battle, "a certain woman" crushes Abimelech's skull with a millstone. Abimelech orders his armor bearer to kill him, lest it be discovered that "a woman killed him" (9:50-57).

    G. *Tola of Issachar* (10:1-2)

    H. *Jair of Gilead* (10:3-5)

    I. *Reiteration of the Religious Problem* (10:6-17; cf. 2:1—3:6)

    J. *Jephthah of Gilead* (11:1—12:7)

Jephthah's rash vow results in the death of his only child, a daughter (11:29-40).

    K. *Ibzan of Bethlehem* (12:8-10)

Ibzan gives his thirty daughters in marriage outside of his clan and brings in thirty young women from outside for his thirty sons.

    L. *Elon of Zebulun* (12:11-12)

    M. *Abdon of Ephraim* (12:13-15)

    N. *Samson of Dan* (13:1—16:31)

A barren woman gives birth to Samson and consecrates him as a Nazirite. His affairs with women bring him into conflict with the Philistines.

III. Conclusion: "No King in Israel"—Cultic and Social Anarchy (17:1—1:25)

    A. *Micah, His Idol, and His Levite* (17:1-13)

Micah's mother makes for him an idol of silver, which he sets up in his own shrine with his personal priest.

    B. *The Levite and the Tribe of Dan* (18:1-31)

    C. *The Levite and the Tribe of Benjamin* (19:1-30)

A Levite's secondary wife is raped. Her body is dismembered and its parts sent to the tribes of Israel.

    D. *Intertribal War* (20:1—21:25)

Six hundred women are seized in a mass rape and given to the tribe of Benjamin (21:15-25)

JUDGES AND METHOD

Historical Criticism: Judges as a Constructed Work

The modern study of Judges is influenced by the various kinds of questions that can be addressed to this book. Perhaps the foremost question asked in the early and middle decades of the twentieth century was, How was this book composed? The answer to this question determined the responses to other fundamental questions regarding the book: How credible was the book as a source of Israel's history, and how reliable was its author as a historian? The stories in Judges were important for the interpreter insofar as they were thought to yield accurate data that could reconstruct a more objective history of Israel's tribal period.

A number of biblical methods (tradition criticism, form criticism, and redaction criticism) have been applied to the book of Judges with these historical or historiographical questions in mind.[4] These methods are generally subsumed under the rubric of *historical criticism.*[5] Historical criticism distinguishes two types of questions in its analysis. The first deals with the historical situation(s) described in the text. The second considers the historical situation(s) that gave rise to the text—the circumstances that produced the work. The book of Judges describes the historical period between the death of Joshua and the tribal bedlam before the birth of Samuel, the final judge in Israel (c. 1250–1020 B.C.E.). Nevertheless, modern scholars have determined that the book did not originate during the tribal period but was composed in stages (both oral and written) much later than the premonarchic era of Israel's history. Depending on which scholar one reads, the final written stage of the book's composition during the exilic or postexilic periods is more than four centuries after the time of the judges (c. 587–398 B.C.E.). Different historical-critical methods examine the various phases of the book's development.

Tradition criticism asks questions about the earlier oral stages of the book. It investigates the places where oral traditions originate (cult centers, tribes, disciples, etc.), how they are transmitted in the various tradent circles,[6] and how they change over time until they are taken up by a redactor and put into written form. Tradition criticism of Judges determined that the book's core comprised an oral collection of stories and legends about the local heroes of various tribes who faced local enemies. For example, the tribe of Benjamin, who was warring against the Moabites, probably revered the judge Ehud. The stories about Samson probably circulated within the tribe of Dan, whose central location near the coast put it into conflict with the Philistines.[7] The didactic cycle of apostasy, oppression, crying out, and deliverance connecting the earlier stories of the Judges could have been imposed upon this collection during its oral stages. However, some critics think that the later deuteronomistic editor (discussed below) was responsible for adding this framework.

Form criticism inquires about the literary genres of pericopes (smaller literary units or sections) that make up a particular biblical work. Some biblical prose forms are sagas, myths, legends, short stories, historical writings, speeches, and letters. Several stories about the Judges could perhaps be categorized as "historical romances."[8] Examples of poetic forms include fables (cf. Judg 14:14). These forms would have circulated orally before being put into writing. Form criticism analyzes the features or patterns that typically characterize a literary form. As an example one may take a present-day oral form: the joke. Although jokes come in different shapes and sizes ("Knock, knock" jokes, "dirty" jokes, ethnic jokes, "Did you hear the one about the . . ." jokes), every joke typically has a feature known as a punch line. Form criticism, moreover, investigates the original oral setting(s) the form would have had within the life of the community, such as a legal or a liturgical setting.[9] Determining the form and setting of a particular passage helps one understand its literary intention. For instance, one assesses the meaning of the joke form and the settings in which jokes are circulated differently from those of religious sermons.

Redaction criticism investigates the process of combining smaller units of tradition and literary forms into larger wholes. It examines how later editors shape the final stages of the book's composition through the frameworks they provide for the smaller units; how they arrange (or rearrange) the smaller sections within the whole; the editorial remarks they make that modify, correct, and even contradict their sources; and the larger units they compose, which add to and complete the work as we have it today. This method studies the religious, political, and cultural agendas of the different editors and how they inform the editors' task of reworking the tradition.

Redaction criticism is of particular interest to students of the book of Judges. Biblical scholar Martin Noth detected affinities between the book of Deuteronomy and the six biblical books that follow it: Joshua, Judges, 1 and 2 Samuel, and 1 and 2 Kings. In 1943 he published an influential study arguing that a major portion of these books was composed by one exilic author during the sixth century B.C.E. and formed a distinct literary complex. Noth labeled this complex the Deuteronomistic History (DH), highlighting the theological relationship between the historical books and the Book of Deuteronomy, which introduces them.[10]

In the original history provided by this exilic author (whom Noth called the Deuteronomist), the period of the Judges begins in Judges 2:6, immediately after Joshua 23. Joshua has just exhorted the people to remain steadfast to God's law and reject the worship of other gods. Judges 2:6-23 describes the actual conduct of the people after Joshua dismisses them. The Deuteronomist lays out a stereotyped pattern of apostasy that characterizes the tribal period, a pattern that would ultimately disintegrate in the book, as each generation behaves worse than its ancestors (Judg 2:19). For his account of the Judges, the Deuteronomist combines two basic traditions: a collection of stories about regional heroes and their exploits and a short list of "minor" leaders (Judg 10:1-5; 12:7-15). The Deuteronomist transforms these local heroes from various tribes into liberators of *all* Israel and its tribes, fitting their stories into a framework detailing the nation's faithlessness.

According to Noth, the core of the book of Judges in the original DH comprises Judges 2:6-11, 14-16, 18-19, and 3:7—13:1. The present book of Judges evolves through a series of postexilic editorial revisions and expansions upon this nucleus. These expansions include another introduction to the book (Judg 1) and the last five chapters, which recount the discord of the tribal period (17–21). Noth was not certain that the Deuteronomist incorporated the Samson stories (13:2—16:31) into his original history.[11] They could have been part of the core; they could have been added later.

Frank Moore Cross modifies Noth's work by positing two major editions of the DH.[12] The first edition (Dtr 1) was produced in the seventh century B.C.E. by a Judean author supportive of King Josiah's religious reform policies. Dtr 1 blames the fall of the northern kingdom of Israel on the allegedly "illegitimate" cult practiced at the shrines of Dan and Bethel, which competed with the temple in Jerusalem. Dtr 1 climaxes its history with the reforms of Josiah, who tried to rid the country of its "idolatrous" cult objects and cult personnel (2 Kgs 22–23). The second edition (Dtr 2) was composed during the Babylonian exile (587–539 B.C.E.). This edition brings the nation's history up to date to include the fall of the southern kingdom of Judah. Addressed to the Judeans in exile, this edition explains the traumatic time of uprooting theologically, by unfolding the people's history of idolatry and faithlessness in both the northern and southern kingdoms.

Cross's theory of the double redaction of the DH is very influential for Robert G. Boling's important redaction-critical analysis of the Book of Judges.[13] The Josianic Deuteronomist (Cross's Dtr 1) adds an introduction to the period and the people's apostasy (2:1—3:6) and a conclusion condemning the illegitimate cult of the northern shrines of Dan and Bethel

(17:1—18:31) as a frame around an eighth-century collection of stories about the Judges (3:7—16:31). The exilic Deuteronomist (Cross's Dtr 2) provides a second introduction about a fragmented and scattered people (1:1-36) and a second conclusion about a people reunited in the face of a devastating civil war (19:1—21:25), creating a "tragic-comic framework" for the book.

Although he acknowledges its connections with the DH, Daniel I. Block regards the book of Judges not as the work of either the Josianic or exilic Deuteronomist, but as an independent, tightly knit composition by another writer, a Judean during the reign of seventh-century king Manasseh. If the book of Judges was originally part of the DH, one would have expected greater integration with the books of Joshua and 1 Samuel, which precede and follow it.[14]

The main focus of the various historical-critical methods is the reconstruction of the historical world the biblical text describes and the different historical stages of the production of this text itself. We have seen that the redaction-critical method has been particularly dominant in the study of the book of Judges. The major complaint against these methods is that they fragment a work into its smaller units of tradition, literary forms, or redactional additions and expansions. The reduction and atomization of a text into its smaller elements fail to deal successfully with the meaning of the text as a whole. Dissatisfaction with the limitations of author-centered historical-critical methods has expressed itself within the past three decades in three major ways: with the shift to text-centered literary-critical methods, with the broadening of historical criticism to include social-scientific approaches, and with a shift to reader-centered approaches, particularly those of the multicultural global reader. We will discuss the first and last of these.[15]

Literary Criticism: Judges as a Unified Work

Reacting against "the (historical-critical) dissection of supposedly composite documents" that dominated the study of Judges, J. P. U. Lilley argues for a "fresh appraisal of Judges as a literary work, starting from the assumptions of authorship rather than of redaction."[16] He points to unities and coherences in the book that would be (dis)missed by historical-critical investigations. Rather than view Judges 1 and Judges 2 as two conflicting introductions to the tribal era added by different redactors, Lilley sees 2:1-5 as a clear transition connecting Israel's inability to stamp out all of the Canaanites (Judg 1) with its defection from God's covenant

to worship Canaanite gods (Judg 2). Moreover, in the body of the book
(3:7—16:31) Lilley observes a "gradual departure from stereotyped for-
mula" and a steady deterioration in Israel's affairs. The narrative of tribal
Israel's progressive disintegration reveals an artistic treatment of the
source material that has not been previously recognized.[17] Finally, rather
than consider the closing chapters of the book (Judg 17–21) as extraneous additions, Lilley thinks that a book about the moral failures of tribal
Israel would be incomplete without these stories. The refrain ("In those
days there was no king in Israel; every man did what was right in his own
eyes") is a biting commentary on the prestate period as a whole and anticipates the establishment of the monarchy in the next phase of Israelite
history.[18]

Other literary-critical reactions to the editorial splintering of the work
point to its internal cohesion and thematic connections. Articles by D. W.
Gooding[19] and Alexander Globe[20] detect chiastic[21] or ring structures that
unify the book. Both regard the stories about Gideon as the center of the
chiasmus or ring (6:1—8:32). By destroying an altar to Baal and building
an altar to YHWH, Gideon embodies the moral integrity of the previous
champions of Israel (6:25-32). Nevertheless, he makes an image out of gold
taken as booty and leads the people back into idolatry (8:22-28). From
Gideon onward, the behavior of Israel's tribal leaders (Abimelech, Jephthah, Samson) progressively becomes more questionable.

Gooding and Globe find thematic links between the two-part introduction (Judg 1, 2) and the two-part conclusion (17–18, 19–21). Judges 1
connects with Judges 19–21 by highlighting the tribe of Judah that YHWH
sends first into battle (1:1-2; 20:18). The Benjaminites fail to drive out the
Jebusites in Jerusalem (1:21). A Levite, reluctant to spend the night in
Jerusalem with the Jebusites, is threatened with rape by inhospitable Benjaminites (19). In Judges 1, a Judean wife (Achsah) secures land with water
for her husband (Othniel). In Judges 19, a Judean wife is raped and tor-
tured when her Levite husband shoves her out into an angry mob. The
amputation of a king's thumbs and big toes (1:6-7) contrasts with the dismemberment of the wife's body (19:29). Judges 2 is linked with Judges 17–
18 in their common focus on an idolatrous cult. While Judges 2 insists
that each successive generation behaves worse than the previous one in its
apostasy, Judges 17–18 discloses that not only the people but the religious
leaders themselves, the Levites, set up idolatrous places of worship.[22]

A literary investigation of Judges is not limited to internal aspects of
the book itself. Besides sorting out the thematic interconnections within
the book and the tensions caused by the framework's disintegration, David
Gunn explores the thematic links between the conclusion of the book of

Joshua (Josh 23–24) and the beginning of the book of Judges (Judg 1–2). Gunn notes a chiastic structuring of their different episodes that emphasizes a pattern of fulfillment/nonfulfillment. The theme of nonfulfillment and failure will characterize the book of Judges.[23]

Three significant book-length investigations adopting literary-critical approaches have been published. Barry Webb argues that Judges is a discrete literary unit, a book, in its own right, and not simply a work in which one finds traces of an original Deuteronomic subtext. Webb provides an "integrated reading" of the work, comparing its unfolding with a musical score. The Book of Judges contains an overture (1:1—3:6), variations (3:7—16:31), and a coda (17:12—21:25).[24] Using another perspective, Lillian Klein studies the literary convention of irony, which she sees permeating the Book of Judges and providing its structural integrity.[25] Irony is particularly manifested in the judges themselves who are called to lead the nation: a left-handed secret agent (Ehud), a woman who commands a male warrior (Deborah), a coward (Gideon), a bastard (Jephthah), and a lover of foreign women who forsakes his Nazirite vow (Samson). Robert H. O'Connell's meticulous literary analysis of the rhetoric of Judges focuses particularly on the unfolding of plot and character. Although primarily a literary analysis, O'Connell has historical interests by arguing that the ideological slant of Judges' rhetoric is a pro-David, pro-Judah, and anti-Saul polemic.[26]

Judges and the Reader

The turn to the text underscores the aesthetic beauty of biblical literature and the religious power of its rhetoric. One encounters the *text* firsthand and not simply the formative historical situations *behind the text*. Nevertheless, text-centered approaches are susceptible to certain problems in their analyses.[27] Severing the text from its author and history could result in an ahistorical inquiry that regards the text primarily as an aesthetic object unto itself rather than a social practice intimately bound to a particular history. Privileging the text overlooks the workings of ideology in the text. It disregards the fact that ideology is *produced* by a particular author who is culturally constrained by historical time, place, gender, class, and bias, among other things. The biblical texts were not written to be objects of aesthetic beauty or contemplation, but as persuasive forces that during their own time formed opinions, made judgments, and exerted changes. Moreover, in all its historical, cultural, and literary constraints, the Bible continues to be a powerful standard for present-day social, as well as religious, attitudes and behavior. Readers inhabiting various social locations will nevertheless understand the biblical text differently.

Particularly since the 1990s, scholars from diverse racial, ethnic, and non-Western groups have asserted their voices in the primarily white Euro-American academic guild. Their influences can be felt in provocative readings of the book of Judges. Robert Warrior interprets the conquered Canaanites of the book from the perspective of the humiliation and genocide of indigenous Native Americans.[28] Koala Jones-Warsaw identifies the victimization of the Levite's wife with the victimization of African-American women.[29] In contrast, Yani Yoo reads the gang-rape of the Levite's wife in light of the forced sexual slavery of Korean women to Japanese soldiers during Japan's colonization of Korea.[30] Giving it still another twist, Patrick S. Cheng examines the story of the unnamed wife from a queer Asian Pacific American perspective that underscores the multiple naming, silencing, oppression, and fragmentation in both experiences.[31] Valerie Cooper draws parallels between Jephthah and his daughter and the racial, gendered, and class-related stresses between black men and women within black families.[32] These essays reveal that the position of the reader with respect to overlapping factors such as gender, sexuality, race, economic class, and colonial history is of critical importance in answering the question What does the text mean? Newer methods continue to appraise such a foundational work as the Bible in light of its powerful (mis)use in the diverse social, religious, and academic communities that have traditionally overlooked such factors.

NEW APPROACHES IN BIBLICAL STUDIES

The contributors to the volume present several of the methods that have come on the scene and that take biblical studies in new directions and address a number of the issues posed above. Each contributor will first introduce the approach by examining the presuppositions of the method: the particular questions it asks of a text and its central characteristics. The specific questions asked by the method will especially foreground its similarities to and differences from the historical-critical approaches. These questions will reveal the kind of information the method provides and what it does not furnish. The contributor will then apply the method to the book of Judges, either to the text as a whole or to certain selections. Brief annotated bibliographies will conclude each chapter.

Richard G. Bowman introduces narrative criticism, a method firmly located in the literary-critical tradition. After presenting the various elements of narrative (narrator, direct and indirect discourse, repetition, structure, plot, setting, point of view, and character), Bowman singles out character for an exposition of the Judges text. The particular "character" he examines in the book is God, someone who is not usually regarded as a separate personality in the Bible. "God is the one who wrote the Bible, 'He' is not a character in the Bible." Bowman's analysis reminds us that depictions of God in the Bible are literary-theological constructions. They do not exhaust all that God is and may not impress or inspire every reader at all times and in all places.

Naomi Steinberg addresses social-scientific criticism, which broadens historical-critical concerns to include the study of Israel's social origins, its customs regarding kinship and marriage, and its social and class structures. This method investigates the modifications and changes in these structures and practices during the course of Israel's history. This introductory chapter began by emphasizing that in spite of their displacement in the text, women are important in the lives of the Judges. Steinberg's analysis of Judges 9 reveals that the detail about the secondary class status of Abimelech's mother in Judges 8:31 is not a trivial or inconsequential one. Having the "correct" mother makes a big difference in one's social, political, and economic position within the community.

Except for the fact that she is a secondary wife and considered a "slave woman" by the offspring of the primary wives (8:31; 9:18), nothing more is known about Abimelech's mother. Feminist criticism raises questions precisely about the marginality or invisibility of women in androcentric texts. According to *J. Cheryl Exum,* feminist criticism employs a number of critical methods (historical, social-scientific, literary) to recover women's lives that are obscured by male texts. It also provides subversive ways to read such texts "against the grain." Opting for a literary-critical approach, Exum focuses on the prominent female characters in Judges: Deborah/Jael; Jephthah's daughter; Samson's mother, his Timnite wife, and Delilah; and the Levite's concubine of the concluding chapters of Judges. She names the nameless women in Judges and reenvisions the stories from their perspectives.

David Jobling organizes his essay on structuralism around the three major questions the approach asks of a text: What are the constant patterns that we find in different stories, and what is their significance? What do the differences that we find among similar stories mean? What general models are useful in analyzing the great variety of literary texts? While illustrating each question with an example from the book of Judges, Jobling focuses his structuralist analysis on a reading of the "fords of the Jordan" incidents in the book (3:27-29; 7:24—8:3; 12:1-6).

Danna Nolan Fewell presents deconstructive criticism, an approach much maligned and misunderstood in critical circles today. Her analogy of the abstract blue painting and its various interpretations does much to make deconstruction accessible to the lay audience. Just as fluid undertones of red complicate and destabilize a painting that seems to be about the color blue, a literary text is a composite of dominant and submerged voices in dynamic tension with each other. Deconstruction is a strategy of reading that allows for all voices in the text to be heard. A text that seems to be about one thing to one reader can mean something else to another. Fewell's deconstructive reading of the deceptively simple story of Achsah in Judges 1:11-15 reveals how meaning in this text oscillates and depends on the specific context of the reader.

In chapter 7, I examine ideological criticism, which integrates sociohistorical and literary criticisms in order to investigate the twofold manifestations of ideology. Sociohistorical criticism uncovers, in an extrinsic analysis, the ideological circumstances involved in the text's production, such as the ideologies themselves, their social location in the dominant and subordinate power groups, the levels of cooperation or conflict among these groups, and so forth. A literary-critical intrinsic analysis studies how ideology is reproduced in the text. It examines a text's absences and rhetoric to determine the relationship between the text and the circumstances surrounding its production. I apply ideological criticism to Judges 17–21, chapters usually discounted as postexilic appendixes to the book. I argue that these chapters are integral to the first edition of the Deuteronomistic History (Dtr 1) as propaganda for Josiah's religious reform program.

In his discussion of postcolonial criticism, *Uriah Y. Kim* argues that just as men relegated women to the status of the inferior Other, Western academic and cultural traditions dichotomize the world into the West and the Rest. The manifold diversity of non-Western nations and their peoples are lumped into a homogeneous mass and deemed second-rate, "primitive," and needing "civilization." Postcolonial criticism foregrounds the Bible as an important text used by the colonizers to legitimate their conquest and exploitation of other lands. Kim lays out how the conquest and colonization of the denigrated foreign Other are embedded and legitimated in the Judges text itself and its interpretations by biblical scholars.

Ken Stone observes that gender criticism not only examines the social construction of gender in the biblical text, but also the instability of categories like man and woman, or masculinity and femininity. Understanding assumptions regarding gender not only between the sexes, but especially among members of the same sex, can provide insights into biblical power plays that scholars who have ignored gender have missed.

Stone argues that in Judges the depiction of Abimelech as falling short of ideals of Israelite "manhood" is part of a pro-Davidic/anti-Saulide polemic that foreshadows and disparages the masculinity of Saul and his son Jonathan in 1 Samuel.

The final chapter of the volume by *David M. Gunn* examines cultural criticism, which acknowledges that readers come to an ancient text like the Bible with many cultural assumptions that are bound to affect their interpretation. Cultures are sets of shared values, beliefs, practices, and artifacts, which are transmitted through generations by imitation and learning, and in which people find social identity. Visual culture may be expressed in traditions of "high" art, like the European oil paintings in art museums, or it may be found in "popular" objects, like clothes, cars, or comics. Gunn uses cultural criticism to examine how the story of the sacrifice of Jephthah's daughter was visualized in family Bibles in the eighteenth and nineteenth centuries. Gunn suggests that a study of the graphic Bible illustrates not only how the text has been received by individual artists and interpreters, but also how culture shapes that reception.

We hope you will notice the interdisciplinary character of all of these new approaches, how they appropriate the best insights of literary theory, the social sciences, postcolonial theory, cultural studies, and the like, to uncover new ways in interpreting the Bible. We also encourage you to see how very much these methods interrelate, as well as how they diverge; for example, how gender criticism can utilize feminist, ideological, and social-scientific criticism in the construction of masculinity and femininity; or how postcolonial criticism can move into the cultural appropriations of the Bible in different colonial contexts. We now invite you to explore these new approaches and new ways of looking at a very old text.

FURTHER READING

General

Davis, Robert Con, and Ronald Schleifer, eds. *Contemporary Literary Criticism: Literary and Cultural Studies*. 4th ed. New York: Longman, 1998. A convenient anthology of essays by exponents of the newer literary-critical theories. For more advanced students.

Eagleton, Terry. *Literary Theory: An Introduction*. 2nd ed. Minneapolis: University of Minnesota Press, 1983. Cambridge, Massachusetts: Blackwell, 1996. An entertaining survey of the major approaches in modern literary theory. Reveals how each has an unconscious ideological agenda and argues for a politically engaged literary criticism.

Rivkin, Julie, and Michael Ryan, eds. *Literary Theory: An Anthology*. 2d ed. Malden
    and Oxford: Blackwell, 2004. An excellent anthology of excerpts covering
    a wide range of important literary theorists, including the more contem-
    porary approaches in cultural studies, post-colonialism, gender studies,
    ethnic studies, and transnational studies.
Selden, Raman, et al. *A Reader's Guide to Contemporary Literary Theory*. 5th ed.
    Harlow, U.K.: Pearson Education, 2005. Offers a "crash course" in contem-
    porary literary theory and theorists who have influenced biblical critics.
    Ranges from Russian formalism to Marxist, structuralist, poststructuralist,
    reader-response, and feminist theories to postcolonial, black British,
    African, Asian American, Caribbean, and queer theory.

Biblical

Alter, Robert, and Frank Kermode, eds. *The Literary Guide to the Bible*. Cam-
    bridge: Harvard University Press, 1987. Different contributors analyze each
    book of the Old Testament from a literary perspective. The editors con-
    sciously exclude from their project the more recent approaches, for exam-
    ple, ideological criticism, deconstruction, and feminist criticism.
Anderson, Janice Capel, and Stephen D. Moore, eds. *Mark and Method: New
    Approaches in Biblical Studies*. 2nd ed. Minneapolis: Fortress. (Forthcom-
    ing 2008.) The New Testament counterpart to the present volume.
Bal, Mieke. *Murder and Difference: Gender, Genre, and Scholarship on Sisera's
    Death*. Translated by Matthew Gumpert. Bloomington and Indianapolis:
    Indiana University Press, 1988. A provocative study that critiques the his-
    torical, theological, anthropological, and literary approaches that have been
    used to interpret Judges 4–5. Shows how these approaches have relied on
    "codes" that allow unconscious judgements to skew the interpretation of
    the text.
Barton, John. *Reading the Old Testament: Method in Biblical Study*. Rev. and
    enlarged. Philadelphia: Westminster, 1996. Not only introduces students to
    the older and newer methods of Old Testament interpretation, but also tries
    to answer questions regarding the *purpose* of practicing these various
    methods.
The Bible and Culture Collective. *The Postmodern Bible*. New Haven: Yale Uni-
    versity Press, 1995. Consciously written to counter Alter and Kermode's *The
    Literary Guide to the Bible,* this book foregrounds what they omit, that is,
    the theory underlying the newer and more controversial approaches to the
    study of the Bible.
Collins, John J. *The Bible after Babel: Historical Criticism in a Postmodern Age*.
    Grand Rapids: Eerdmans, 2005. Deals with the impact of the newer
    approaches on biblical interpretation and theologizing. Although he situ-

ates himself more on the modern side of the debate, Collins recognizes the importance of bringing the postmodern "voices from the margin" into the conversation.

Gorman, Michael J. *The Elements of Biblical Exegesis: A Basic Guide for Ministers and Students*. Peabody, Mass.: Hendrickson, 2001. A "user-friendly" guide to the basic steps of exegetical interpretation. Excellent charts of the exegetical methods, their goals, and the questions they ask of the text, along with helpful annotated bibliographies of the basic tools of exegesis.

Hayes, John H., and Carl R. Holladay. *Biblical Exegesis: A Beginner's Handbook*. 3rd ed. Atlanta: John Knox, 2007. Familiarizes the student with the standard historical-critical methods and with literary criticism, structuralism, and canonical criticism. Contains a chapter on exegesis from cultural, economic, ethnic, gender, and sexual perspectives, plus an appendix on electronic technologies in exegesis.

Holladay, Carl R. "Contemporary Methods of Reading the Bible." In *The New Interpreters Bible*, vol. 1. Edited by Leander E. Keck, 125 49. Nashville: Abingdon, 1994. A helpful overview of biblical methods according to three paradigms: the divine oracle paradigm, the historical paradigm, and the literary paradigm.

McKenzie, Steven L., and Stephen R. Haynes, eds. *To Each Its Own Meaning: An Introduction to Biblical Criticisms and Their Application*. Revised and expanded. Louisville: Westminster John Knox, 1999. Includes discussions of social-scientific, structural, narrative, reader-response, poststructuralist, feminist, and socio-economic criticisms with applications to texts in either Genesis or Luke-Acts.

Methods of Biblical Interpretation. Foreword by Douglas A. Knight. Nashville: Abingdon, 2004. Excerpted from the *Dictionary of Biblical Interpretation*. Edited by John H. Hayes. Nashville: Abingdon, 1999. A handy, concise overview of traditional and cutting-edge exegetical methods with excellent bibliographies for further study.

Schwartz, Regina M., ed. *The Book and the Text: The Bible and Literary Theory*. Cambridge: Basil Blackwell, 1990. A collection of essays designed to complement studies such as Alter and Kermode's *The Literary Guide to the Bible* by engaging the more "controversial" approaches in literary theory, such as structuralism, deconstruction, semiotics, feminist criticism, ideological criticism, and psychoanalytic interpretation. For the advanced student.

Soulen, Richard N., and R. Kendall Soulen. *Handbook of Biblical Criticism*. 3rd ed. Revised and expanded. Louisville: Westminster John Knox, 2001. A useful dictionary of terms and concepts involved in biblical exegesis. This edition includes precritical and postcritical interpretation and a practical diagram of biblical interpretation.

Vander Stichele, Caroline, and Todd Penner, eds. *Her Master's Tools? Feminist and Postcolonial Engagements of Historical-Critical Discourse*. Global Perspectives in Biblical Scholarship 9. Atlanta: Society of Biblical Literature, 2005.

> A fine collection of essays that explore the encounter between historical
> criticism and feminist, gender, and postcolonial criticisms in discourses on
> the Bible.

For the most up-to-date studies incorporating the more recent critical
approaches to the Bible, consult the monographs in the Semeia Studies
series published by the Society of Biblical Literature, the monographs published by Sheffield Phoenix Press, and the annual journals *Biblical Interpretation* and *The Bible and Critical Theory.* Also helpful are the past issues
of the discontinued journal *Semeia.*

2

NARRATIVE CRITICISM

Human Purpose in Conflict
with Divine Presence

RICHARD G. BOWMAN

A classic *New Yorker* cartoon shows two ancient scribes, one peering over the shoulder of the other, who is seated at a writing table, pen in hand. The overseeing scribe has the stern, superior look of a self-assured lecturer, while the face of the seated scribe expresses surprise and incredulity. The seated scribe says, "You mean when I use a phrase like 'Pharaoh *dreamed* seven cows came up out of the Nile,' or 'God *remembered* Noah,' or David's wife Michal *'despised him in her heart'*—that's speculative journalism?"[1]

For a narrative-critical approach to interpretation such comments are not regarded as "speculative journalism." Instead they are understood as indications of the narrator's omniscient assessment of the events that are related through the story. As such, these comments are regarded as information that is essential for a more complete understanding of the story.

This example illustrates only one feature of narrative criticism, which focuses on an analysis of the literary features of biblical texts. Narrative criticism seeks to discover and disclose the narrative's own intrinsic points of emphasis, thereby facilitating its interpretation and consequently helping to discriminate among various possible interpretations.

The basic presuppositions of narrative criticism are that (1) the final, present form of the text functions as a coherent narrative; (2) this narrative has a literary integrity apart from circumstances relating to the compositional process, the historical reality behind the story, or the interpretive agenda of the reader; and (3) an analysis of the literary features of this narrative will reveal an interpretive focus. The questions asked of the text follow from these presuppositions and concern how the general elements of narrative are manifested in a particular narrative to yield a meaningful and meaning-filled story.

19

ASSESSMENT

No single reading strategy or interpretive method accounts for all the important literary or historical data, either textual or extratextual. Different methods approach the text with different presuppositions and for different purposes. As a result, readers ask various kinds of analytic questions of the story and seek a variety of answers. The asking of certain questions precludes the asking of others and consequently excludes obtaining certain information. No one method is, therefore, sufficient for a comprehensive interpretation of any narrative. Each approach has its own advantages and disadvantages. Often, benefits of one method are limitations of another, and likewise weaknesses of one method are strengths of another. Here are what I regard as the inherent limitations as well as the essential advantages of narrative criticism.[2]

Advantages

The first advantage is that narrative criticism focuses on the present form of the text. Interpretations are based on empirically observable data within the text, not on the speculated intentions of the author, the hypothetical reconstructions of the historian, or the ideological agenda of the reader. By focusing on the narrative itself, the reader discovers the dynamics of the story itself. The division of the text into its component sources and the historical reconstruction of previous versions assist us in discovering issues important to earlier communities and in understanding the process by which the present form of the text was created. They do not, however, help us understand the final form of the story. The final form is as important as earlier versions, because it is the text that has been preserved for us and is the one most accessible to us.

A second advantage is that narrative criticism focuses on making constructive sense of the text. This method recognizes that a literary text cannot be completely consistent and free from all contradictions. However, instead of exploiting these inconsistencies in a deconstructive or ideological reading, narrative criticism chooses to explicate them in favor of constructive reading. It focuses on the constructive continuities of sense rather than the deconstructive discontinuities of nonsense.

Another advantage of narrative criticism is that it focuses on literary conventions inherent in Hebrew narrative. Identifying the conventions of composition is helpful in establishing and understanding the coherence and therefore the meaning of biblical narrative. An analysis of these conventions uncovers the dynamics of the story and signals the story's own internally generated emphasis. Through an understanding of these conventions the interpreter can show that the biblical narrative is not, to paraphrase Shakespeare, a tale redacted by an idiot, full of sound and fury, signifying nothing.

A final advantage is that it protects against overinterpretation[3]—the practice of assigning meanings to a story that exceed the possibilities generated by the data in the story itself. Because narrative criticism emphasizes textual data, it prevents the inclusion of extratextual information that alters the focus of the text in favor of the extraneous material.

One way in which narratives are overinterpreted is through the recent fascination with narrative gaps, that is, places in the story where desired information is missing and must allegedly be filled in by the reader's imagination in order to make sense of the story. Gaps are regarded as significant interpretive clues in that they provide evidence of inconsistencies and contradictions inherent in the narrative. However, for narrative criticism, gaps are not hermeneutical invitations to speculate on the motivation of character, the meaning of events, or the concealed ideology of the author. Instead, they are indications of what is important to the narrator in the development and presentation of the story. What is omitted—that is, the missing material that creates the gap—is not important. Gaps are nonetheless of interpretive significance because they point to what is important— that is, the material that is included. Therefore, narrative criticism ignores rather than explores narrative gaps, thereby avoiding overinterpretation.

Limitations

The first limitation of narrative criticism is that it is not particularly concerned about the historical reality behind the text or in its reconstruction. Yet, narrative criticism is not in principle opposed to historical criticism and does not preclude the importance of historical information for an understanding of the present form of the text. Such information is extremely important in understanding certain features of a text and avoiding misinterpretation. An analysis of the literary dynamics of the story reveals when historical information is useful and even necessary to clarify the meaning of the story. For example, an understanding of the procedure for conferring a blessing in ancient Israelite society adds an important interpretive dimension to the story of Achsah.

The second limitation is that narrative criticism does not specifically take into account the agenda of the reader. This is to be expected, since the method focuses on generating data from the narrative rather than on filtering the data through political, social, or aesthetic convictions of the reader. Yet, narrative criticism is compatible with reader-oriented approaches, for example, feminism, because it does provide narrative data that can then be analyzed from the perspective of the reader.

A final limitation is that narrative criticism is not particularly sympathetic to deconstruction and its relentless quest for indeterminate and undecidable meanings. Focusing on the coherence and continuity of the story and the portrayal of its characters, it does not typically attempt to account for data that do not fit a consistent interpretive scheme. Yet the method does acknowledge ambiguities and even multiple meanings, but it attributes them to the complexities of character and the intricacies of events, complexities and intricacies that do not create unresolvable confusion and irretrievable significance.

THE ELEMENTS OF NARRATIVE

A narrative, by definition, "requires a story and a story-teller."[4] The central elements of a story are plot, setting, point of view, and character. The storyteller is often referred to as the narrator. In developing the plot of a story and in presenting its characters, the narrator draws on a wide repertoire of compositional techniques, such as the use of narrated discourse versus direct discourse and repetition. These compositional techniques are integrated into the overall organizational structure of the narrative that the narrator supplies. This framework provides the story with coherence and thematic unity according to the conventions of ancient Hebrew narrative. In the following pages I shall offer a brief theoretical discussion of these elements and then give a more substantive interpretive illustration from Judges.

The Narrator

Narrators are usually either first-person or third-person narrators.[5] If the narrator is the first-person, "I" narrator, the story can be told only from the limited position of what the narrator has experienced or observed. If, on the other hand, the narrator is an omniscient, third-person narrator ("he," "she," "they," or a person's name), the story can be related from any number of perspectives. The story can follow the actions of any of the characters; it can move from place to place and jump from a present time to a past or even a future time; and it can present the thoughts and feelings of any character or the narrator. Biblical narrators are usually third-person, omniscient narrators who reliably and accurately relate their stories, though not without an interpretive perspective.[6]

Narrated Discourse and Direct Discourse

The biblical narrator employs a variety of compositional techniques through which the narrative is conveyed and the thought of the story expressed. Central to the narrator's presentation of the story is the choice of narrated discourse (narration) or direct discourse (speech).[7]

Direct discourse or speech refers to occasions where the narrator reports the utterances of a character in the story. It usually occurs as part of a dialogue between two characters but occasionally appears as a monologue. In the development of the story, the use of direct discourse either as dialogue or monologue serves two functions:

1. It develops the story by dramatizing significant aspects.
2. It emphasizes certain features through the dramatization.

Narrated discourse or narration refers to those occasions when the narrator speaks and relates aspects of the story. The use of the narrator's own voice to develop a particular aspect of the story serves four functions:

1. It summarizes developments in the story instead of dramatizing them through direct discourse.
2. It provides necessary background information on events or characters through exposition or description.
3. It allows the narrator's use of an omniscient perspective to reveal the internal thoughts and emotions of characters.
4. It provides the narrator with a means to comment on the story for explanatory or evaluative purposes.

The narrator's choice of either direct discourse, narrated discourse, or some combination of the two in the presentation and development of the story suggests important, internally generated points of emphasis. For example, the use of direct discourse interrupts what would otherwise have been a continuous narrative thread, thereby placing an organizational emphasis on the information contained in the speech. That an incident is dramatized through speech instead of summarized also indicates its significance within the organizational structure of the story, because it is presented more directly and with greater detail. Similarly, the narrator's use of omniscient perspective to acquire and report on the thoughts or emotions of a character provides important information on a character's motivation. This utilization of omniscient perspective in the narrated discourse portions also supplies contextual information necessary in understanding those portions of the narrative dramatized through direct discourse.

The biblical story of Achsah in Judges 1:11-15 provides examples of the alternating use of narrated and direct discourse. The narrative comprises two parts, which portray Achsah initially as object and subsequently as subject:

1. Judges 1:11-13   Achsah as Object
2. Judges 1:14-15   Achsah as Subject

The narrator begins the first part of the story with an expository narrated report that the Judahites were launching a divinely sanctioned attack against the inhabitants of Debir. Caleb, a leader of earlier preconquest ventures, is apparently commanding this exploit as well. The aging hero is not, however, personally going to lead the assault. Narrated discourse yields to direct discourse as Caleb issues an invitation for battlefield leadership: "Whoever attacks Kiriath-sepher [Debir] and takes it, I will give him my daughter Achsah as wife" (Judg 1:12).[8] This speech defines and even emphasizes the traditional roles of women as daughter and wife by its interruption of a narrated discourse sequence. It further points out an interconnection between the two: as a possession of the father, the daughter is a viable resource to be bartered in exchange for military conquest.

Having thus defined the accepted and expected status of Achsah, the narrator resumes narrated discourse to report Othniel's acceptance of Caleb's offer. In so doing the narrator uses omniscient perspective to further identify Othniel as the son of Kenaz, Caleb's younger brother. The marriage is thus between two Hebrews, thereby maintaining their ethnic integrity.

In vocabulary that repeats that of the invitation, the narrator further observes that Othniel "took" Debir, and that Caleb honored his commitment and "gave him his daughter Achsah as wife" (Judg 1:13). Through this repetition the narrator's report emphasizes the roles Achsah is expected to fulfill as the daughter of Caleb and the wife of Othniel. The subordinate status of Achsah is further reinforced because she is twice presented as the grammatical object of the verb "to give," initially in Caleb's speech and then in the narrator's subsequent report.[9]

At this juncture, however, the narrator, surprisingly, shifts the focus of the story. In the reorientation of the second part, Achsah becomes subject instead of object, active instead of passive, vocal instead of silent.[10] These changes are chronicled in encounters between Achsah and her husband and between Achsah and her father.

The story resumes with an encounter between Achsah and Othniel. The narrator uses narrated discourse to report, "When she came to him [i.e., Othniel], she urged him to ask her father for a field" (Judg 1:14). The grammar of this sentence places Achsah as the subject of the verb. Contrary to traditional expectations, Achsah not only acts but acts assertively with her husband. However, without specifically reporting the result of this encounter or formally noting a change in setting, the narrator abruptly continues the story by reporting another encounter, this time between Achsah and Caleb.

Whereas the encounter between Achsah and Othniel was related in summarizing narrated discourse, the confrontation between Achsah and Caleb is presented in dramatizing direct discourse. The inconclusive nature of the encounter between Achsah and Othniel and the contrasting use of direct discourse to report the encounter between Achsah and Caleb combine to stress the importance of the second encounter. The narrator conveys the climactic encounter as follows: "As she dismounted from her donkey, Caleb said to her, 'What do you wish?' She said to him, 'Give me a blessing; since you have set me in the land of the Negeb, give me springs of water'" (Judg 1:14-15).[11]

Achsah is again portrayed as making a request of a dominant male in her life. The grammar of the sentence again makes Achsah the subject. She is shown as acting and acting assertively a second time, here as the initiator in relationship to her father. She directly requests from him a blessing, a gift typically bestowed by the father on the firstborn son.[12] Achsah not only demands her own blessing, but she also continues her speech with a justification for her request. With this justification we probably learn in retrospect the result of Achsah's request of Othniel. It appears that her father had only halfheartedly complied with her previous appeal, giving only an arid portion of land. Achsah then circumvents male posturing and power plays and demands, under the aegis of the paternal blessing, springs of water so that her land might be productive and useful.

Narration concludes the story, reporting Caleb's compliance with Achsah's request: "And Caleb gave her the upper springs and the lower springs" (Judg 1:15). In this instance we learn immediately, albeit without elaboration, the result of her request. However, the narrator only reports Caleb's compliance and does not reveal his motivation. The absence of this information suggests that the narrator's stress is the assertiveness of Achsah and not the motivation for her father's compliance. The curious reader is left only to conjecture whether Caleb was persuaded by her presence, her argument, or both.

In part through the alternating use of narrated and direct discourse, the narrator portrays Achsah in unexpected relationships with both her father and her husband. The initial phase of the story shows her in a submissive role as the possession of her father. Her only option is to be offered as the wife of a warrior as compensation for a successful military campaign against the enemy. Yet, the final phase of the story portrays her differently. Once she becomes the wife of Othniel, Achsah assumes an assertive stance vis-à-vis her husband and her father. She asserts herself with her husband, asking him to acquire from her father a suitable plot of land to cultivate. When his effort apparently fails to achieve all she desires, she acts in his place and confronts her father directly, demanding arable land under the rubric of the paternal blessing. Thus, she is portrayed as the initiator of action in these relationships, a role inconsistent with the expected submissive postures of obedient wife and dutiful daughter. Instead of assuming these traditional stances, she expects her husband to heed her request and her father to fulfill his own bequest.

Structure

The narrator imposes order and coherence on the recounted events through the organizational structure of the story. A description of the narrative structure, therefore, is central to discerning the narrator's internal, interpretive emphasis. Narrative structure can be determined on the basis of both form and content.

A three-part structure of Judges can be described as follows:[13]

1. The Prologue – Judges 1:1—3:6
2. The Era of the Judges – Judges 3:7—16:31
3. The Epilogue – Judges 17:1—21:25

The Prologue takes place "after the death of Joshua" (Judg 1:1) and relates various attempts to continue the conquest of the land. After a few initial successes, these attempts largely fail. Unifying this section of the narrative is a common content that centers on various attempts to take possession of the land (Judg 1:1-36) and subsequent explanations for the failure to do so (2:2—3:6). A formal feature of the narrative, which also serves to unify the section as well as thematically characterize it, is the tenfold repetition of the verbal phrase "did not/will not drive out" (1:19, 21, 27, 28, 29, 30, 31, 32, 33; 2:3).

The failure to drive out the inhabitants of the land inaugurates the Era of the Judges. This central section is further divided into six episodes, each of which is introduced by the thematically as well as structurally significant phrase "the Israelites [again] did what was evil in the sight of the Lord" (Judg 3:7, 12; 4:1; 6:1; 10:6; 13:1). Each episode relates the career of a major judge, as follows:[14]

Episode I	Judges 3:7-11	Othniel
Episode II	Judges 3:12-31	Ehud
Episode III	Judges 4:1—5:31	Deborah
Episode IV	Judges 6:1—10:5	Gideon (and Abimelech)[15]
Episode V	Judges 10:6—12:15	Jephthah
Episode VI	Judges 13:1—16:31	Samson

Again after some initial successes (Othniel, Ehud, and Deborah), the judges begin to show serious character flaws (Gideon and Abimelech, Jephthah, and Samson). As a result, Samson, the last judge in the sequence, is described as only "beginning to deliver Israel from the hand of the Philistines" (Judg 13:5).

The unsuccessful Era of the Judges in turn yields to an apparently leaderless time, which is recounted in the Epilogue. The formally distinguishing and unifying feature describing this period is the fourfold repetition of the phrase "in those days there was no king in Israel" (Judg 17:6; 18:1; 19:1; 21:25). The first and last repetition of the phrase is coupled with supplemental clarifying information: "all the people did what was right in their own eyes" (17:6; 21:25). The two stories included in this section, Micah and the Danites and the Rape of Levite's Concubine, suggest that what was regarded as "right" resulted in various murders and assorted mayhem.

The structure of the book of Judges thus reflects a coherent literary unity. The narrator's use of repetition in each of the three parts presents an important thematic focus: the progressive deterioration in the relationship between the Hebrew people and God as well as among the Hebrews themselves.

Plot

Plot is similar to structure but refers more specifically to a sequence of events that are related in terms of their causes and consequences.[16] An analysis of the plot includes an identification of the tension motivating the action of the story and an understanding of the circumstances that resolve this tension. In assessing the dynamics of a story, it is often helpful to describe the conflict generating the story and to discern how the conflict is resolved.

Each episode of the central section follows, albeit with important variations, a fourfold plot schema that is conveniently outlined in the Prologue (Judg 2:6-19):

1. Israel is unfaithful in relationship to God.
2. Israel is consequently oppressed by her enemies.
3. Israel petitions God for divine assistance.
4. God appoints a judge to deliver Israel.

This recurring sequence of actions illustrates another type of repetition and functions to emphasize the nature of Israel's relationship with God. The tension that generates the action revolves around Israel's unfaithfulness to God and her consequent subjugation by external enemies. The plot climaxes when Israel repents and requests divine help. The conflict is finally resolved when God appoints a judge who defeats the enemy.

Each episode nuances this basic plot configuration in different ways. Whereas the episode involving Ehud presents a left-handed hero who deceptively assassinates the enemy king, the episode relating the story of Deborah turns upon friction caused by having a woman as judge. By way of contrast, Gideon doubts his own ability, Jephthah doubts the ability of God, and Samson overconfidently abuses his talents.

Repetition

As the preceding sections on structure and plot indicate, repetition is an important compositional technique used in organizing a story as well as in presenting and emphasizing its themes. The concept has been illustrated in these sections, but it would now be helpful to catalog the types of repetition and summarize their functions.

Several types of repetition are available to the biblical narrator: that of (1) words or phrases, (2) motifs or themes, or (3) a sequence of actions.[17] The first type is the most obvious and involves the repeated use of single words or phrases; for example, the phrases used to unify each section of narrative. The second is more abstract and involves the repeated use of images or the recurrence of central ideas; for example, the theme of irresponsibility in relationship to God. The final type represents a patterned sequence of actions; for example, the recurring components of the plot.

Three of the several functions of repetition in biblical literature are as follows:

1. Repetition indicates the structure of the narrative.
2. Repetition signals key themes.
3. Repetition provides emphasis to central ideas.

An example of the first function is the division of the central section into six episodes, each of which begins with an introductory restatement of the evil committed by the people. The repeated reference to the failure of the Hebrews to drive out the inhabitants of the land in the first section is an example of the second function. The third function is exemplified by the reiterated lack of a king in the final section.

Setting

Narratives take place in specific locales that are often significant for a more complete understanding of the story.[18] For example, much of the story about Samson, a man designated prior to birth as a judge, takes place not in Hebrew territory but among the Philistines in a variety of Philistine cities, as Samson pursues sexual liaisons with Philistine women. Such foreign settings reinforce the portrayal of Samson as an irresponsible judge who betrays his own heritage.

Point of View

Point of view refers to the perspective from which the story or portions of the story are told.[19] Even though a story is related from the vantage point of a third-person, omniscient narrator, this narrator can, on occasion, surrender this privilege and convey portions of the story from the more limited perspective of one of the characters. In so doing the narrator can show how a specific character understands certain events or how different characters have varying perceptions of the same event.

Seemingly contrasting accounts regarding the defeat of the Anakim and the capture of the Canaanite cities of Hebron and Debir provide an example from the books of Joshua and Judges. Included among the exploits of Joshua is the assertion that "Joshua came and wiped out the

Anakim from the hill country, from Hebron, from Debir, from Anab, and from all the hill country of Judah and from all the hill country of Israel; Joshua utterly destroyed them with their towns. None of the Anakim was left in the land of the Israelites" (Josh 11:21). However, a subsequent account relates that "according to the commandment of the Lord to Joshua, he gave Caleb . . . Hebron. . . . And Caleb drove out from there the three sons of Anak: Sheshai, Ahiman, and Talmai" (15:13-14). Yet, in the Prologue of Judges, the defeat of the Anakim and conquest of Hebron is attributed to the tribe of Judah: "Judah went against the Canaanites who lived in Hebron; and they defeated Sheshai and Ahiman and Talmai" (Judg 1:10). Finally, a summary of the Hebrew conquests in Canaan notes that "Hebron was given to Caleb, as Moses had said; and he drove out from it the three sons of Anak" (1:20). Whether Caleb himself actually leads the assault on the city is questionable, because he had previously commissioned Othniel to attack Debir, and Othniel, not Joshua, is credited with its capture (1:12-13).

These ambiguities blur the historical issue of who defeated the Anakim, but they can be understood literarily when one realizes that the narrator is providing several different perspectives on these military escapades. From Joshua's point of view, he is the hero; from Caleb's point of view, he is the hero; from a nationalistic point of view, the collective tribe of Judah is the hero.

The alternating presentation of these points of view can be construed as demonstrations of the stereotypical male zeal for competition and exaggeration that is embedded within and integral to the various conquest stories of early Israel. These shifts in perspective thus present claim versus counterclaim in the quest for recognition. First Joshua, then Caleb, and finally tribal Judah are portrayed as contending with each other for the accolades of success by claiming victory in military campaigns against their enemies. Ironically, however, the goal of their claims and counterclaims appears to be elusive. Despite the militaristic posturing of Israel's leaders, their attacks on the inhabitants of the land appear to have failed. This failure to drive out the inhabitants of the land then becomes the predominant theme of the Prologue of Judges. The dominant and evaluative perspective belongs to the narrator who presents each perspective, yet each stresses the repeated failure of Israel to achieve its military goal.

Character

What a narrative expresses is as important as the ways it organizes and conveys its story. An analysis of how a narrative is structured and which compositional techniques are used to relate the story provides clues to the narrative's own internally generated points of interest. Once these interpretive clues have been isolated, one investigates the information they disclose. A primary method through which this information is presented is the narrative portrayal of character.

Characters and their actions generate the conflicts that create the plot events of the story. Characters' speeches dramatize the events in which the characters are involved. Therefore, a character cannot be portrayed apart from events involving that character, and the events that involve a character cannot be separated from a depiction of the character. As a theoretician as well as practitioner of narrative literature, Henry James has rhetorically observed, "What is character but the determination of incident? What is incident but the illustration of character?"[20] His comment also applies to the biblical portrayal of character and event.

In biblical literature, character is revealed in four ways:[21]

1. through a character's actions and interactions with other characters—most open to speculative interpretation, therefore most problematic and least authorative for evaluating a character;
2. through a character's own speeches—in the middle with respect to speculative interpretation, therefore midrange problematic and midrange authorative for evaluating a character;
3. through other character's speeches about a specific character—in the middle with respect to speculative interpretation, therefore midrange problematic and midrange authorative for evaluating a character;
4. through the narrator's comments about a character—least open to speculative interpretation, therefore least problematic and most authorative for evaluating a character.

These techniques for characterization fall along a continuum of accuracy and dependability. Whereas a character's actions are ambiguous and subject to critical appraisal, the narrator's assessment of a character emerges from an omniscient perspective and is therefore more authoritative. Although less open to multiple explanations than a character's actions, a character's own speeches or the comments of other characters about him or her are still more problematic than the narrator's assessment. Because they occupy the center of the continuum, these speeches need to be the subject of careful evaluation.

In analyzing character it is also often helpful to distinguish between static and dynamic characters. Some biblical characters do not change over the course of the story, whereas others exhibit considerable change. Some show a single facet of their literary personality, and others reveal a complex array of traits.

Othniel, the first judge, is an example of a static, single-faceted character. In the brief, narrated discourse account of his tenure as judge, we learn only that he went to war against Aram and that he was successful in this venture.

Samson, by way of comparison, is a dynamic, multifaceted character. In the lengthy chronicle of his exploits, we learn that in spite of his prenatal designation as the deliverer of Israel from the Philistines, he spends his youth courting the Philistine women instead of conquering the Philistine men. Only after he is betrayed by one of his paramours does he gain insight into his mission and pray that God assist him in his campaign against the Philistines. Although he is given considerable talents, he uses them more for mischief and malice than for the vindication of his people and the implementation of a vision.

Further illustration of the techniques for character portrayal will be discussed in the expository section that follows. Any one of the elements of narrative could have been developed at length, but I have chosen character, because it allows us to focus on an often neglected feature of biblical narrative—that is, the character of God.

HUMAN PURPOSE IN CONFLICT
WITH DIVINE PRESENCE

The book of Judges offers characterizations not only of individual humans but also of God and the Hebrew people as a whole. The narrator portrays God and the divine involvement with humans in three ways:

1. God intervenes to punish human transgressions.
2. God appoints or somehow attempts to use human leaders to deliver the Hebrews from external political/military oppression.
3. God bestows the potential for human success but otherwise refrains from intervention, thereby allowing the exercise of human freedom but limiting the divine exercise of power.

Whereas the narrator offers a more nuanced portrayal of some of the judges and other characters, the storyteller characterizes both God and the Hebrew people more precisely and unambiguously. In contrast to Achsah, who is revealed through actions and speech, God and the Hebrew people are directly conveyed through the narrator's comments and evaluations.

God Portrayed as Punishing Human Transgressions

That God intervenes to punish transgressions is a major contention in the book of Judges. The narrator relates the paradigm for this divine activity in an expository section toward the conclusion of the Prologue (Judg 2:11-15). The situation is one in which the people "did what was evil in the sight of the Lord and worshiped the Baals"; consequently, "the anger of the Lord was kindled against Israel." The narrator then describes the result of this divine anger in three ways: (1) God "gave them over to plunderers who plundered them"; (2) God "sold them into the power of their enemies all around"; and (3) "the hand of the Lord was against them to bring misfortune."

These three punishments are reported in detail in the second part of the book, which relates the Era of the Judges (Judg 3:7—16:31). The following chart summarizes for each succeeding episode the narrator's characterization of the divine response to the "evil" committed by Israel.

Divine Response to Transgressions

Judge	Divine Response to the People's Transgressions
Othniel	Sold into the hand of King Cushan-rishathaim
Ehud	Strengthened Eglon, the king of Moab
Deborah	Sold into the hand of King Jabin of Canaan
Gideon	Given into the hand of the Midianites
Jephthah	Sold into the hand of the Philistines/Ammonites
Samson	Given into the hand of Philistines

In relating the specific instances that illustrate the general paradigm, the narrator reports three times that God "sold" Israel into the hand of its enemy. This characterization of divine activity begins the sequence of six episodes and continues in an alternating pattern.

As the narrative episodes progress, the transgressions of Israel escalate. Prior to the tenure of Othniel as judge, the "evil" attributed to the people by the narrator is specified as the worship of the Baals and the Asherahs. By the time of Jephthah, divine anger is provoked by the people's worship of five other national gods as well as the Baals and the Asherahs. The divine response is likewise intensified, and the people are "sold" into the hand of two enemies instead of one.

Twice toward the end of the sequence, again in alternating fashion, God is portrayed as "giving" Israel into the hand of its enemy. Both reports are equally concise, although an intensifying of divine displeasure is implied by the length of time the Israelites are given over to oppression, which increases from seven to forty years.

In the second episode, the story of Ehud, the narrator cites the third divine response option from the original paradigm. Rather than take direct action against Israel, in which the Hebrews are "sold" or "given" to their enemy, God intervenes indirectly against Israel by strengthening the power of its enemy.

Through the paradigm in the Prologue and through repeated illustrations of the paradigm in the episodes of the six major judges, the narrator portrays God as capable of intervention. This intervention is further portrayed as the divine punitive response to Israel's transgressions. These interventions specifically take the form of a transaction between God and Israel's enemies, in which God either strengthens Israel's enemy or "sells" or "gives" Israel into the hand of its foes.

God Portrayed as Delivering from Oppression

The narrator of Judges not only portrays God as intervening to punish transgressions but also as being involved in deliverance from oppression. Again, the paradigm is related in an expository section toward the end of the Prologue, when the narrator writes, "The Lord raised up judges, who delivered them out of the power of those who plundered them" (Judg 2:16). The paradigm suggests that the rescue process involves two phases: (1) a divine action by which God selects a judge and (2) a human action through which the chosen leader delivers the people.

A summary of the way the narrator specifically fills out the paradigm in each episode from the Era of the Judges is presented in the following chart.

Deliverance from Oppression

Judge	Divine Action	Human Actions
Othniel	raised up	delivered (N)*
Ehud	raised up	delivered (N)
Deborah	was judging (use by God implied)	gave into hand (C)
Gideon	negotiated with God	delivered (C, G)
Jephthah	negotiated with people (use by God implied)	fight with/defeat (C, G)
Samson	God chose prior to birth	began to deliver (G)

Judge	Result
Othniel	Lord gave into hand (N)
Ehud	Lord gave into hand (C)
Deborah	Lord gave into hand (C) Lord routed; God subdued (N)
Gideon	Lord set every man's sword against his fellow (N)
Jephthah	Lord gave into hand (N)
Samson	Implied that God responded to a prayer for revenge (N)

*N indicates that the narrator makes the comment, C that a character makes it, and G that God makes it.

As the episodes progress from Othniel to Samson, God is portrayed as taking a more active role in obtaining leaders. Whereas God initially "raised up" Othniel and Ehud, God uses existing leaders with Deborah and Jephthah, and finally the deity directly negotiates with Gideon and appoints Samson from birth.

Ironically, however, this progressive involvement seems to result in more limited success. The deliverances achieved by Othniel, Ehud, and Deborah are portrayed as unqualified successes. This is not the case with Gideon, Jephthah, and Samson.

Gideon is as successful as the previous judges. However, his success only encourages the people to make him their permanent leader. Even though Gideon rejects their offer for theological reasons, he requests the golden earrings of the spoil, which he fashions into an ephod. The narrator then observes that "all Israel prostituted themselves to it, and it became a snare to Gideon and his family" (Judg 8:27). His victory is thus compromised.

Jephthah is equally successful in his battle against the Ammonites. Yet, his success comes at the expense of his daughter's life, and it also leads to internal conflict with the Ephraimites.

Samson is successful in spite of himself. In seeking personal vengeance he inadvertently defeats a national Israelite foe. Even then his victory is not complete, but only partial. As the narratives in 1 Samuel show, Israel continues to battle the Philistine oppressors.

In these episodes the narrator portrays God as capable of intervening in human affairs by designating a human leader to deliver the Hebrews from oppression. However, deliverance is contingent on the action of these human leaders, actions that may or may not be consistent with divine intentions. As a result these episodes indicate that divine involvement does not necessarily guarantee overall success, and they hint that the divine power of intervention is constrained by the exercise of human freedom.

Human Freedom and the Limits of Divine Power

The limitations of divine power become more apparent in three other references to divine activity and involvement. These are (1) the narrator's attribution of divine presence with someone, (2) the narrator's comment that the divine spirit is conferred on an individual, and (3) a character's acknowledgment of the divine presence. The attributions of divine presence either by the narrator or by a character are conveniently summarized in the following chart:

Attributions of Divine Presence

Judge/Character	The Lord Is with "X"	Spirit of God	Acknowledgment by Character
Judah	X		
Joseph	X		
Judges	X		
******			
Othniel		X	
Ehud			X
Deborah			X
Gideon	X (x2)	X	
Jephthah		X	
Samson		X (x4)	

The phrase "The Lord is with [someone]" occurs primarily in the Prologue, but it is also used in relationship to Gideon. In the Prologue the narrator relates various incidents pertaining to the ongoing conquest of the land after the death of Joshua. As specified by divine instruction (Judg 1:1-2), Judah initiated the assault, whose success is attributed to God: "Then Judah went up and the Lord gave the Canaanites and the Perizzites into their hand" (1:4). After reporting a series of successful ventures, the narrator notes that "the Lord was with Judah" (1:19). The extent of the conquest by Judah is then summarized: "And he took possession of the hill country, but could not drive out the inhabitants of the plain, because they had chariots of iron" (1:19). Whatever the presence of God with Judah signifies, it apparently does not guarantee victory. The story thus functions to suggest the limitations of God's power to ensure success.

Also among the first to launch an attack on the land was the clan of Joseph, with whom the narrator notes the presence of God: "The house of Joseph also went up against Bethel; and the Lord was with them" (Judg 1:22). As before, God's presence with the house of Joseph does not presuppose victory. God may be with them, but they nevertheless send out spies to reconnoiter the area, where they encounter a resident willing to betray his city. Covert negotiations with this man, not reliance on divine strength, yield a successful assault on the city. Even this success is qualified by the narrator's report that the betrayer moves to another locale, rebuilds the city, and names it Luz, after the one he betrayed. This story, too, hints at the limitations of divine authority insofar as it is represented by divine presence.

Another assertion of divine presence occurs toward the end of the Prologue in the paradigmatic statement that typifies the dynamics of the divine/human relationship in Judges. After recounting the formulaic disobedience of the people, and God's anger with and punishment of them, the narrator writes, "Whenever the Lord raised up judges for them, the Lord was with the judge" (Judg 2:18). The narrator then explains the motivation for divine presence: "For the Lord would be moved to pity by their groaning because of those who persecuted and oppressed them" (2:18). From the statements made in this passage, it would appear that divine presence guarantees victory. However, in the passage immediately following, the narrator reveals Israel's persistent transgressions and reports God's consequential decision not to drive out the remaining nations through a dramatizing, direct discourse speech. In the speech God proclaims, "I will no longer drive out before them any of the nations that Joshua left when he died" (2:21). The narrator uses authorial omniscience to explain the significance of the action: "In order to test Israel, whether or not they would take care to walk in the way of the Lord as their ancestors did, the Lord had left those nations, not driving them out at once" (2:22-23). This speech and its explanation again suggest that divine power is constrained by the human response to it.

The final use of the phrase "the Lord is with [someone]" occurs in the Gideon episode. As part of the negotiations between Gideon and God regarding Gideon's assumption of the role of judge, Gideon is told twice that God would be with him (Judg 6:12, 16). Initially, Gideon is addressed by an angel of God as "a mighty warrior," and is assured that "the Lord is with you." Gideon responds with a skeptical question, "If the Lord is with us, why then has all this happened to us?" (6:13). His question reflects the perhaps prevailing notion that divine presence automatically guarantees success. However, the angel's original salutation, "mighty warrior," suggests that the basis of success actually resides in human abilities. Resuming the "mighty warrior" motif, God instructs him, "Go in this might of yours and deliver Israel from the hand of Midian" (6:14). This speech elaborates on the importance of human abilities and suggests that possession by the divine spirit is not sufficient. Gideon must be willing to use his own skills if he is to be successful. God then reassures Gideon that "I will be with you, and you shall strike down the Midianites, every one of them" (6:16). However, such assurances and reassurances do not completely convince Gideon, who acts with extreme caution when he does act and who continues to seek repeated demonstrations of God's favor and authority.

These examples from the Gideon episode again suggest that divine presence only seems to confer the potential for human success; it does not confirm success as an inevitable result. Instead divine power is limited by the exercise of human freedom to obey or disobey God, to use or misuse human skills.

More common in Judges than the phrase "the Lord is with [someone]" is the bestowal of the divine spirit on someone. It is first used in the Othniel episode, where the narrator writes that after God raised up Othniel as a deliverer, "the spirit of the Lord came on him, and he judged Israel; he went out to war, and the Lord gave King Cushan-rishathaim of Aram into his hand; and his hand prevailed over Cushan-rishathaim" (3:10).

In this instance, the conferring of the divine spirit seems to be associated with the activity of judging, which in turn is associated with the waging of war against Israel's enemies, a venture that on this occasion is successful. To whom the narrator attributes this success is significant. In part, the storyteller ascribes it to God: "The Lord gave King Cushan-rishathaim of the Aram into his hand." Yet, Othniel exercised his own skill in achieving it as well: "And his [i.e., Othniel's] hand prevailed over Cushan-rishathaim." The brief story of Othniel thus presents the paradigm for successful divine/human interaction and cooperation. The presence of God confers the potential for human success, but faithful human action is also necessary to acquire that success.

The narrator does not explicitly state that the spirit of God is given to either Ehud or Deborah, the two succeeding judges. Yet, both successfully deliver Israel from the oppression of its enemies, and both voice their own conviction that God gave them their victories. Although divine involvement is not neglected in the portrayal, the narrator does emphasize the confident leadership ability and tactical skills of both human judges. Thus, Ehud is characterized as a clever assassin who uses his intelligence to outwit the Moabite king and then uses this success to summon support from the people. Likewise, Deborah is portrayed as an assertive female leader who is able to command male soldiers and successfully lead them into battle against their enemies. Even though both of these judges credit God with the victory (3:28; 4:9), their stories stress the importance and necessity of the human involvement in the achievement of success.

In the succeeding episode about Gideon, the narrator explicitly notes that "the spirit of the Lord took possession of Gideon" (6:34). Yet, as previously discussed and by way of contrast with Ehud and Deborah, Gideon doubts his ability to deliver, and twice demands additional signs of divine assistance. This episode continues to develop the theme that divine presence can be compromised by a limited human capacity to believe and to act on those beliefs.

The subsequent story of Jephthah is similar to the story of Gideon. Both men possess the spirit of God and both negotiate additional assurances of success. After negotiations for a peaceful settlement with the Ammonites break down, the narrator writes that "the spirit of the Lord came on Jephthah" (11:29) as he prepared militarily to confront the Ammonite oppressors. However, immediately following the report of the conferring of the divine spirit and before the account of the battle is a scene in which Jephthah makes a vow to God. The narrator writes, "And Jephthah made a vow to the Lord, and said, 'If you will give the Ammonites into my hand, then whoever comes out of the doors of my house to meet me, when I return victorious from the Ammonites, shall be the Lord's, to be offered up by me as a burnt offering" (11:30-31). As in the story of Gideon, the conferring of the divine spirit has limited effect. Jephthah still doubts his ability to be successful and makes an additional vow.

However, Jephthah's doubt and his consequent vow result in the victimization of his innocent daughter. Apparently following a custom for victory celebrations, Jephthah's daughter comes out "to meet him with timbrels and dancing" (11:34). Seeing her, Jephthah realizes the horror of the situation and makes a mourning gesture by tearing his clothes. However, he mourns not for his daughter but for himself. He berates her: "Alas, my daughter! You have brought me very low; you have become the cause of great trouble to me. For I have opened my mouth to the Lord, and I cannot take back my vow" (11:35). The speech not only suggests the extent of his daughter's victimization, since her father laments his own misfortune and not his daughter's, but it also suggests the belief that once initiated, a human course of action cannot be altered, even by God.

The narrator's portrayal of the conflict in this story suggests that the father's act of self-preservation results in the death of his daughter. This human action is the cause of innocent suffering. When human freedom to act in destructive ways is exercised, God does not intervene and compromise the exercise of this freedom. Instead, the deity allows divine power to be constrained.

The phrase "the spirit of the Lord" occurs four times in the climactic Samson episode. Initially, it occurs in the narrator's summary at the conclusion of the narrative relating the circumstances of Samson's birth: "And the boy grew, and the Lord blessed him. The spirit of the Lord began to stir him" (13:24-25). At this point no action of any kind follows.

The second reference occurs during one of Samson's journeys to Timnah. The narrator reports that "suddenly a young lion roared at [Samson]. The spirit of the Lord rushed on him, and he tore the lion apart barehanded" (Judg 14:5-6). In this instance the spirit of the Lord seems to allow Samson to defend himself against an attacking lion. However, the carcass of the lion later becomes the source of a riddle Samson uses to taunt the Philistines at his marriage feast. The riddle in turn becomes a source of conflict that eventually occasions the third use of the phrase.

After Samson's wife betrays her husband by telling her countrymen the answer to the riddle, the narrator writes, "Then the spirit of the Lord rushed on him, and he went down to Ashkelon. He killed thirty men of the town, took their spoil, and gave the festal garments to those who had explained the riddle" (Judg 14:19). In this instance the spirit of the Lord seems to facilitate Samson's revenge against the Philistines as well as his acquisition of the resources to pay off his lost wager. Once again, however, Samson's actions are motivated by concerns that are personal, not political.

The final conferral of the divine spirit also enables Samson to defend his personal safety. As the narrator recounts the incident, Samson sets fire to the Philistines' wheat fields because his wife has been given to someone else. When the Philistines respond by attacking Judah, the men of Judah persuade Samson to surrender himself. Samson is bound with "two new ropes" and left for the Philistines at Lehi. As the Philistines approach him, the narrator writes, "The spirit of the Lord rushed on him, and the ropes that were on his arms became like flax that has caught fire, and his bonds melted off his hands. Then he found a fresh jawbone of a donkey, reached down and took it, and with it he killed a thousand men" (Judg 15:14-15).

In these instances, possession of the spirit of the Lord seems to result only in the personal protection of Samson from a variety of threats, some of which are caused by his own antics. Granted, Samson kills many of the Philistine oppressors, but he does so only inadvertently as he pursues personal vengeance. Given the extensive preparations for the birth of Samson and the frequent references to his possession by the spirit of the Lord, such limited results seem surprising. It again appears that divine power is constrained by the exercise of human freedom, a freedom that on these occasions is used for personal protection rather than national defense.

Although the narrator of Judges portrays God as actively intervening in the life of the Hebrew people, the narrator shows God acting without constraint and with complete success only when authorizing punishment for human transgressions. The narrator's portrayal also shows God intervening to initiate a process of deliverance from oppression. The initial step in this process is the divine selection of a human leader. However, this exercise of divine authority is not unqualifiedly successful. Success depends on the subsequent actions of the human leader.

This portrayal, furthermore, suggests that the presence of God with the human leader, or the leader's possession by the spirit of the Lord, does not guarantee success. Divine success appears contingent on an appropriate human response. Hence, the exercise of divine power is limited by the exercise of human freedom, the exercise of which frequently misuses and abuses human potential. Accordingly, the deity can influence but not command human actions; God will act to punish transgressions, but not to prevent them.

Whether these constraints on divine authority are inherent or self-imposed is beyond the purview of this essay, if not the parameters of the biblical literature. What this literary analysis of God's portrayal in Judges does emphasize, though, is that divine power is limited in its effectiveness by actions resulting from human freedom. Divine presence seems to confer only potential for success; it does not confirm success as an inevitable result.[22]

Divine and Human Portrayals in the Epilogue

The Epilogue is usually regarded as a secondary, disruptive supplement to the book of Judges. However, from a literary perspective, this section not only continues to develop themes from the Prologue and the Era of the Judges, but it also intensifies them.

Consistent with the emerging portrayal of a constrained divine authority, the narrator relates two stories that reflect the unrestrained exercise of human freedom. The narrator specifically and repeatedly notes that these stories take place when there was no king in Israel, a time when everyone did what was right in his or her own eyes. Not only is there an absence of human leadership during this era, but there is also a conspicuous lack of divine involvement.

In the first narrative, the story of Micah and the Danites (Judg 17–18), the process recounted in the section on the Era of the Judges is reversed. Instead of God's arranging for human leadership, human beings attempt to secure divine favor. An Ephraimite named Micah makes an ephod and teraphim, installs them in his personal shrine, and designates one of his sons as priest. When a Levite priest wanders by his house, Micah acquires his services for ten pieces of silver a year. Certain now that he has acquired for his personal worship an adequate facility and an appropriate functionary, Micah concludes, "Now I know that the Lord will prosper me, because the Levite has become my priest" (17:13).

Micah's manipulative attempts to acquire favor are not successful. When a band of Danite warriors seeking to acquire land of their own pass by Micah's house, they steal his icons as well as persuade the Levite priest to join them. Proceeding to the city of Laish, whose inhabitants the narrator describes as "quiet and unsuspecting," the Danites "put them to the sword, and burned down the city" (Judg 18:27). At this juncture the narrator makes the ironic comment, "There was no deliverer, because it was far from Sidon and they had no dealings with anyone" (18:28).

In situations where the exercise of human freedom attempts to manipulate divine favor, either through the manufacture of sacred objects and the purchase of priests or through the theft of another's icons and coercion of his priest, divine power is limited and constrained. In such circumstances there will be no deliverer, whether of divine or human origin. This story establishes a context for the following tragic story of the rape of the Levite's concubine (Judg 19–21).

The conflict that generates this story's action begins when the Levite's concubine "became angry with him, and she went away from him to her father's house" (Judg 19:2). The Levite "sets out after her," and the narrator explicitly states his purpose: "to speak tenderly to her and bring her back" (19:3). However, these intentions are not fulfilled, and their nonfulfillment results in the innocent victimization of the Levite's concubine.

On the return journey, the Levite seeks refuge for the night with an old man from Gibeah. During the evening, the men of the city, whom the narrator describes as "a perverse lot," demand that the old man send out his guest so they may sexually violate him. The old man counters by offering his own daughter and the Levite's concubine. When the men reject the offer, the narrator reports that the Levite "seized his concubine, and put her out to them. They wantonly raped her, and abused her all through the night until the morning" (Judg 19:25). The extent of the concubine's brutalization is revealed in the Levite's callous response to her the next morning. Seeing her "lying at the door of the house, with her hands on the threshold," he commands her, 'Get up, we are going'" (Judg 19:27-28).

The Levite's lack of concern for his concubine's well-being is further indicated by his own desire for personal revenge. He again disregards the sanctity of her person, this time by dismembering her body and sending the pieces "throughout all the territory of Israel" with the message, "Has such a thing ever happened since the day that the Israelites came up from the land of Egypt until this day? Consider it, take counsel, and speak out" (Judg 19:30). Thus summoned, the people of Israel seek and achieve vengeance on the men of Gibeah. The Levite is thus avenged for whatever indignity he believes he experienced, but the concubine remains forever victimized.

Like that of Jephthah's daughter, this story suggests that a human act of self-preservation results in innocent suffering. When human beings are irresponsible in exercising their freedom, God does not intervene. Instead God allows divine power to be constrained.

The Epilogue thus confirms and intensifies the emerging portrait of God in Judges, one in which the deity refrains from intervention in order to preserve the exercise of human freedom, even if that exercise results in innocent victims. It also confirms and intensifies the emerging portrayal of human beings as flawed in the exercise of their freedom. The narrator's portrayals stress human responsibility, not divine accountability, and emphasize responsible human interaction, not responsive divine intervention.

The Epilogue also continues to portray God as involved in the punishment of transgression. Following the rape and murder of the Levite's concubine, the people of Israel, from Dan to Beer-sheba, assemble to seek vengeance on Gibeah. They decide to "go up against [Gibeah]" so that they might "repay Gibeah of Benjamin for all the disgrace that they have done in Israel" (Judg 20:9-10). When the Benjaminites decide to protect Gibeah, the tribes formulate their battle strategy by consulting God. They inquire of God, "Which of us shall go up first to battle against the Benjaminites?" (20:18).

The query is similar to one made at the beginning of the Prologue, where the people inquire of God, "Who shall go up first for us against the Canaanites, to fight against them?" (Judg 1:1). In the Prologue, however, the issue is not internal vengeance but external conquest. Also, there the people do not initiate the battle and then consult God, as they do in the Epilogue. On the contrary, God has sanctioned the assault prior to the people's inquiry about strategy. The circumstances surrounding the two consultations themselves portray the progressively deteriorating relationship between God and the people.

In both the Prologue and the Epilogue, the divine response to the people's query is similar: "Judah shall go up [first]" (Judg 1:2; 20:18). However, in the Prologue, God adds, "I hereby give the land into his hand" (1:2). The narrator subsequently affirms that "Judah went up and the Lord gave the Canaanites and the Perizzites into their hand" (1:4).

In the Epilogue, however, divine assurance of success is missing. Accordingly, the Benjaminites inflict substantial casualties on the assembled army. Before continuing the assault, the people consult God a second time: "Shall we again draw near to battle against our kinsfolk the Benjaminites?" (Judg 20:23). Again, the answer is, "Go up against them" (20:23). Once more, the Benjaminites inflict heavy casualties.

The tribes then inquire a third time, "Shall we go out once more to battle against our kinsfolk the Benjaminites, or shall we desist?" (Judg 20:28). God again responds affirmatively but this time adds the assurance of victory missing from the previous answers: "Go up, for tomorrow I will give them into your hand" (20:28). This time they are successful, and the narrator attributes the victory to God: "The Lord defeated Benjamin before Israel" (20:35).

Thus the narrator not only portrays God as punishing Benjamin but implies judgment against the rest of Israel as well. By encouraging their attack without assurances of success, God, in effect, sets them up for defeat. Given the background description of the story as a time in which each person did what was right in his or her own eyes, and given the particular details of the story relating the brutal rape and murder of the Levite's concubine, the narrator seems to be implying judgment on the people as a whole for allowing a climate of violence in which events such as these take place. What each person regards as right in his or her own eyes, especially as it involves interpersonal and even intertribal violence, is not, in fact, right in the eyes of God. Although God does not prevent the transgression, God does punish the transgressors.

Illustrating various concepts of narrative criticism, my reading identifies three central interrelated themes in the book of Judges: (1) the progressive deterioration of the relationship between God and the Hebrew people; (2) the limitations imposed on divine power by the exercise of human freedom; and (3) the misuse and abuse of human freedom. Even so, this is only *a* reading of Judges, not *the* reading. Although there is no one definitive reading, mine is, I hope, a useful one. However, readings, like stories themselves, are received by the larger interpretive community according to the predisposition of the individuals who compose it. Some readings can hurt, some can heal. Whether an interpretation hurts or heals depends on how the story and a particular reading of it is adopted by the individual, or even on how the individual is forced to adapt to it. To paraphrase the narrator of Judges, there are in the contemporary reading environment no authoritative interpreters or absolute interpretations of the Bible; each reader interprets and appropriates interpretations according to what is meaningful in his or her own eyes.

FURTHER READING

General

Abbott, H. Porter. *The Cambridge Introduction to Narrative.* Cambridge: Cambridge University Press, 2002. A useful volume in Cambridge's "Introduction" series, which presents narrative concepts from the perspective of secular literary criticism. Illustrated with examples from fiction and nonfiction narratives.

Cobley, Paul. *Narrative.* London and New York: Routledge, 2001. An introductory history of narrative literature from its early Hellenistic and Hebrew origins through the rise of the novel, concluding with its postmodern forms.

Biblical

Alter, Robert. *The Art of Biblical Narrative.* New York: Basic, 1981. A pioneering study on the elements of narrative as they occur in biblical narrative. Includes helpful examples as well as theoretical discussions.

————. *The World of Biblical Literature.* New York: Basic, 1992. A sequel to *The Art of Biblical Narrative.*

Amit, Yairah. *Reading Biblical Narratives: Literary Criticism and the Hebrew Bible.* Minneapolis: Fortress Press, 2001. A readable introduction to the concepts of Hebrew narrative by a Tel Aviv University professor. Illustrated with a variety of examples from the Hebrew Bible.

Bar-Efrat, Shimon. *Narrative Art in the Bible.* Sheffield: Almond, 1989. A helpful introduction to the concepts of the narrator, the characters, and the plot. Theoretical concepts are amply illustrated with biblical examples.

Berlin, Adele. *Poetics and Interpretation of Biblical Narrative.* Sheffield: Almond, 1983. A useful introduction to the concepts of character and point of view. Good examples and an insightful comparison of literary methods with historical-critical methods.

Fokkelman, J. P. *Reading Biblical Narrative: An Introductory Guide.* Louisville: Westminster John Knox, 1999. An introduction for the general, inexperienced reader by one of the more accomplished practitioners. Narrative concepts such as narrator, hero, plot, time and space, repetition, and point of view are helpfully discussed and consistently illustrated with twelve stories from the Hebrew Bible.

Sternberg, Meir. *The Poetics of Biblical Narrative: Ideological Literature and the Drama of Reading.* Bloomington: Indiana University Press, 1985. An advanced and technical discussion of the compositional techniques of biblical narrative.

3

SOCIAL-SCIENTIFIC CRITICISM

Judges 9 and Issues of Kinship

NAOMI STEINBERG

WHAT SOCIAL SCIENTISTS STUDY

Many possibilities for misunderstanding arise when we seek to comprehend situations we don't understand. What typically happens is called projection—that is, interpretation based on the individual's own circumstances. Let me illustrate my point with two examples that come from personal experience in teaching about religion. One must know something about Judaism in order to understand why men, and sometimes women as well, cover their heads with a cap when entering a synagogue or why some men even keep their heads covered at all times. The reason is to show respect for God; covering the head is a way to demonstrate human awareness that there is a higher being. If, however, a person has no background in Judaism, he or she may draw conclusions about the significance of head covering that have nothing to do with religion and that are humorous as well. A student once told me that she believed Jewish men covered their heads because they were self-conscious about their baldness and tried to hide it by wearing a hat; she was under the impression that baldness was a genetic trait in all Jewish men. On another occasion a Jewish student expressed her belief that Christians worshipped money; while attending a Sunday morning church service, she noticed that after the collection plate was brought to the altar, the entire congregation stood and the minister offered a blessing over the money. With no comparable ritual from her Jewish background to help her understand this experience, the student misunderstood the significance of the blessing of the gifts by the church members for the work of the church.

Just as we must have a prior awareness of modern religious rituals in order to understand religious acts, so we must have knowledge of ancient social structures and institutions in order to fully comprehend the world depicted in the Hebrew Bible. Without such knowledge, we may wind up imposing contemporary Western models and attitudes onto an ancient society with a social structure different from our own. We call this way of thinking "ethnocentrism." To avoid ethnocentrism, scholars depend on a number of approaches based in the social sciences.[1] Using social data, the researcher attempts to recover the dynamics of social organization in ancient Israel. The aim of this chapter is to identify some of the general presuppositions of a social-scientific study of the Hebrew Bible and to demonstrate the usefulness of this approach through an in-depth study of Judges 9.

The book of Judges recounts the story of the Israelites' escape from slavery in Egypt and their efforts to settle in the land of Canaan after wandering through the wilderness. Then, some process of social reorganization moved the tribes to form from what are reported to be loosely organized tribes a tighter social structure based on a unified state organization. Can some theory of social change or a model of social organization shed light on how and why this transformation took place? Careful investigation of the narratives of Judges reveals that rather than being eyewitness accounts of Israel's early experience in Canaan, or the promised land, the texts were heavily edited at a later time (see chapter 1 of this volume). Specifically, after years of living in this land that Israel took over from the local population, foreigners entered and expelled the Israelites to Babylon. This expulsion prompted Israel to examine its past in order to try to explain why, in light of the treaty Israel had made with God at Mount Sinai, a treaty that promised Israel God's protection, Israel suffered military defeat at the hands of an enemy nation and was sent into exile. Judges simultaneously explains how Israel took possession of the land and why Israel eventually lost it.

Later individuals edited this material, with the result that these possession stories repeat a pattern of God's people continually breaking their end of the covenant, such that God had no choice but to expel Israel for its transgressions. Given the double purpose that these narratives serve, how can the modern reader attempt to understand how Israel came to control a land of its own? Is it possible to move beyond the revision of earlier narratives in order to reconstruct the origins of Israel in Canaan?

Israel's Social Origins

Recently, scholars have come to recognize the value of turning to models provided by the social sciences for addressing the question of Israel's origins. Past efforts by scholars to understand this process focused on questions of religion and history. Instead of asking about the dating of the Israelites' entry into the land, or when they first encountered their God, Yahweh, scholarship oriented toward sociology and anthropology now raises questions about the social structures and social circumstances that lie within the text, as well as those behind the text, that is, the ones in which the Israelites actually lived. This methodological approach shapes the questions asked of the biblical text. In the broadest sense, the methodology of the social sciences asks, "What social structures and social processes are explicit or implicit in the biblical literature, in the scattered socioeconomic data it contains, in the overtly political history it recounts, and in the religious beliefs and practices it attests?"[2] Yet the investigator must let questions arise from the issues raised by the biblical literature rather than imposing research agendas on the text that are neither relevant nor appropriate to the material. The comparative perspectives provided by the social sciences demonstrate that, in the case of ancient Israel, the answers to questions about social organization and social structure differ from those that arise out of our own Western, industrialized society.

The biblical tradition presupposes an all-Israelite conquest of the land, but the extent to which this perspective has been superimposed on the texts by later compilers and editors must be addressed. Specifically, we must ask: Who migrated into the land and who settled there? What self-identity and religious unity existed among these tribes? Finally, how did the tribes come to occupy the land of Canaan?

The biblical texts themselves provide conflicting accounts of how this occupation took place. Some texts claim that a lightning campaign brought Canaan under Israelite control (Josh 10:40; 11:16-17), while other accounts (e.g., Judg 1) present a less glorified picture of what happened when Israel attempted to gain entry into the land. Scholarship suggests that the description of a swift, successful occupation comes from later editors, while the earlier biblical traditions present the less glorified account.

Additional data on this issue come from archaeology. However, it provides inconclusive results if one aims to "prove" the Hebrew Bible. Sometimes the archaeological material lends support to the biblical account, but at other times it conflicts with what the Bible tells us. One group of scholars argues that the archaeological evidence reveals a wave of destruction in the thirteenth and twelfth centuries B.C.E., which can be attributed to Israelite invasion of the land under Joshua. These scholars contend that there was indeed a conquest of Canaan by the Israelites. In contrast to this perspective, certain German scholars working in the twentieth century maintain that Judges 1 reflects what actually happened, that is, that there was a peaceful infiltration of the land over a long period of time. The occupation took place in two stages: nomads looking for summer pasturage for their flocks settled in Canaan, and then later expanded their control to other unsettled areas. Scholars of this line of thinking believe that the archaeological destruction attributed to the Israelite invasion actually reflects the incursion of the Sea People, or the Philistines.

More recently, several scholars have interpreted the biblical data in light of cross-cultural models that suggest the so-called conquest was actually caused by a decaying political system maintained by the upper classes in Canaan that weighed heavily on the lower classes. A group of lower-class individuals entering Canaan met people of similar economic status, to whom they brought a message of economic liberation. The groups joined forces and the locals rose up against their oppressive overlords. Thus the conquest was from within—an overturning of the hierarchical system of Canaanite overloads by the disenfranchised.

Many believe that the circumstances of Israel's origins are a combination of the conquest and the revolt models. A group of individuals came into Israel from outside the land and fused with sympathizers within, who willingly converted to this new message, thereby throwing off the old system of domination and oppression. The complex picture presented by archaeology indicates that the same conclusions cannot be drawn throughout Syria-Palestine. At some sites the local Canaanites were replaced by Israelites and at others by the Philistines. Different parts of the country experienced different patterns of occupation.

The means of conquest of the land can be directly related to the type of organization that ties one group of Israelites to another. In fact, the reader must continually ask what size group is being referred to when the name "Israel" appears in a text in Judges. We must be careful not to assume automatically that every reference to "Israel" should be read as including the twelve-tribe system that the biblical text later defines as normative.

The material in Judges provides no clear answer to the question of what unified Israel in its early occupation of the land. Were they in fact a unit, or merely separate tribes? Until recently, the work of the German scholar Martin Noth provided the answer most accepted among biblical scholars. Basing his opinion on analogies from ancient Greece and Italy, Noth believed that early Israel was an amphictyony, "a community of those who dwell around" a sacred shrine. The amphictyony was a social unit linked to a common religious center where the tribes gathered for purposes of celebrating sacred festivals.[3] Recently, biblical scholars have reevaluated the amphictyonic thesis and have rejected its theory of unification.[4] By carefully examining the biblical texts, we see a lack of unity among the tribes prior to the existence of centralized leadership under David and Solomon (1000–922 B.C.E.)

Leadership in the tribes was typically local and, as currently edited throughout the texts, comes only through the inspiration of Yahweh. Although Judges reads as a chronological flow from one leader to the next, the texts are believed to convey information about individuals who were originally unconnected to each other and who are of different personality types. These narratives were later edited together to present a picture of the divine spirit of God leading Israel in its time of need. Yet, Israel continued to follow other deities. So, we need to look at other models of social structure to help us better understand the social organization assumed in the texts.

Biblical scholar Norman K. Gottwald set the stage for a discussion of these issues by refuting the argument that early Israel was based on pastoral nomadism. Gottwald believes that early Israel has its origins within Canaan, as the disenfranchised peasants "conquered" the land from within by revolting against the hierarchical ruling structure, thereby achieving autonomy from it. Instead of city-states providing social organization, people were grouped in extended family systems that were concerned with economic self-sufficiency. Thus, he reconstructs the origins and so-called occupation of the land in a fashion quite different from earlier scholars. Gottwald relies heavily on social models of economic life for nomads and peasants, and on an understanding of the social processes of interaction between rulers and those who are ruled by them—in this case, bureaucrats ruling peasants, or the upper classes dominating and subjugating the lower classes. It is a model that interrelates religion, politics, and economics. Gottwald understands the religion of Yahwism as a message addressing concerns for equality among the disenfranchised. He concludes, "The name 'Israel' referred not merely to a religious community but to a sovereign retribalizing society concerned with fundamental issues of survival and the good life."[5]

The period of the formation of Israel can be understood as based on the tension between city-states and rural life, between hierarchical systems of taxation and kinship systems of social organization. The text under consideration here, Judges 9, can be analyzed from the perspective of power politics between the king and the assembly who put him into office. There appears to be tension between how much power the latter will allot the former, and how much the former expects the latter to sacrifice.

Kinship and Marriage

In order to better reconstruct the social organization of ancient Israel as reflected in Judges 9, we must first understand the kinship system. Ancient Israel traced kinship on the basis of patrilineal descent; that is, the social system connected generations through fathers and sons. Moreover, men were polygamous; one man could marry more than one woman (the reverse does not appear to be true) though the social standing of these different wives might differ depending on the economic terms that initiated the marriage and on the offspring produced by it. In addition, the social system gave preference to endogamous marriages, or marriage within certain boundaries of the kinship system, as opposed to exogamous marriages, or marriage outside certain boundaries of the kinship system. Endogamous marriages functioned to perpetuate the lineage from father to son, rather than to form alliances between groups. Put another way, a preference existed for marriages based on patrilineal endogamy because ancient Israel's social structure depended for its continuance on a relationship between the choice of marriage partners and patrilineal descent as a function of such marriages. This particular pattern of marriage served to keep family inheritance within the lineage of the groom and his father.

Although monogamy is the type of marriage most familiar in our society, it may be a rather ineffective arrangement for perpetuation of the family, owing to various obstacles that may interfere with reproduction. In fact, historically, there have been several different options by means of which a family can address the problem of absence of progeny. Serial monogamy occurs when a man divorces a barren woman in order to marry a fertile one. Even more effective than serial monogamy for producing heirs is either polygyny or polycoity. Polygyny is defined as taking additional wives of equal status to one another, as opposed to polycoity, which is the addition of concubines or handmaids, that is, women of lower status than the primary wife, to the household.[6] An option other than adding women is for a husband to add a child or children through adoption. The choice made among these options is determined by issues such as custom, economics (property considerations), and the ages of the parties to the primary marriage. In the case of the ancestral stories of the biblical book of Genesis, the relationship between these options and the designation of a family heir depended on both the man and the woman, whether a primary or a secondary wife, being descendants of the Israelite lineage begun by Terah back in Genesis 11. With regard to adoption in the biblical texts, the adopted individual was required to be able to trace his lineage back to Terah in order to be a family heir.

In this scheme, a concubine was a woman whose continued presence within the family was not dependent on economic arrangements. Typically, a concubine was a secondary wife, whose involvement with the husband represented a secondary union, both in terms of being an additional wife and of having a lower status than the legal wife. Her function was to provide sexual enjoyment in a situation where the man already had off-spring by his primary wife. If he did not have a child by his primary wife, a man could take a secondary wife to produce a child.

A family unit can include both a wife and a concubine, or slave wife, and still be labeled a monogamous marriage. In fact, concubinage is typically associated with monogamy, not polygyny.[7] In a union between a man and a barren woman, a concubine may be used to obtain an heir because she does not threaten the economic basis of the marriage. Her secondary status as a slave wife is separated from the status of her child, who is considered a legitimate heir to the biological father and to the primary wife.

Social Structure

It is important to discuss the place of the family within the structure of Israelite society. The smallest unit of society is the *bêt ʾāb,* the family household. The family household refers to both social organization and residency; it fulfills both social and economic purposes, and is the locus for both production and reproduction. A family household is a domestic unit, or a group of persons living together who are related by birth or marriage (though servants may also be included in this unit), and who depend on each other for economic survival. Although biblical scholars have attempted to better understand the organization of the Israelite household, the texts themselves provide conflicting evidence on this issue; even the archaeological data can be ambiguous. Whereas modern interpreters have information on how ancient homes were laid out and on how public buildings or utilities were placed, it is still difficult to be certain how the people who inhabited these spaces utilized them. Moreover, social scientists inform us that in any society no one form of household organization predominates. The biblical texts present information on a variety of household forms. Owing to the breakup of families, residential forms are never static but give rise to new configurations in the course of the evolution of the family household.[8]

The next distinct level of social organization in ancient Israel after the family household is the lineage, a descent group that is composed of a number of residential groups. The *mishpāḥâ* or clan, is the enlargement of the kinship circle to include lineages related by marriage for purposes of protective association. On a daily basis, an individual in ancient Israel would be less directly affected by the *mishpāḥâ* and more acutely aware of his or her position within the *bêt ʾāb*. Possibly the *mishpāḥâ* served protective functions in the time frame presupposed in the book of Judges.[9] The social structure of kinship relates to the exercise of power within the larger organization. The level of social organization above the *mishpāḥâ* would be the *shēbeṭ,* or tribe.[10]

Social Class

A consideration of social life in ancient Israel requires that we pay attention to economic matters. Increasingly, biblical scholars have come to recognize the interpretive value of economic status for the analysis of the biblical texts.[11] It is clear that social classes can and do change, hence the importance of studying issues of economic development over time and place. Attending to matters of wealth and power and the interconnection between these two dimensions of social structure raises the question, "Who gets what and why?"[12] Reconstruction of the economic dynamics of biblical texts helps the modern interpreter understand matters of power and social class. Yet these categories of social analysis need not be seen as separate from each other; in the case of Judges 9, a relationship appears to exist between how kinship structures social relations and, particularly, how it legitimates power and can be invoked in the interest of accumulating wealth. The rules of social organization may require that specific behavior be displayed in recognition of kinship ties. An individual may be expected to provide hospitality, loyalty, economic aid, or assistance in military contexts based on kinship ties. Kinship links are most commonly stressed when an individual can gain something through the family connection. Economic obligations imposed through marriage—whether to a primary wife or a secondary one—are also relevant.

In order to investigate the complexity of these socioeconomic relations, cross-cultural models are potentially relevant for illuminating obscure aspects of social life. The modern interpreter must bear in mind that neither the ancient world nor the modern one can always be expected to conform to the rules; there are always exceptions, and we must recognize that the biblical text may preserve evidence of both the exception and the rule.

Once we are aware that patterns of social structure are not consistently upheld, we can be careful not to impose a neat sense of order where the ancient Israelite may not have experienced one.

To demonstrate the benefits of social-scientific methodology as a means of interpreting the Bible, we turn now to an extended analysis of Judges 9. The general outline presented above for interpreting the "conquest" based on economic concerns and a rejection of the hierarchical ruling structures dictated by Canaanite overlords provides the context for focusing on one particular text. How does analysis of Judges 9 shed additional light on the process of assuming economic independence from a power structure that disadvantaged the underclasses? Do economic concerns provide a context for understanding the dynamics of the text? Before we begin our work, let us remember that the methodological approach shapes the questions we may ask of the text. We are interested in what error, from the perspective of social organization, Abimelech committed, and in why it is an error.

JUDGES 9: MOTHER'S KIN/FATHER'S KIN—
DOES IT MAKE A DIFFERENCE?

Judges 9 relates the events that take place when Abimelech, a son of the prior judge Jerubbaal, decides to assume the responsibility of leadership over the city of Shechem at the expense of the lives of his seventy half brothers, sons born to Jerubbaal by a woman who was a primary wife to him. By contrast, Abimelech's mother was his secondary wife (8:31).

Abimelech successfully seizes leadership over Shechem through the support of his mother's kin, who are from Shechem. Abimelech convinces his maternal kin to support him in his bid for rulership by arguing that the city will benefit from leadership by one individual within their family group, rather than suffering under the hand of Jerubbaal's seventy sons by another woman; the Shechemites believe that it would be to their advantage to be ruled by an insider, a kinsman, rather than by a group of outsiders, nonkinsmen (Judg 9:1-3). Abimelech hires an army and with them he kills his half brothers. Having demonstrated his leadership abilities to the citizens of Shechem, Abimelech becomes king of the city (9:6).

Jotham, Jerubbaal's youngest son, survives the massacre and denounces Abimelech's actions. Jotham delivers his denunciation through a parable, or a speech made through the use of analogy, about trees seeking to appoint a king for themselves (Judg 9:8-15). Neither the olive tree, the fig tree, nor the vine is willing to take the position because, all three argue, they already serve a useful function and cannot abandon their responsibilities. Only the bramble, who seemingly has no special function, will agree to become king over the other trees, provided that the position has been offered to him in good faith. Jotham concludes by suggesting that the Shechemites did not act in good faith when they supported Abimelech's massacre of his half brothers, because the father of all these men, Jerubbaal, is dishonored through this behavior toward his family (9:16-20).[13]

Despite the initial favor that Abimelech is offered by the Shechemites, their sentiments turn against him. The Shechemites station men on mountaintops who rob passing travelers (Judg 9:25). For reasons that are not made clear to us, this action appears to cause harm to Abimelech.

Introduced into the story at this point is the figure of Gaal, son of Ebed. Gaal takes up residence in Shechem, where the locals become sympathetic to his words against Abimelech. Specifically, Gaal questions whether the Shechemites owe their loyalty to Abimelech, and Gaal expresses his wish to organize the people under his own leadership so that they can overthrow Abimelech (Judg 9:28-29). Interestingly, the text tells us that Gaal has moved to Shechem with his kinsmen. Verse 31 repeats that Gaal and his kinsmen have moved to the area and that *they* are stirring up trouble against Abimelech. Whereas Abimelech appears to want to rule not only Shechem but the surrounding area as well, Gaal appears satisfied with the idea of leadership over Shechem alone.

Abimelech is alerted by Zebul, the ruler of Shechem, to the fact that Gaal is stirring up the citizens against him. The text assumes Zebul's loyalty to Abimelech. Thus, Zebul informs Abimelech of the growing support for Gaal and suggests that Abimelech launch a surprise attack on Gaal's forces when they come out of the city gate in the morning (Judg 9:32-33). Gaal spots the men of Abimelech waiting to ambush him and goes out against the enemy, but ultimately is defeated and forced out of Shechem by Abimelech. Meanwhile, Abimelech resides at Arumah, a city southeast of Shechem (9:41).

The following day, after learning that some of the citizens of Shechem are working in their fields, which lay outside the city gate, Abimelech attacks and kills these people. To finish off the city completely, Abimelech burns it to the ground (Judg 9:42-45).

Leaders from Shechem's group hear of these events and come together in an attempt to overthrow Abimelech. Abimelech reacts to this challenge to his leadership by instructing his followers to do as he has done: to cut some firewood in order to burn down Shechem's stronghold. The success of Abimelech's plan results in the death of approximately one thousand citizens (Judg 9:46-49).

Abimelech's final battle is fought against the city of Thebez, inside of which is a fortress where all Thebez's citizens are gathered. The people move onto the roof of the fortress, a vantage point from which they are able to see Abimelech attempting to burn down their city. A woman throws a millstone, or a stone used for grinding grain, from the top of the tower down on Abimelech.[14] The millstone is described as "only" crushing his skull, although Abimelech is certain to die from the wound (Judg 9:43). Lest anyone say he met his death at the hands of a woman, Abimelech instructs his sword-bearer to kill him. The era of Abimelech ends when all his army returns home (9:55). The details of the narrative paint a picture of Abimelech as dividing the geographic area against itself when those outside of Shechem fight him. An editorial conclusion inserted by later revisionists interprets these events as the punishment Abimelech and the lords of Shechem justly deserved for the deaths they unjustly caused to the seventy sons of Jerubbaal, and as the fulfillment of Jotham's curse on them (9:56-57).

Despite the lack of certain geographic data within the text, that is, the exact location of Arumah and Thebez, the dynamics of the events fall into place. Verse 22 reports that Abimelech's reign over Israel lasted for three years; although we have no reason to doubt the length of his reign, Abimelech's authority was not over all Israel, but rather was localized in the area surrounding Shechem. The events described in Judges 9 pertain to a very limited geographic area.

Abimelech attempted to establish his leadership through the kinship system. He assumes his right to leadership as one based in inheritance, from his father Jerubbaal to him as son, despite the existence of seventy half brothers (Judg 9:2a) whose claim to rulership is based on their mother's status as a primary wife of Jerubbaal, whereas in contrast Abimelech's mother was a secondary wife. On the other hand, his greatest base of support comes not from his paternal kinsmen but from his maternal kinsmen. Abimelech tries to establish leadership through maternal kinship, emphasizing his mother's lineage (Judg 9:2b). Initially, his maternal kin at Shechem, which appears to be a non-Israelite city, support him in his efforts and supply him with funds to hire an army. However, despite the backing of the Shechemite lords, Abimelech uses another city southeast of Shechem as his base of operation. Abimelech's decision to take up residence elsewhere suggests that Shechem may not have been the center of his power operation and may not have been as important to him as his kinsmen had hoped. Ultimately, the Shechemites refuse to consider Abimelech their supreme leader. Abimelech strikes out against the Shechemites, burns their city to the ground, and attempts to extend his authority to other cities in the area. His so-called reign ends only when he is killed attempting to seize the tower at Thebez.

Abimelech's story raises many questions. How are we to interpret the events of this chapter? The later editing of the story and throughout the book of Judges leads the reader to believe that the problem caused by Abimelech was a theological one: at this time in history, the ideology of Yahweh as divine king was in place, and temporary human leadership came in the form of individuals singled out by God to provide military intervention. These human leaders functioned solely because God chose them. Of course, in the case of Abimelech, human initiative results in the selection of Abimelech as "king."

The events in the story of Abimelech presuppose that his father, Gideon—called only Jerubbaal in Judges 9—saved the Shechemites from the Midianites, and that for this reason the Shechemites owe loyalty to Gideon's son(s). In Judges 9:16-17, Jotham, son of Jerubbaal, says to the Shechemites, ". . . if you have dealt well with Jerubbaal and his house, and have done to him as his actions deserved—for my father fought for you, and risked his life, and rescued you from the hand of Midian. . . ." In other words, the text introduces loyalty based on kinship issues—loyalty to the patrilineage of Gideon.

How does knowledge of the general workings of the kinship system in ancient Israel illumine our understanding of Judges 9? What specific social structures support Abimelech in his expectation of receiving the backing of his mother's kin at Shechem? To answer these questions and to understand the details of Abimelech's actions, we must refer to the discussion outlined above of social organization in ancient Israel. Despite the ambiguity in the Hebrew terms themselves, social structure in Judges appears to be based on kinship grounded in the *bêt ʾāb*, or father's house.[15] Larger groupings of these houses are called lineages, which are grouped together into a *mishpāḥâ,* or clan. These clans are grouped together into the *shēbeṭ,* or tribe, although the biblical texts suggest that the reality of twelve tribes operating together—the organization referred to as "Israel"—did not exist until the development of a centralized monarchy, that is, until after the time period under consideration in Judges.[16] Each of the Hebrew words above appears to have more than one possible translation, but all appear to refer to socioeconomic organization.

Scholars argue that Abimelech's error is his attempt to assume leadership based on human initiative; this is an affront to God's ability to rule the people. Reasoning from the perspective of social organization based on kinship structure, I maintain that the central problem plaguing Abimelech lies less in the realm of divine versus human leadership and more in his attempt to undermine the legitimate ancient Israelite societal norms of patrilineal kinship.

In the United States, kinship is traced through both parents of an individual. Each of us is related equally to both our mother's and our father's side of the family. By contrast, the Hebrew Bible recounts a system of kinship organization traced exclusively through the father's line. Once we recognize that the author of Judges 9 assumes the system of patrilineal descent, we can immediately recognize that Abimelech acted without legitimate authority when he attempted to base his leadership on kinship traced through bilateral descent, the form of social organization in which descent is traced through both the mother's and the father's lineage. The problem can be stated thus: "The Shechemites make Abimelech king because he is their kin through his mother's line. However, the legitimate societal norm is kinship traced solely through the father's relations." Interestingly, in Judges 8:19, Gideon acts on behalf of his half brothers (his brothers through his mother's lineage). The texts do support the perspective that there is a tension between descent traced through the father and descent traced through the mother. All the same, in the case of Abimelech, the situation becomes more complex. Gideon had numerous wives. Thus all his sons had the "appropriate" father, but not all his sons—in particular, Abimelech—had the correct mothers, that is, primary wives of Gideon. Abimelech's mother is on a lower rung of the socioeconomic hierarchy than Gideon's other wives, and the story is about the legitimate kinship structure for the organization of society. Abimelech dies as punishment for his attempt to rule based on bilateral kinship assumptions rather than the legitimate societal norm of kinship traced through only the father's line.

Studying only the Hebrew terms used to designate Abimelech's mother's status in isolation from their social context provides limited information on how kinship affects social structure. We need a social context in which to locate words referring to the status of women. The problem of interpreting the text of Judges 9 exists because after so many thousands of years modern scholars are unable to be certain of the range of meaning intended in any one word, and must recognize that this range may have changed over time. In particular, the word *pilegesh,* used to characterize the relationship of Abimelech's mother to his father Gideon, traditionally means secondary wife. Whether this term has sociological significance, beyond that of the secondary legal and social status of a concubine, or secondary wife, remains open to debate. As is often the case in polygamous marriages, the secondary wife or wives may live separately from the primary wife and the husband (8:31).

Mieke Bal argues that the key to understanding Judges 9, as well as other texts in Judges, lies at the domestic, rather than the political, level, and that it has to do with the place of residence of women after marriage. In society nowadays, newlyweds need not reside with either the bride's or the groom's family of origin. Most newlyweds prefer to set up residence apart from both sets of parents, a pattern of living known as neolocal residence. In ancient Israel, because of the interest in retaining land within one family so that it could be passed down from one generation to the next, newlyweds typically lived with the groom's father. This pattern of residence after marriage reinforced the patrilineal system of descent. Bal believes that the topic of residence for women after marriage is relevant for understanding Judges 9. She argues that Judges points to a time in Israelite history when residence patterns were shifting from the bride's living with her father to the bride's moving away to live with the groom's family. Bal contends that at an early stage in Israelite history *pilegesh* referred to a woman who continued to live with her father after her marriage, but that later on *pilegesh* meant a woman who lived with her husband's family. To argue that the word refers to residence patterns after marriage rather than to sociolegal status[17] is to ignore cross-cultural data on polygyny that indicates that no one residence pattern is normative in this type of marriage.

In the situation of polygyny, different patterns of residence for a man's wives may be understood in economic terms. A wealthier man can support wives in separate homes, while a less wealthy individual often takes a secondary wife who lives under the same roof as his primary wife, in order that he may benefit from their combined economic contribution to his income. The distinction between a woman living with her father after marriage and living with her husband's father is less a function of historical change or feminist ideology on autonomy for women, and more closely related to economic matters. Moreover, even in the case of polygamous wives dwelling in the same household, occasions such as arguments between the women or between the husband and the wife may result in a woman's returning to her father's home as a strategy for obtaining her wishes. She disrupts her husband's household in order to get his attention and to convince him of the validity of her request. Again, the basis for the entire marriage and residence arrangement is economic.

One cannot generalize about residence patterns in Judges 9 based solely on historical periods. In any historical time frame there will always be a variety of living arrangements that can be explained through economic circumstances. In contemporary Western society, there are cases where newlyweds move in with either the bride's or the groom's family, owing to lack of financial resources or a housing shortage, even though we might consider it more typical, and more desirable, for the couple to start their life together in their own apartment or home.

Repeated usage of kinship terms serves to emphasize that issues of social organization through kinship structure hold the key to the problems plaguing Abimelech's attempt to govern. Abimelech uses these kinship ties to gain something from the Shechemites, something which they later do not want him to have. Abimelech retaliates for this disloyalty by killing them. Kinship through his mother originally provides him with the power base needed to assume control, yet ultimately his actions are understood as an abuse of the kinship system, that is, he acts with power but without legitimate authority. This is not the case in Judges 8:19, where Gideon avenges the death of his brothers through his mother—his maternal kinship line—by the hands of Zebah and Zalmunna, Midianite kings.

In the case of Abimelech, the killing of his seventy half brothers compensates for Abimelech's biological origin through a secondary wife of Gideon, and establishes him as the social descendant of his father, that is, as one entitled—in his own mind, anyway—to assume leadership on the death of his father. If such an interpretation is correct, Abimelech bases his power on kinship through both his mother's descendants and his father's kinship line. He murders his paternal brothers because they are the only ones who could legitimately oppose his right to rule; if they were no threat to him, their murder would be impossible to understand. Thus, although connected to each other, these men are distinguished from each other. Moreover, Abimelech says to the Shechemites, it is better for me than for the seventy sons of Gideon to rule over you. Thus one explanation for the events in the text rests on the sociological distinction between power and authority. Power depends on might, while authority is determined by legitimate rights. Abimelech demonstrates his power and subsequently the Shechemites give him the authority to rule.

What rewards does this loyalty to Abimelech and his kin bring to the Shechemites? A shift in perspective to economic matters may help us understand what is going on here and will allow us to answer questions such as the following: What social realities lie behind Gaal's comment that the Shechemites no longer look with favor on Abimelech? What are the Shechemite men doing to the passersby in the hill country that is detrimental to Abimelech, and how does their behavior explain Abimelech's initial motives for demanding authority in the area? What is Zebul receiving from Abimelech as head of the city—and what is he giving back in return—that explains why he does not join the rebel forces of Gaal? Why are other cities in the area surrounding Shechem uninterested in the leadership provided by Abimelech—that is, what is the cost to them of such leadership?

To answer these questions, let us consider the following reconstruction of events. The Shechemites were in league with and conducted caravanning trade with the Midianites, who were exploiting them. Possibly the Midianites were also exploiting Gideon with the aid of the Shechemites. Thus the hierarchy from the top down would be Midianites, Shechemites, and Gideonites. Gideon succeeds in ridding the people of the Midianites, leaving the Shechemites to ambush people and caravans again as they travel through the hill country. The return of Shechemite dominance would bring on the enmity of Abimelech, who may have been attempting to place himself in the role formerly held by the Midianites. Abimelech may have expected a share of this caravan booty as a result of being proclaimed leader of the Shechemites, and failure on the part of the Shechemites to pay up could have brought retaliation against them. Zebul may have been Abimelech's paid informant or official, placed over the Shechemites to see that they paid their share of booty to Abimelech. As Abimelech's paid official, Zebul's loyalty would be to him, and so Zebul reported the Shechemite's planned insurrection.

We may even speculate that individuals traveling in the hill country were killed by Gaal and his men. Notice the patriotic tone of Gaal's speech explaining why the Shechemites should not follow Abimelech: "We are strong men who have a long history and are superior to him" (9:28). So earlier, while Gideon was alive, the Midianites were the foes against which the allies Shechem and Israel united; in the time of Abimelech, with the Midianites out of the picture, the former allies became enemies. What the Midianites had earlier attempted to do—control, tax, raid, and kill hill country travelers or traders—Israel now attempts to do. Because the Shechemites initially agreed to take Abimelech's side against his seventy half brothers, it is reasonable to assume that more lies behind this choice than simple kinship loyalties and that the decision must have been sweetened with the promise of economic gain.

It appears that Gideon's seventy sons exercised some power within the region of Shechem, based on heredity through their father. However, Abimelech's right to rule stems not from his place in his father's lineage. Abimelech ultimately seizes the throne in Shechem as a result of the intervention on his behalf by his mother's kinsmen with the notables of the area. It appears that the latter, who should probably be considered the equivalent of the local ruling assembly, have the authority to designate Abimelech as their leader.[18] Thus, Abimelech manipulates the norm regarding legitimate kinship, resulting in an impact on social organization.

We may understand Gaal as the leader of a group of mercenaries hired by the Shechemite assembly to organize resistance to Abimelech.[19] Once these rebels are defeated, Abimelech moves on to murder other resisters. Even if Abimelech had survived the attack against Thebez, for all intents and purposes, his attempt to establish himself as king through an illegitimate manipulation of the kinship system fails. Leadership could no longer remain in his hands. Events would come to no good for him. He could only continue to murder all those who opposed him and wanted to overthrow him.

Yet another dimension of social organization that social-scientific study may shed light on concerns types of leadership. The situation is the same as that of kinship: study of words alone cannot tell us enough about the social location of these words in ancient Israel. We must guide our analysis with the theoretical perspectives provided by cross-cultural study. The text reports that Abimelech ruled for three years as *sar.* In addition to this word for leadership, one must remember that other words for leadership are included in the text: *mālak, māshal.* Although these words may be synonymous for each other, scholars believe that each of these words represents a different concept of rulership from different historical times.

The interconnection between leadership and kinship guarantees that "stability of the social system depends on the lineage's being able to curb its natural tendency toward disunity."[20] In other words, lineage support brings stability to the social structure, while a breakdown in lineage support leads to disorder and even chaos in social organization. Kinship is a means of organizing social structure based on the emphasis of a particular relationship between individuals, especially in contexts where there is economic gain, or property, involved.

The final editing of the text within the Deuteronomistic History, which is designed to explain that the Babylonian exile was inevitable given Israel's disobedience to Yahweh's will from the beginning of its existence, places the blame for the events in Judges 9 on Abimelech's attempt to seize what should be divine initiative. Scholars believe that Jotham's parable derives from this late editing and that it reflects this theological perspective. The parable has been inserted as a means to assist the reader in interpreting the events surrounding Abimelech as reflecting the abuse of the monarchy and human leadership. The parable speaks of the bramble's offering something that sounds attractive and advantageous to the other trees, but which the bramble is actually unprepared to give.[21] Once we move beyond this editing framework, which explains events as being caused by an evil spirit sent from Yahweh (9:23), and consider the events from the perspectives provided by the social sciences, the dynamics of the text can be explained based on the kinship system that appears to be the basis for social organization in ancient Israel. As we have seen, the text illustrates not the ideal on kinship but serves as an example—a warning—of what can happen when an individual wrongfully manipulates the social structure to his personal advantage.

In conclusion, the events recounted in Judges 9 provide a sociology of culture; they inform us about how the breakdown in legitimate kinship organization ultimately results in the abolition of leadership at Shechem. This information is embedded within a narrative that was revised to conform to a new historical context which understands that leadership is grounded in God, and that any violation of this pattern leads to disaster.[22]

FURTHER READING

Carter, Charles, and Carol L. Meyers, eds. *Community, Identity, and Ideology: Social Scientific Approaches to the Hebrew Bible.* Winona Lake, Ind.: Eisenbrauns, 1996. Reprints pioneering articles on social-scientific study of the Bible as well as more recent works.

Chalcraft, David. J., ed. *Social-Scientific Old Testament Criticism: A Sheffield Reader.* Sheffield: Sheffield Academic Press, 2006. A collection of essays applying social-scientific methodology to the study of biblical texts.

Clements, Ronald, ed. *The World of Ancient Israel: Sociological, Anthropological, and Political Perspectives.* Cambridge: Cambridge University Press, 1989. Contributors investigate diverse aspects of life in ancient Israel.

Gottwald, Norman K. *The Tribes of Yahweh: A Sociology of the Religion of Liberated Israel, 1250–1050 BCE.* Maryknoll, N.Y.: Orbis, 1979; reprinted Sheffield: Sheffield Academic Press, 1999. This study presents the peasant model of revolt advocated by the author. In the new introduction to the 1999 edition, Gottwald reflects on how social-scientific study of the Hebrew Bible has changed since he first wrote his volume, and he assesses these changes in biblical studies.

———. "Social Class as an Analytic and Hermeneutical Category in Biblical Studies." *Journal of Biblical Literature* 112 (1993): 3–22. A study of the relevance of wealth and power of one group over another in light of the social relations of production.

Lemche, Niels Peter. *Early Israel: Anthropological and Historical Studies on the Israelite Society before the Monarchy.* Vetus Testamentum Supplements 37. Leiden: E. J. Brill, 1985. A highly detailed investigation of ancient Israel before the time of King David.

Lenski, Gerhard, and Patrick Nolan. *Human Societies: An Introduction to Macrosociology.* 10th rev. and updated ed. Boulder, Colo., and London: Paradigm, 2006. The section on agrarian societies and the relationship between producers and non-producers is of importance for understanding pre-monarchical and monarchical Israel.

McNutt, Paula. *Reconstructing the Society of Ancient Israel*. Library of Ancient Israel. Louisville: Westminster John Knox, 1999. A synthesis of research until 1999 focusing on reconstructions of society in ancient Israel.

Meyers, Carol. *Discovering Eve: Ancient Israelite Women in Context*. New York: Oxford University Press, 1988. Recovers data on the lives of women in early Israel after demonstrating that the biblical texts and their interpretations are male-centered and cannot be taken at face value.

Overholt, Thomas. *Channels of Prophecy: The Social Dynamics of Prophetic Activity*. Minneapolis: Fortress Press, 1989. Examines the social processes that enabled biblical prophets to carry on their work.

Perdue, Leo G., et al. *Families in Ancient Israel*. Louisville: Westminster John Knox, 1997. Includes discussion of family life over the course of ancient Israelite history.

Petersen, David L. "The Social World of the Old Testament." In *The Oxford Study Edition of the Revised English Bible*. Edited by J. Suggs, et al. New York: Oxford University Press, 1992, 68–78. An introduction to social structure in ancient Israel and to the place of religion within this structure.

Simkins, Ronald A., and Stephen L. Cook, eds. *The Social World of the Hebrew Bible: Twenty-five Years of the Social Sciences in the Academy. Semeia* 87 (1999). A collection of essays all applying social-scientific methodologies to biblical texts and topics.

Smith, Daniel L. *The Religion of the Landless: The Social Context of the Babylonian Exile*. Bloomington, Ind.: Meyer-Stone, 1989. Based on social analysis of oppressed groups removed from their land in the contemporary world, this work provides models of how Jews adapted to life after they were removed from Israel by the Babylonians in 587 B.C.E.

Stager, Lawrence. "The Archaeology of the Family in Ancient Israel." *Bulletin of the American Schools of Oriental Research* 260 (1985): 1–35. Uses archaeological data to reconstruct family life in premonarchical Israel.

Steinberg, Naomi. *Kinship and Marriage in Genesis: A Household Economics Perspective*. Minneapolis: Fortress Press, 1993. An analysis of Genesis 12–50 from the perspective of cross-cultural patterns of kinship and marriage.

Wilson, Robert R. *Sociological Approaches to the Old Testament*. Philadelphia: Fortress Press, 1984. A critical introduction to how the social sciences can inform contemporary study of the Hebrew Bible.

4

FEMINIST CRITICISM

Whose Interests Are Being Served?

J. CHERYL EXUM

Feminist criticism takes many forms. By nature, it tends to be interdisciplinary, for it regards disciplinary boundaries as artificial and confining, and it resists the limitations that the use of any single methodology imposes on interpretation. The starting point of feminist criticism of the Bible is not the biblical texts in their own right but the concerns of feminism as a worldview and as a political enterprise. Recognizing that in the history of civilization women have been marginalized by men and denied access to positions of authority and influence, feminist criticism seeks to expose the strategies by which men have justified their control over women. And because women's cooperation in this state of affairs is necessary, to varying degrees, feminist criticism also seeks to understand women's complicity in their own subordination: What factors have encouraged women to accept a subordinate position, and how have women both adapted to and resisted the constraints of a world where men are in charge?

Some feminist critics have taken a historical approach to these issues. As Gerda Lerner observes, to understand women's subordination as the result of historical processes and not as something "natural" is to recognize that it can be ended by historical process.[1] She points out that in the building of civilization and in the preservation and transmission of culture from one generation to the next, women have shared equally with men. Yet women's contributions and concerns do not receive equal treatment in the historical record, for, until recently, the writers of history have been men, and men have recorded only those events they considered important and have interpreted them from their point of view. Moreover, women have been excluded not only from the historical record but also from the vital process of interpreting that record, the process of assigning

---

* Throughout this essay, translations from the Hebrew are mine; in most cases, they are close to the NRSV.

meaning to the past. History, so the saying goes, is told by the winners, and increasingly in modern times groups whose experiences have been suppressed are laying claim to their own version of the story; in the United States, the African American experience is a prime example. But whereas class or race or ethnicity has been responsible for the exclusion of various groups from the historical record, men have never been excluded simply because they were men. Only women have been excluded because of their sex.[2]

Lerner responds to this situation by attempting to document the creation of patriarchy and its subordination of women from earliest times, treating the biblical period as a stage in this complex process. She defines "patriarchy" as the institutionalization of male dominance over women and children in the family and, by extension, in society in general. In this chapter, I will be using the term "patriarchy" to refer both to a social system and to an ideology in which women are subordinated to men.

Although it is only one stage in the process by which men have established hegemony over women, the biblical period represents an important stage, for perhaps no other document has been so instrumental as the Bible in shaping Western culture and in influencing ideas about the place of women and about the relationship of the sexes. Indeed, because its influence has been so extensive and because it continues to play an important role for many people, women and men, the Bible needs to be approached from a critical feminist perspective.

It is fairly obvious that the Bible is about men, and that the biblical writers are not particularly interested in women and their experiences. When they appear in the biblical material, women almost always are in a subordinate role, usually as someone's wife or mother or daughter—for socially women were under the authority of their fathers before marriage and of their husbands after marriage. Their "stories," such as they are, are recounted in fragments, as snatches of the larger stories of men. Even the books that bear women's names are not necessarily concerned with women's experiences. There are, of course, exceptions, as there have always been exceptions: the extraordinary woman whose achievements receive recognition in a man's world (usually those achievements are in male-identified, and thus positively valued roles). Deborah, in the book of Judges, is an example of the exceptional famous woman—prophet, judge, and military leader—and we shall look at her "story" below.

If the Bible is so obviously about men, what about its authors and its intended audience? It is reasonable to assume that the Bible was produced by and for men. Perhaps women were responsible for some of the traditions that found their way into the biblical story; possibly they sang some of the songs recorded in the Bible, or told some of the stories to their sons, who later wrote them down.[3] But even if the Bible's authors were not all male, it is the male worldview that finds expression in the biblical literature, for, as the dominant worldview of the time, it was shared by men and women alike.

It is also the case that, in the long history of biblical interpretation, men have traditionally set the agenda for interpreting the Bible. They pursued formal study of the Bible, and they decided what sorts of questions should be addressed to the text and what sort of answers were "legitimate."[4] This is not to deny women's engagement with the Bible; I am speaking here not of individual use of the Bible but about public use and the institutions— such as the academy, the synagogue, or the church—that "authorize" interpretation. Only recently have women been in positions to challenge established doctrines and to influence the course of biblical interpretation.

Given this state of affairs, it is easy to see why feminist criticism of the Bible does not take the biblical text itself as its starting point. If the Bible presents us with men's views of women—what men thought women were like, or what they wished them to be—the feminist critic must ask how, if at all, a woman's perspective can be discovered in, or read into, this androcentric literature. As long as we remain within the androcentric ideology of the biblical text—that is, as long as we accept the male-centered worldview that is inscribed in the biblical literature—we can do no more than describe ancient men's views of women. Many feminist critics thus find it necessary to step outside the ideology of the biblical texts and raise questions not simply about what the text says about women but also about what it does not say—questions about its underlying assumptions about gender roles (the roles society assigns to men and women on the basis of their sex),[5] about its motivation for portraying women in a particular way, about what it conceals and unintentionally reveals about the fact of women's suppression.

In approaching the Bible on their terms rather than on its terms, many feminist biblical scholars have drawn on anthropology, sociology, and literary criticism for their methodological point of departure. Anthropological and sociological models can help us in reconstructing the lives of ordinary women in ancient times,[6] or in investigating sources of power available to women and factors that influenced the status of women in Israelite society, such as class or urbanization.[7] Much can be learned about women's lives in biblical times by examining kinship patterns and the role played by women in the family,[8] or by inquiring into the particularities of women's religious experience.[9] Various literary approaches have been adopted to expose strategies by which women's subordination is inscribed in and justified by texts.[10] Subversive readings or counterreadings can be produced by using the clues most authors provide (even if unconsciously) to alternative ways of reading the stories they narrate.[11] A feminist critic may choose to focus on women as characters, on women as readers, or on gender bias in interpretation (that is, how commentators read sexual stereotypes and their own gender biases into the biblical literature).[12] By exposing male control of the production and interpretation of literature, feminist criticism attempts to subvert the hierarchy that has dominated not only readers but also culture itself.

In what follows I will be pursuing a literary approach to the stories of women in Judges. It needs to be stressed, however, that historical, anthropological, sociological, and literary approaches are interdependent, complementary rather than alternative ways of dealing with the biblical evidence. The gap between historical and literary concerns characteristic of earlier studies is being narrowed as more and more critics turn their attention to ways that texts construct social reality even as they are shaped by it. Nor are these by any means the only methodological options. Increasingly, feminist biblical critics are moving beyond and outside the world of the text and drawing on contemporary resources (e.g., fiction, poetry, art, letters) and experience in order to engage a range of social, political, and theological issues. The social location of the critic plays an important role in determining these issues. Perhaps nowhere is this more evident than in womanist criticism, with its own distinctive agenda, and in the growing emphasis on interpretation in a global perspective,[13] with postcolonial criticism, in particular, promising to be especially influential in shaping the direction of feminist criticism.[14]

SOME FEATURES OF FEMINIST LITERARY CRITICISM

Feminist literary criticism is remarkably pluralistic and diverse. It not only recognizes the gains to be had from a variety of approaches—because it is suspicious of the notion that there is a "proper way" to read a text as an expression of male control of texts and male control of reading—it also encourages multiple, even contradictory, readings of the same text. Reading is not disinterested. Our interpretation of a text is the result of the kinds of questions we ask, and those questions are determined by our interests (acknowledged or not). It is a good idea, therefore, to ask of any interpretation: What reading strategy is being adopted and what kind of conclusions does it allow the interpreter to reach?

Among the questions feminist literary criticism might raise are:

- Is there a woman or a woman's point of view in this text? (The places where women do not appear in the text can be as significant as the places they do appear.)
- How are women portrayed in this text? Do they speak? Are we given access to their point of view?
- Who has the power in this text? How is power distributed? How do women get what they want (if they do)? And (Freud's famous question), what do women want?
- How does the text represent uniquely female experiences, such as childbearing, or traditionally female experiences, such as child rearing?
- How have women's lives and voices been suppressed by this text? Are women made to speak and act against their own interests?
- What hidden gender assumptions lie behind this text (for example, that women lead men astray, or that women cannot be trusted)?

One of the questions I have found especially useful in my own work is, Whose interests are being served? I view women in the biblical literature as male constructs—that is to say, they are the creations of androcentric (probably male) narrators, they reflect androcentric ideas about women, and they serve androcentric interests. Since in androcentric texts like the Bible women often speak and act against their own interests, a strategic question to ask is, What androcentric agenda does this text promote? Does it, for example, function to keep women in their place, under the control of men? Does it show male control of women as something necessary for society to function smoothly, or as something women desire? What buried and encoded messages does this text give to women? Consider an example from the realm of fairy tales: the story of Sleeping Beauty. This tale does not encourage women to take control of their own lives. It recommends passivity—waiting patiently for the day your Prince Charming will come and bring happiness into your life. Marrying a socially superior man is a means to attain a higher social status. He will fulfill your dreams and provide for all your needs. For generations, women internalized the buried and encoded gender message of this tale and made their life choices in anticipation of marrying their hero and living happily ever after. Men, too, are given a subtextual message: they are expected (and the expectations are projected onto women) to fill the shoes of the hero who can offer his passive dream girl a new and better life. And, of course, she should be beautiful and he should be rich.

A FEMINIST APPROACH TO JUDGES

It is generally agreed that Judges is a collection of stories that are only loosely connected to one another (see chapter 1). For the main part, the book presents a series of self-contained stories about individual deliverers (Othniel, Ehud, Deborah, Gideon, Jephthah, Samson) as well as about a few unsavory characters (Abimelech, Micah, the unnamed Levite of chapters 19–21). Taking our cue from the structure of the book of Judges itself, we can focus on the individual stories in which women play a role and consider in each case what androcentric interests these stories promote. As in the case of Sleeping Beauty, we shall look for the implicit messages these stories convey about gender roles and expectations. Since in what follows I will be more concerned with the messages given to women than with those given to men, I will focus on the stories in which women figure prominently: Deborah and Jael (Judg 4, 5); Jephthah's daughter (Judg 11); Samson's mother, his Timnite wife, and Delilah (Judg 13–16); and the nameless woman of Judges 19.

Deborah/Jael (Judges 4–5)

This story, in which a male warrior is eclipsed by a woman (warrior), provides a good opportunity both to explore constructions of masculinity and to observe the way male ideology co-opts a woman's voice. Interpretations of this text influenced by its political ideology approve the "heroes," those on the "right" side—Deborah, Barak, the Israelite troops, and Jael (even though they have difficulty condoning Jael's way of contributing to Israelite victory)—and criticize those on the "wrong" side—the Canaanites, Sisera, and Sisera's mother. Since the gender code operates independently of the question of who is on which side or which side is the "right" side, we shall read this story not in terms of the Israelites-versus-Canaanites dichotomy but rather with a view toward clarifying the gender positions occupied by the characters. In terms of the roles they play in this story, what do the men have in common and what do the women have in common?

What is expected of a man? Not just in these chapters but in Judges as a whole, men are warriors; they are expected to fight and to be brave. We find this ideology succinctly presented at the beginning of Judges in the paradigm story of the model judge, Othniel (Judg 3:7-11), and in one way or another it informs the way the other judges are presented. Othniel is inspired by God, he judges Israel, he goes to war, he is victorious, and he brings security to the land. Like Othniel, Barak and Sisera are leaders of men, generals who rally their troops to battle. Sisera commands "nine hundred chariots of iron, and all the men who were with him, from Harosheth-ha-goiim to the river Kishon" (Judg 4:13), and Barak has ten thousand men (4:14) "at his heels" (5:15). In the male ideology of war, the winner destroys his enemies until none are left (as Judges 4:16 has it), or he leads away captives humiliated in defeat (5:12). For all their military might, however, both Sisera and Barak fall short of what is expected of a hero-warrior. Barak is hesitant; he refuses to go to war unless Deborah goes with him. His reluctance is implicitly reprimanded when Deborah replies that she will go but he will not get the glory. Men fight for glory, for acclaim, and to have their valor praised in victory song (like the *Iliad,* or the Song of Deborah, for instance). But, so Judges 4 implies, because Barak behaved in a womanly way, showing uncertainty (cowardice?), he will suffer an insult to his male pride: a woman will snatch his glory from him (4:9).[15] Similarly, Sisera fails to be genuinely heroic: he flees the battle scene on foot rather than fighting to the end with his army.

Who is Barak? What image stands behind his portrayal? In his dependence on Deborah, he seems almost childlike. He is the little boy who still needs his mother—Deborah, the "mother in Israel" (5:7). Without her, he won't fight: "If you will go with me, I will go, but if you will not go with me, I will not go" (4:8). Sisera, too, resembles a frightened little boy, seeking the security his mother provides. He won't fight either, once the odds are against him, so he runs away. He finds refuge with a woman who, for all appearances, is a nurturing mother, but who turns out to be a cunning assassin.

If the men in this story are in the symbolic position of little boys, the women are their mothers. Deborah is the good mother. Before she "arose as a mother in Israel" (5:7), conditions were wretched. Deborah delivers her children from danger and makes their lives secure. She is the life-giving mother. Jael, on the other hand, is the death-dealing mother. Her behavior is maternal: she offers Sisera security ("turn aside to me") and assurance ("have no fear," Judg 4:18). The picture of Jael covering Sisera and giving him milk to drink suggests a mother putting her son to bed. She even watches over him while he sleeps to protect him from harm ("Stand at the door of the tent, and if any man comes and asks you, 'Is anyone here?,' say 'No,'" Judg 4:20). But the nurturing, protective mother can suddenly, unexpectedly, turn deadly. The bad mother is cold and bloodthirsty. She may attack her son in his sleep, when he is utterly defenseless (4:21). Or she may turn on him in the essential motherly act of feeding him (5:25-27). The differing descriptions of Jael's assassination of the unsuspecting Sisera in Judges 4 and 5 are different expressions of anxiety about the mother's threatening side.

According to much psychoanalytic theory, the mother's body is the source of desire and fear, of love and hate. The nurturing mother offers security and protection. But the mother is also a source of anxiety and frustration, because she may deny her body to the infant. Or the child may feel smothered by her. Her presence may be perceived as overwhelming, threatening the child's identity and making the child's differentiation from the mother difficult. Anxiety over this duality in the mother gives rise to a fundamental ambivalence toward her. The text projects its anxieties onto the women, who are all mother figures.

The dangerous mother and the nurturing mother are one and the same (thus my title "Deborah/Jael" for this section, not "Deborah and Jael"). Although at first glance it may seem that the text separates the two aspects of the mother, making Deborah the good mother and Jael the sinister one, actually it demonstrates that it is not possible to experience only one side of the mother and not the other. Jael is both nurturing and deadly. Deborah not only gives life to Israel but also sends her "sons" off to war, where many of them will die. Moreover, as Sisera shows, you can never be sure when the good mother may turn into the bad mother.

The infant's desire for the mother's body has a sexual aspect, which explains the mixture of erotic imagery and maternal imagery in the account of Sisera's encounter with Jael. Jael invites Sisera into her tent, much as the "strange" woman of Proverbs invites the young man to "turn aside" to her. While he sleeps there, she "comes to him," a description that calls to mind the phrase "come to/unto her," used of a man having sexual intercourse with a woman. He bends over between her legs, falls and lies there. The verb "to lie" can also refer to sexual intercourse. Mieke Bal observes that the entire scene can be read as a reversed rape.[16] Danna Fewell and David Gunn's reading of Judges 5:6 produces the even more graphic image of the woman approaching the man and thrusting a phallic tent peg into his mouth:

> She reached out her hand to the tent peg,
>   her right hand to the workman's hammer;
> She hammered Sisera,
>   she smashed his head,
>   she pierced and struck through his mouth.[17]

That the erotic imagery does not extend to Deborah may reflect patriarchy's attempt to deny the mother's sexuality, especially in the case of the good mother. The good mother is not a sexual mother, as we shall see in the case of Samson's mother.

There is another mother in the story, Sisera's mother (Judg 5:28-30). She is anxious about her son's well-being, but she cannot protect him. She so desperately desires his success that she tries to convince herself of it by imagining that his delay is caused by taking and dividing the spoils of battle.

> Are they not finding and dividing the spoil?
> A female, two females for every hero;
> spoil of dyed stuff for Sisera,
> spoil of dyed stuff,
> dyed embroidery, two embroideries for my neck as spoil?
>   (Judg 5:30)

This mother serves as the mouthpiece for the male ideology of war, in which pillage and rape go together. To the victor belong the spoils: the victorious men get to rape the defeated enemy's women, and the victorious men's women get the defeated enemy's finery. The androcentric narrator who places these words in the mouths of Sisera's mother and her female attendants thus suggests that men go to war to plunder for the sake of their women, and that this is something women want ("two embroideries for my neck as spoil").[18] He also has a mother endorse the rampant rape of other women and their daughters—the Hebrew reads, "a womb or two for every hero."

As Fewell and Gunn recognize, placing these words in the Canaanite women's mouths puts them in the position of approving their own imminent rape.[19] (According to Judges 4:16, all the men in Sisera's army are killed, so the captives led away in 5:12 are women and children.) The narrator who puts words in the Canaanite women's mouths puts their words in Deborah's mouth. The result is a victory song in which Deborah, a woman, a mother in Israel, sings about another woman, Sisera's mother, who sings (this is a poetic text) about women being raped in war. By means of this song within a song, not only Sisera's mother's voice but also that of the good mother, Deborah, is appropriated to advocate the male ideology of war in which rape is taken for granted as a weapon of terror and revenge. This is not Canaanite ideology; it is male ideology.

If one wished to argue that the narrator is using Sisera's mother's speech to condemn rape, one would have to say he is also condemning plunder, and thus condemning war. Israel's mission, however, is to dispossess and despoil the Canaanites, and this is what the Song of Deborah and the book of Judges are about. There is no reason to expect the Israelite victors to treat the defeated men's women any better than their Canaanite counterparts are pictured as doing. Indeed, Israelite men took women prisoners for their sexual use, as we know from the law in Deuteronomy 21:10-14. This law attempts to place restrictions on male behavior toward female captives, but does not deal with women who were raped on the spot and abandoned or killed.

It is true, I think, as Fewell and Gunn observe, that we lose sympathy with the Canaanite women when they callously imagine the rape of innocent women. Should we not also lose sympathy with Deborah, who imagines Sisera's mother and her attendants imagining the rape of innocent women? And should we not hold the narrator accountable, who, in the interests of his ideology, exploits women's voices to accept rapists who exploit women's bodies?

Bat-jiftah (Judges 11)

Jephthah's daughter is one of many anonymous female characters in Judges. One way to restore her to the subject position she is denied in the story is to give her a name. Mieke Bal calls her "Bath," which in Hebrew means "daughter," to remind us of the role that defines her: she is bath-Jephthah, "the daughter of Jephthah."[20] Following Bal's lead, but using the fuller form of the name, I call her Bat-jiftah (Bat-jiftah is a closer approximation to the Hebrew than Bath-Jephthah and is easier to pronounce).

Bat-jiftah's story is shocking. She is offered by her father as a human sacrifice to God in fulfillment of a vow. Incredibly, she makes no protest; she accepts the fate to which her father's vow consigns her with alarming composure. What is more, God does nothing to stop the sacrifice. There is no divine staying of the father's hand and provision of a ram as a substitute for the child, as was the case when Abraham was prepared to sacrifice his son Isaac (Gen 22). There is no narratorial condemnation of the sacrifice either, no "Now the thing that Jephthah had done was evil in the sight of the Lord," such as we find in the framework of Judges.[21] All these features make for a strange and disturbing story.

We do not know who or what Jephthah has in mind when, in return for victory, he vows to sacrifice to God "the one coming forth who comes forth from the doors of my house to meet me, when I return in peace from the Ammonites" (Judg 11:31). But his reaction (verse 35) indicates that he did not expect to be met by his daughter. First he rends his garments in an act of mourning. Then he speaks, displacing the blame onto the victim in an effort to express his sense of not being solely responsible for this horrible outcome: "Ah, my daughter, *you* have brought me very low and *you* have become the source of my trouble."[22]

The narrator does not tell us how Bat-jiftah knows or surmises the terms of her father's vow. She simply responds to Jephthah's speech with a speech of her own, in which she surrenders her volition, submitting to the authority of the father: "My father, you have opened your mouth to the Lord; do to me according to what has gone forth from your mouth, now that the Lord has granted you vindication against your enemies, the Ammonites"(verse 36). Notice how the narrator has the young woman speak against her own interests here. She neither questions the man who has consigned her to death nor blames him for her misfortune. Like her father, she accepts the vow as irrevocable and unalterable.[23] In encouraging her father to fulfill his vow, she subordinates her life to her community importance, accepting her role as sacrificial victim so that the sacrifice might be performed. The seriousness of the vow is thus upheld, the sacrifice promised to the deity is performed, and paternal authority goes unchallenged.

The paternal word is not to be countermanded but simply postponed: Bat-jiftah asks only for a two-month reprieve before the vow is carried out—a period of time that she will spend in the mountains with her companions. According to most translations of verse 37, the young woman goes away to "bewail my virginity," but the meaning of the phrase is far from clear. The word translated "virginity" does not indicate a physical state but rather the point of transition from child to marriageable young woman. It may refer to some type of puberty rite that signifies her physical maturity and readiness for marriage—some experience she wants to have before she dies. In other words, the issue for Bat-jiftah may be participation in this rite with her friends and not regret over never having experienced sexual intercourse.[24]

Virginity is, however, an issue for the androcentric narrator, who emphasizes Bat-jiftah's tragic plight in dying so young by adding that she died a virgin ("she had not known a man," verse 39). In the androcentric economy, bearing children was a woman's most important function and the thing for which she was most valued. To die without offspring meant to die unfulfilled and incomplete. But the unnamed daughter who leaves behind no children as a legacy is not forgotten. Her memory is kept alive by the ritual remembrance of women. Because she does not protest her fate, Bat-jiftah poses no threat to patriarchal authority. And because she voluntarily performs a daughter's duty, her memory may be preserved. The narrator rewards her for her submission to the paternal word by memorializing her in a yearly ritual: "It became a custom in Israel that the daughters of Israel went year by year to commemorate Jephthah the Gileadite's daughter, four days each year" (Judg 11:39-40). Patriarchal ideology here co-opts a woman's ceremony in order to glorify the victim. The encoded message this story gives to women is: submit to paternal authority. You may have to sacrifice your autonomy; you may lose your life, and even your name, but your sacrifice will be remembered, even celebrated, for generations to come. In my opinion, we find here the main reason Jephthah's daughter's name is not preserved: because she is memorialized not for herself but *as a daughter*. The phrase translated above "it became a custom in Israel" could also be translated "she became an example in Israel"—a rendering that would further underscore Bat-jiftah's value to the patriarchal system as a model for proper, submissive female behavior.

The precise nature of the ritual held by the women of Israel in honor of Bat-jiftah is not clear. The rare word that the NRSV translates "to lament" in verse 40 occurs only one other time in the Bible. In Judges 5:11 it refers to recounting the victories of the Lord. This usage suggests that the women recite Bat-jiftah's story, and for this reason I translated it above as "to commemorate." Significantly, however, these other women are not actually permitted to speak in the narrative. They are there to remember, and their yearly ritual is used by the narrator to keep alive the memory of the victim.

If we allow the women's ceremonial remembrance to encourage glorification of the victim, we perpetuate the crime against Bat-jiftah. How, then, do we reject the concept of honoring the victim without also sacrificing the woman? Recognizing that the narrator uses the women of Israel to elevate the willing victim to honored status allows us to expose the text's valorization of submission and glorification of the victim as serving androcentric interests. Acknowledging the victim's complicity in the crime enables us to move beyond a simplistic view that sees Bat-jiftah as an innocent victim. She does not resist (which is to say, the narrator does not allow her to resist). She speaks on behalf of the sacrificial system and patriarchal authority, absolving it of responsibility.

Even as the narrator controls Bat-jiftah's words, however, imprisoning her within the confines of the patriarchal word, her speech bears traces of her attempts to assert herself.

She said to him, "My father, you have opened your mouth to the Lord; do to me according to what has gone forth from your mouth, now that the Lord has vindicated you against your enemies, the

Ammonites." And she said to her father, "Let this thing be done for me, let me alone two months that I may go and wander upon the hills and bewail my nubility, I and my companions." (Judg 11:36-37)

Whereas Jephthah shifts the blame to his daughter when he calls her the source of his trouble (verse 35), Bat-jiftah reminds him—and us—of his responsibility: "*You* have opened *your* mouth to the Lord; do to me according to what has gone forth from *your* mouth" (verse 36, emphasis added). More important, though she surrenders her volition in the first part of her speech, in the second part, her speech transports her to a point of solidarity with her female friends. Unlike her father, who faces this ordeal alone, she has companions with whom to share her distress (where are the Israelites who returned victorious from battle with Jephthah?). *Ra'yotay*, "my companions," is her last spoken word in the narrative; *'abi*, "my father," was her first. Symbolically, through speech, she journeys from the domain of the father who will quench her life to that of the female companions who will preserve her memory. This image is too powerful to be controlled fully by the narrator's androcentric interests. The androcentric text segregates women: the daughter spends two months with female companions, away from her father and the company of men; the ritual of remembrance is conducted by women alone. But the rite of passage, which Bat-jiftah observes with her friends, and the women's ceremony, in which Bat-jiftah is commemorated, transform female segregation into female solidarity.[25] By resisting the androcentric agenda that motivates this story, and by engaging in some feminist symbol-making of our own, we can redefine its images as images of female solidarity.

Samson's Women (Judges 13–16)

There are two kinds of women according to this story: the good (safe) woman and the bad (threatening) woman. The good woman is usually placed on a pedestal, as a mother or a virgin. She is idealized in her non-sexual role. The bad woman is defined by her sexuality: she is the sexually available, "wanton" (from the perspective of male ideology) woman, who arouses in men both desire and animosity (men blame *her* for *their* lust). This stereotype is still with us today. The distinction, like the double standard in which it finds expression, applies only to women; men are not judged respectable or disreputable on the basis of their sexual behavior. Delilah is often referred to as a "loose woman" but no one calls Samson a "loose man."

Samson's mother belongs to the category of "good woman." The story highlights her role and underscores her virtues. For example, she receives more information from the divine messenger about the child's destiny than her husband, she alone is told that the boy's hair may not be cut, and she alone learns that he will be the first to deliver Israel from the Philistines (compare verses 3-5 with verse 7 and verses 13-14). In addition, she is more perceptive than Manoah: she senses something otherworldly about the visitor from the start (verse 6), whereas it takes a miracle for Manoah to recognize him (verses 16, 21). Finally, she understands the divine intention better than Manoah (verses 22-23).

But if she is more favorably portrayed than her husband, it is because she poses no threat. She does nothing on her own, which is a trait that patriarchy finds desirable in a woman. Unlike the Timnite and Delilah, who pry into Samson's secrets, she does not ask questions of the mysterious visitor: "I did not ask him from where he came, and he did not tell me his name" (Judg 13:6). In spite of the fact that the messenger appears to her on two different occasions when she is alone, she makes no attempt to engage him in conversation. Rather, both times she runs off to tell her husband, who will ask all the questions in this family. She may be more perceptive than her husband, but she does not challenge Manoah's position of authority. Significantly, we are not told the woman's view of her situation (does she long for a child?) or her circumstances (is her sterility a source of misery?) or even her name. (We don't even know if the news makes her happy, though some commentators are convinced that she is overjoyed.) By suppressing information about her, the narrator focuses our attention on her role as a mother. I suggested above that Jephthah's daughter's name is not preserved because she is remembered as a *daughter*. Similarly, this woman's name is not preserved because she is remembered as a *mother*. She, too, needs to be given a name in order to restore her to her full subject position. A rabbinic text calls her Hazzelelponi, and I shall borrow this name.[26]

To see how the positive portrayal of Hazzelelponi serves male interests, we need to interrogate the ideology that motivates it. Texts like this could serve as a means of social control. Thus we need to ask: What is it about this woman that would make women in ancient Israel want to be like her? What is it about the image of the *mother* that makes those responsible for maintaining the social and symbolic order want to manipulate it?

Patriarchy could not exist without women's cooperation. Force and fear are often relied upon to keep women in their place. But rewarding women for their complicity is one of patriarchy's most successful strategies, because it can often achieve a level of cooperation that force or threat cannot guarantee. Motherhood is patriarchy's highest reward for women; it offers women one of the few roles in which they can achieve status in patriarchal society. It is also in the interests of patriarchy that women should want to be mothers, and thus motherhood is presented as something women themselves most desire (witness the many biblical accounts of sterile women who desperately desire and finally give birth to a long-awaited son).[27]

If motherhood confers honor and status, what areas of women's experience does it fail to address? Patriarchal literature, with its underlying attitude toward woman's sexuality as something to be feared and therefore to be carefully regulated, severs the relationship between eroticism and procreation. It affirms motherhood but denies the mother's sexual pleasure. Judges 13 not only denies the mother's sexual pleasure, it goes so far as to dissociate her pregnancy from the sex act, not even acknowledging, in typical biblical fashion, "Manoah knew his wife and she conceived." Instead it begins with the (male) emissary telling the woman she is pregnant. Indeed, the miraculous birth of a child to a sterile woman demonstrates that the deity controls her reproductive ability. The absence of sex from this chapter is particularly remarkable when viewed against Samson's sexual liaisons in Judges 14–16. The erotic is associated not with the mother but rather with another kind of woman—the disreputable woman, the bad woman, the foreign ("other") woman.

None of the three women with whom Samson becomes amorously involved ever becomes a mother. (Motherhood redeems women and these women are irredeemable.) Although the text specifically identifies only one of these women as Philistine (Samson's wife from Timnah), most readers assume all three are Philistines. Is the harlot whom Samson visits in Gaza a Philistine simply because she lives in a Philistine city? She could be a "foreign woman" who happens to live in Philistia—an Israelite woman, for example. Few commentators raise the possibility that Delilah, who has a Hebrew name and lives on the boundary between Israelite and Philistine territory, might be Israelite. Most take her for a Philistine, just as they assume the other women are Philistine, for surely an Israelite woman would not betray Samson to his enemies!

Though the text does not identify Delilah as a harlot, it is often assumed that she is one (perhaps because Samson visits a harlot in Judges 16:1-3?). Because she is not identified in terms of her familial relationship to a male—she seems to have her own house, and Samson is apparently her lover though she is not his wife—other possibilities for understanding her position in society are rarely entertained. Another assumption one frequently encounters not only about Delilah but also about the Timnite woman is that the women used sexual wiles to discover Samson's secrets.

Are readers who make such assumptions and draw such conclusions about these women simply reading in accordance with the ideology of the text, picking up on the latent message about the danger of women's sexuality? Or do they create this association from their own biases, which they project onto the text?

I would argue that both these processes are at work, and that the story encourages us to read in accordance with an ideology that classifies women according to negative and positive images: the foreign woman and the mother. Both the negative image of the foreign woman and the positive image of the mother (legitimate wife) are well established in the Bible, and our narrator therefore does not need to set up this contrast. He simply assumes it and builds upon it, and he counts on us to accept it and apply it when we read. We are led to assume that Israelite women behave respectably, while foreign women are disreputable and treacherous.

Why does Samson reveal his secrets to a woman? His riddle, "Out of the eater came something to eat, out of the strong came something sweet" (14:14), offers the key. The answer to it is another riddle, "What is sweeter than honey? What is stronger than a lion?" (14:18), whose answer is "love," whatever other sexual meanings can be found in it. Love is Samson's weak point, his Achilles' heel. The story expresses the male's fear of surrendering to a woman. It also recognizes the temptation a woman offers, the male's attraction to her. Samson sees women as desirable but chooses to ignore their danger, even with three chances to learn. Delilah does not betray Samson so much as he betrays himself by telling her the secret of his strength. She does not disguise her intentions. By the fourth time she inquires about Samson's strength, it is clear what she will do with this information. In psychoanalytic terms, if Samson tells her anyway, it can only be because he has a subconscious need to tell her—that is, a subconscious need to give in to woman's sexual power. He needs to prove his love by surrendering something uniquely his, a part of himself—the answer to his riddle (Judg 14), the source of his strength (Judg 16)—something that gives the woman power over him. Surrender is both attractive and dangerous—too dangerous, according to our story, since it threatens a man's distinctness as male and thus his superior status (women are supposed to surrender to men, not the other way around). The text's message to the Israelite male is, "Don't do it!" Women rob men of their strength. The man who surrenders is emasculated; he loses his potency. At another level, this is the male fear of losing the penis to the woman, an anxiety that finds representation in Samson's symbolic castration, which takes place when his hair is cut and he is blinded.

Like the book of Proverbs, this text teaches the Israelite male a lesson about the dangers of foreign women. Nationalism reinforces its gender ideology. Philistines are by definition bad. The reader identifying with the ideology of the text is predisposed to think the worst of women who are allied with them. The women do not have to be specifically identified as foreign women but only to *behave* like foreign women to *be* foreign women and therefore dangerous, capable of robbing a man of his vitality. The text complicates the nature of the male–female relationship by casting it in terms of Israel's relation to foreigners. The only good woman is an Israelite woman, but the text is uneasy about the Israelite woman, for she is good only to the extent that her sexuality is controlled. Thus the only Israelite woman in the story appears in the role of mother. Beneath the apparent, surface distinction between Israelite and foreigner lies the gender issue of nonsexual (and thereby nonthreatening) woman versus sexual (and threatening) woman.

The threat posed by women's sexuality can be reduced by regulating women's behavior. In popular notions of the tale, women are blamed for Samson's downfall, although in the biblical story both the Timnite woman and Delilah act as they do because they are manipulated by the Philistines. Their power over Samson is appropriated by men, in the interests of an androcentric agenda. In teaching its lesson about the danger of women, the text uses the strategies patriarchy has historically relied upon to control women. One is reliance on female fear of male aggression; in other words, by intimidation, as in the case of the Timnite, who tells her countrymen the answer to Samson's riddle because they threaten to set fire to her and her father's house (14:15). The threat of physical harm has traditionally been an effective means by which men control women. But it is not always the most desirable. Often a better way is by reward, as Delilah's example indicates. There are more subtle forms of reward than outright bribery, of course, as Samson's mother illustrates: patriarchy rewards women with honor and status in return for their assent to their subordination and cooperation in it.

The division of women into respectable women and disreputable women also works to regulate female behavior by making gender solidarity impossible. (What might have happened if Samson had brought his wife from Timnah to his parents' house and she had met his mother?) We can now see why Samson is not endangered by the harlot at Gaza (16:1-3) as he is by his wife and by Delilah. The harlot is no threat to the patriarchal system; she already appears in an inferior, subordinate, and carefully regulated role in society. The women to whom men are inclined to make a commitment are the ones they must beware of; Samson gave in because he loved.

The notion that women are not to be trusted enables patriarchy to justify their subjugation. Women, as the account of the Timnite shows, are
easily intimidated and manipulated, and, as Delilah shows, morally defi-
cient. Even Hazzelelponi is not above suspicion. She, after all, does not tell
Manoah the whole message concerning Samson's future. Nor does
Manoah really trust her, since he is not content with her account of the
visitation but prays for the messenger to come "to us" to "teach us" about
the boy. Even though Manoah never gets as much information as
Hazzelelponi about their son's future, he does receive confirmation of
Hazzelelponi's story from the (male) messenger. If the text teaches men a
lesson about the dangers of women and justifies patriarchy's control of
women's sexuality, its lesson to women depends upon women's accepting
its distinction between respectable and disreputable women. The story
encourages women to become lawful and loyal mothers. This is the only
role in which they can achieve status. The only alternative this text offers
to the image of mother is that of the disreputable woman.

In Judges 13–16, the Philistine oppressors are represented by women,
and the oppressed Israelites by Samson. Whereas the narrator wants to see
Israel's situation of oppression reversed, the oppression of women is taken
for granted. Women's subordination to men is, after all, considered to be
the natural state of things. But the recognition in the story that something
is wrong with the structure of power relations between Israelites and
Philistines opens the possibility that other power relations (such as those
between men and women) may also be imbalanced. In order to deny that
this is the case with the position of women and to justify patriarchy, the
narrator portrays women as either esteemed in (Hazzelelponi) or deserving of (the three "foreign women") their inferior status. But the fact that
Samson loses his life in the process of establishing his superior position
over the threat posed by woman's sexuality shows how costly the struggle
to maintain supremacy is.

Bat-shever (Judges 19)

In Judges 19, we meet another unnamed woman, a victim of gang rape
whose anonymity distances the reader by making it harder to view her as
a person in her own right. On the analogy of the name Bat-jiftah, I call
her Bat-shever (daughter of breaking)—a name that recalls her treatment
by the men of Gibeah and her subsequent dismemberment by her husband. In addition to meaning "breaking" or "fracture," the Hebrew word
shever also refers to interpretation in the phrase "breaking of a dream"

(Judg 7:15). Thus the name also signifies the role feminist interpretation plays in breaking open the text's androcentric ideology and exposing the buried and encoded messages it gives to women.

The English translation "concubine" gives the impression that this woman is not legally married, whereas the Hebrew word *pilegesh* refers to a legal wife of secondary rank. According to the Hebrew text of verse 2, the Levite's wife "played the harlot against him." Because the text provides no evidence of sexual misconduct on the woman's part, most translations follow the versions in translating verse 2 as she "became angry with him." This reading also makes more sense in light of what follows in verses 2-3, for it seems unlikely that she would become a prostitute and go to her father's house. It is even more unlikely that the Levite would go after her to bring her back if she had become a prostitute.

But what if the Hebrew phrase means something else altogether? Bat-shever leaves her husband and returns to her father's house. That sounds more like divorce than adultery, but Israelite law did not recognize divorce on the part of a wife. Let us assume, therefore, that Bat-shever's assertion of autonomy is tantamount in the narrator's eyes to an act of harlotry.[28] The concept of "harlot" or "whore" has meaning only within an ideology according to which women's bodies are the property of men. Only women are harlots or whores; if the terms are applied to males it is only in an extended or figurative sense.[29] At issue in Judges 19, then, is male owner-ship of women's bodies, control over women's sexuality. A woman who asserts her sexual autonomy by leaving her husband—and whether or not she remains with him is a sexual issue—is guilty of sexual misconduct. This is the ideology that determines the way gender relations are under-stood and evaluated in this story. In the end, the woman is raped by a mob and dismembered by her own husband. As narrative punishment for her sexual "misconduct," her sexual "freedom," she is sexually abused, after which her sexuality is symbolically mutilated.

It is not clear at what point the woman died or even that she is dead when the Levite dismembers her. Why is the dismemberment, a super-fluous act of violence, necessary? It conveys to women an implicit mes-sage about sexual behavior. By leaving her husband, the woman makes a gesture of sexual autonomy so threatening to patriarchal ideology that it requires her to be punished sexually in the most extreme form. But it is not enough that the woman who has offended sexually, by acting as if she and not the man owned her body, is abused sexually, by having her body possessed by many men. Because it has offended, the woman's sexuality must be destroyed and its threat diffused by scattering. Cut-ting up the woman can be viewed on a psychological level both as an expression of male fear of women's sexuality, which must therefore be destroyed, and as an attempt to discover the secret of woman's sexuality. Because woman is the seductive and dangerous other, her mystery must be opened up by force.[30]

If one man, her husband, cannot possess her, then many men will. But in the end, no one can possess her. What is the husband to do with his damaged goods? He destroys the evidence of the rape in a manner that symbolically repeats it, by sharing the woman's body among men, but that at the same time desexualizes the female body, by dismembering it and scattering the parts. He also destroys the evidence of the crime against the woman by giving a different account of what happened when he offers his testimony to the Israelite assembly.

In this story, the men of Gibeah are portrayed as intending to rape the Levite: "Bring out the man who came into your house, that we may know him" (verse 22). Rape is a crime of violence, not of passion, and the men of Gibeah want to humiliate the Levite in the most degrading way, by forcing him into a passive role, into the woman's position. But instead of the man, they get a woman. Moreover, they are offered two women, and get only one. Since they could easily overpower the host and his guests, why do they settle for only Bat-shever? I believe two impulses are at work here: male-male rape is too threatening to narrate, and, in terms of the gender-motivated subtext, it would leave the woman unpunished. The narrative possibility of the Levite's rape by the mob is therefore abandoned. How are we to explain the fact that, although both Bat-shever and the host's daughter are offered to the mob, only Bat-shever is thrown out? If we understand Bat-shever's abuse as her narrative punishment, then the sparing of the virgin daughter makes sense: she is not mistreated because, unlike Bat-shever, she has not committed a sexual offense against male authority. Decoded, the message the story of Bat-shever gives to women is that any claim to sexual autonomy (presented as unfaithfulness or misconduct) has horrendous consequences. Male violence is something every woman fears. The best defense is, stay out of the way; maybe you won't be noticed. The survival of the host's daughter illustrates that sometimes this stratagem works.

In cases of rape, the issue of the woman's responsibility is often raised. Why was she dressed like that? What was she doing alone at night in that neighborhood? Had Bet-shever stayed in her place, under her husband's authority where she belonged, she would not have ended up at the wrong place—Gibeah of Benjamin—at the wrong time. By insinuating that women, by the way they behave, are responsible for male sexual aggression, the narrator relies on a fundamental patriarchal strategy for exercising social control over women. Using women's fear of male violence as a means of regulating female behavior is one of patriarchy's most powerful weapons. And it remains effective. If the message to women encoded in the story of Jephthah's daughter was: yield to the paternal word and you will be remembered and celebrated for generations to come; and that of the Samson story was: there are only two kinds of women, and you don't want to be the wrong kind; the message in Judges 19 is a cautionary one: if you do anything that even remotely suggests improper sexual behavior, you invite male aggression.

Do the crimes against Bat-shever go unpunished? The other Israelite tribes go to war against Benjamin (the tribe to which Gibeah belongs) to avenge crimes against a man and his property. Notice that they do not know what we know; they have only the Levite's account of events in Gibeah (Judg 20:4-7), and his version is different from the earlier account of the horrible crimes against the woman, both the gang rape and the dismemberment. The Benjaminites are punished for siding with the rapists and would-be murderers. The mutilation of the woman's body by the Levite, in contrast, is neither redressed nor explicitly censured. The fate of her dismembered body seems to be forgotten as intertribal warfare breaks out. This does not mean that the mutilation is unproblematic, however. After the Levite dismembers Bat-shever and sends the parts of her body throughout Israelite territory, we read: "All who saw it said, 'Such a thing has never happened or been seen from the day that the people of Israel came up out of the land of Egypt until this day; consider it, take counsel, and speak'" (Judg 19:30). What is meant by "such a thing" that has never happened or been seen before? Since only later does the Levite tell the tribes what happened at Gibeah, "such a thing" can only refer to the dismemberment and parceling out of the woman's body. When the tribes assemble at Mizpah, they ask the Levite: "Tell us, how did this evil come to pass?" (20:3). Here, too, the only obvious referent for "this evil" is the dismemberment. These oblique references hint at some lingering guilt on the narrator's part about the dismemberment, and we may view these signs of his dis-ease as evidence of a guilty narrative conscience.

In three days of fighting, the Israelites kill all but six hundred Benjaminite men. They also kill noncombatants, including all the Benjaminite women, when they destroy the Benjaminite towns. When they realize that they have almost wiped out an entire Israelite tribe, they have a change of heart. To rebuild the tribe of Benjamin, wives are needed for the surviving Benjaminite men, but because the other Israelites have sworn not to give their daughters in marriage to the Benjaminites, they procure wives for these men by destroying the town of Jabesh-Gilead, killing all the men and all the women except for four hundred young women who are virgins. These adolescents, spoils of war like the rape victims mentioned in Deborah's Song (Judg 5:30), are "awarded" to the Benjaminite men and forced to become their wives. The sexual violence does not end here. Because still more wives are needed for the Benjaminite men, the Israelites commission them to capture wives from the dancers in the yearly festival at Shiloh. As the book of Judges draws to a close, male violence reinscribes the story of female violation, with Israelite men repeating on a mass scale the crimes of the men of Gibeah.

FEAR OF AND VIOLENCE AGAINST WOMEN

What do the stories we have examined have in common? In one way or another, they all betray a fear of women and of women's sexuality, and they are all aimed at circumscribing and controlling women's behavior. Women in biblical times were under the control of men—fathers, husbands, brothers—and these stories justify and inscribe women's subordination to male authority. One of the few roles in which women could achieve status was that of mother. Much as patriarchy might like to represent itself as natural and necessary, it cannot conceal the traces of its anxieties and inherent contradictions. The story of Deborah/Jael unsettles the patriarchal ideal of the mother as nurturing and self-sacrificing by recognizing the mother's threatening side. The mother cannot be controlled. The power of the mother is patriarchy's Achilles' heel.

Something else our stories have in common is violence. Fear of women's sexuality leads to violence against women as a means of control. According to Andrea Dworkin, men become advocates of violence in order to master their fear of violence. They *do* violence in order not to be victimized by it, in order not to be weak and powerless like women.[31] One of the ways men deny their responsibility for violence is by scapegoating women, blaming women for violence of which they are the victims. We can see this tactic at work in the texts we have examined. But the violence unleashed against Bat-shever is not her fault, anymore than it was Bat-jiftah's fault (as Jephthah implies) that she became the sacrificial victim, or the Timnite woman's fault that the Philistines retaliated against her when Samson burned their fields, or Delilah's fault that Samson was captured by the Philistines (he didn't *have* to tell her his secret). Attention to the gender politics of Judges enables us to expose the phenomenon of scapegoating women for what it is: a strategy patriarchy uses to avoid facing and having to deal with its own violent legacy.

In the book of Judges, violence against women is part of the larger problem of social and moral decay in Israel. The breakdown of social and moral order is presented as if the gender of the victims of violence were irrelevant. Yet the fact that the final illustration of Israel's descent into lawlessness is the gang rape and dismemberment of a woman calls attention to the role gender plays, on a deeper level, in the presentation. And the book ends with women, again, the objects of male violence. Only recently have we begun to distinguish ethnically or racially motivated violence from other kinds of violence. That violence is also gender-motivated may soon become not just something we know but a legal issue as well. Exposing gender-motivated violence in a biblical text is, of course, far removed from the real-life issue. But recognizing gender-motivated violence, even in a biblical text—and perhaps especially in a biblical text, because of the Bible's continuing influence on our society— is a contribution feminist biblical criticism can make to the work of feminism as a political enterprise.

FURTHER READING

General

Bach, Alice. *Religion, Politics, Media in the Broadband Era.* Sheffield: Sheffield Phoenix Press, 2004. A thought-provoking, accessible study of the Bible and religion in contemporary American society. One chapter discusses the story of the Levite's wife in Judges 19–21 in the context of contemporary violence.

Bird, Phyllis. *Missing Persons and Mistaken Identities: Women and Gender in Ancient Israel.* Minneapolis: Fortress Press, 1997. A collection of influential articles, written over a period of more than twenty years, dealing with various facets of women's roles in the Bible and in ancient Israelite society.

Camp, Claudia V., and Carole R. Fontaine, eds. *Women, War, and Metaphor: Language and Society in the Study of the Hebrew Bible. Semeia* 61 (1993). Articles in this collection treat the relationships of images of women and war, a topic particularly relevant to the study of Judges in view of its representation of warfare and violence against women. An essay by Gale A. Yee deals with Judges 4; Alice A. Keefe deals with Judges 19; and there are scattered references to Judges throughout the volume.

Exum, J. Cheryl. *Plotted, Shot, and Painted: Cultural Representations of Biblical Women.* Sheffield: Sheffield Academic Press, 1996. A chapter on Delilah looks at her cultural afterlives, noting the way the biblical ideology is reinscribed in retellings of the story of Samson and Delilah in literature, music, and art. Other chapters discuss Bathsheba, Michal, Ruth, the women of the exodus, and prophetic pornography.

Fuchs, Esther. *Sexual Politics in the Biblical Narrative: Reading the Hebrew Bible as a Woman.* Sheffield: Sheffield Academic Press, 2000. Indispensable reading for anyone interested in feminist biblical criticism. Stories of mothers, brides, wives, daughters, and sisters are analyzed, including, from the book of Judges, Jephthah's daughter, Samson's mother, and the Levite's wife in Judges 19.

Lerner, Gerda. *The Creation of Patriarchy.* Oxford: Oxford University Press, 1986. Investigates the origins of patriarchy and women's complicity in it. Impressive in its scope and breadth, it begins with the origins of civilization and traces the development of patriarchy (as social system and ideology) through the biblical and classical Greek periods. There is also a second volume, *The Creation of Feminist Consciousness from the Middle Ages to Eighteen-Seventy.* Oxford: Oxford University Press, 1993.

McKinlay, Judith E. *Reframing Her: Biblical Women in Postcolonial Focus.* Sheffield: Sheffield Phoenix Press, 2004. A trenchant feminist and postcolonial reading and an outstanding example of the influence of a reader's social location on interpretation.

Schroer, Silvia, and Sophia Bietenhard, eds. *Feminist Interpretation of the Bible and the Hermeneutics of Liberation.* Sheffield: Sheffield Academic Press, 2003. Articles in this collection provide a good introduction to biblical interpretation in global perspective.

Vander Stichele, Caroline, and Todd Penner, eds. *Her Master's Tools? Feminist and Postcolonial Engagements of Historical-Critical Discourse.* Atlanta: Society of Biblical Literature, 2005. Articles in this volume reflect multiple postmodern positions and illustrate ways postcolonial criticism is shaping the feminist agenda.

Feminist Criticism of Judges

Ackerman, Susan. *Warrior, Dancer, Seductress, Queen: Women in Judges and Biblical Israel.* New York: Doubleday, 1998. Analyzes different roles played by women in Judges and related texts and the place such "types" played in ancient Israelite religion.

Bal, Mieke. *Death and Dissymmetry: The Politics of Coherence in the Book of Judges.* Chicago: University of Chicago Press, 1988. A brilliant counterreading of Judges in terms of its gender-bound violence and the social revolution that gives rise to it. Daughters who are the victims of male violence (Jephthah's daughter, Samson's wife, and the Levite's wife—called Bath, Kallah, and Beth) are avenged by Jael, the Woman-with-the-Millstone, and Delilah, symbolizing the displaced mother. Not readily accessible to beginners, but worth the effort.

———. *Lethal Love: Feminist Literary Readings of Biblical Love Stories.* Bloomington: Indiana University Press, 1987. Contains a provocative psychoanalytic reading of the story of Samson and Delilah; also treated are Bathsheba, Ruth, Tamar, and Eve. A good point of entry into Bal's work.

————. *Murder and Difference: Gender, Genre, and Scholarship on Sisera's Death.* Trans. Matthew Gumpert. Bloomington: Indiana University Press, 1988. Discusses the Deborah/Jael story in terms of differences between the "masculine" prose account in Judges 4 and the "feminine" song in Judges 5, and criticizes the way commentators read sexual stereotypes and their own gender biases into the biblical literature.

Brenner, Athalya, ed. *A Feminist Companion to Judges.* The Feminist Companion to the Bible 4. Sheffield: JSOT Press, 1993. *Judges: A Feminist Companion to the Bible (Second Series).* Sheffield: Sheffield Academic Press, 1999. Collections of articles, some previously published, dealing with Judges from a range of feminist perspectives.

Exum, J. Cheryl. *Fragmented Women: Feminist (Sub)versions of Biblical Narratives.* Sheffield: Sheffield Academic Press; Valley Forge: Trinity Press International, 1993. Asking what androcentric interests these stories promote, one chapter deals with the women in the Samson story; another reads the story of Jephthah's daughter against that of David's wife, Michal; another reads the Levite's wife against Bathsheba. Other chapters discuss Sarah, Rebekah, Rachel, and Leah.

Fewell, Danna Nolan. "Judges." In *The Women's Bible Commentary.* Edited by Carol A. Newsom and Sharon H. Ringe, 67–77. Louisville: Westminster John Knox, 1992. A survey of the book of Judges concentrating on the women characters.

Thompson, John L. *Writing the Wrongs: Women of the Old Testament among Biblical Commentators from Philo through the Reformation.* Oxford: Oxford University Press, 2001. A fascinating survey of the way early Jewish and Christian interpreters dealt with the stories of biblical women. One chapter deals with Jephthah's daughter; another, with the Levite's wife and the host's virgin daughter in Judges 19, together with Lot's daughters. The other biblical woman considered is Hagar.

5

STRUCTURALIST CRITICISM

The Text's World of Meaning

DAVID JOBLING

"Structuralism is a philosophical view according to which the reality of the objects of the human or social sciences is relational rather than substantial."[1] This definition indicates the wide scope of structuralism's claim—to offer the most appropriate orientation to all the fields of study having to do with human individuals and societies. But it is also very open-ended, suggesting that the many efforts to define structuralism more precisely are unhelpful or even wrong.

According to this view, we do not come to terms with the world of experience as a set of isolated items, but as a set of relationships among items. It is the recognition of these relationships that makes the world intelligible. Our minds develop through the awareness of these relationships (so that it is not possible to say whether the relationships are "in" the world or "in" our minds—they are at once the condition and the developing product of our mental activity).[2] All the products of human minds, including literary texts, express meaning through the structured patterning of the elements of which they are made. Structural analysis of texts is the process of moving from their perceived patterning to the "messages" they carry. The patterning need not represent the conscious intention of the producer of the text; indeed, the linguistic analogy to which I shall turn in a moment suggests that it probably does not. And the patterning *I* find in a text is at the same time something my individual mind has *achieved,* and it will not be identical to what anyone else finds.

I shall return to the implications of these critical issues, and to the question of where structuralism is located on the map of biblical methods (see below, "Structuralism and Criticism"). First, I shall review the development of literary and biblical structuralism, with illustrative examples taken, when possible, from work on Judges. I shall not offer a comprehensive proposal for how to do structural analysis—how to get from text to message—although I shall make reference to some such proposals and try to put them into a framework that will enable the reader to understand and use them critically.

THE ANALOGY OF LANGUAGE

We sometimes ask of a text, "What is it trying to say?" This seems an odd question—presumably, what it is trying to say is what it says. Yet we do ask the question, which suggests that we perceive a "message" in the text different from the words themselves, a message for which the text is, perhaps, only one possible vehicle. We may even, paradoxically, sense a "message" in the text that the text does not clearly or fully convey; we think we know what it's "getting at," even when this isn't identical to what it says! What is the nature of this peculiar relationship of text to meaning?

Structuralism deals with these questions by analogy with ordinary language as it is studied in the science of linguistics. It is with linguistics that structuralism began, and this is where we must begin in trying to understand it. We must put aside for the moment issues having to do with an extended *text* like Judges, for linguistics works primarily with language on a much smaller scale—from the smallest units of sound (phonemes) up to the level of the sentence.

Suppose, in a conversation, I speak an English sentence to another person, and she accepts it, and responds. By "accepts," I do not mean she agrees with what I say, simply that she recognizes my sentence as a properly formed English sentence. What has happened here? Something very complex and, on both our parts, mostly unconscious. It is not on the basis of experience or memory that I speak or that she understands. In all likelihood, neither of us ever spoke or heard that identical sentence; indeed, it may never before have been spoken or written by anyone. Yet my interlocutor dealt with it easily as I pronounced it.

We were both, quite unconsciously, drawing on our knowledge of English. But what exactly is "English"? It consists of a vast *system* of relationships among English words, some relationships having to do with differences of meaning, other relationships having to do with correct word order.[3] It is by reference to this system that both I and my hearer measure the correctness of my sentence. But there are some odd facts about this system. First, I need no *conscious* awareness of it in order to speak or understand English. For instance, English speakers who couldn't say what a noun or an adjective is still put adjectives in front of nouns, as English syntax requires, rather than behind them. Second, the system has no existence separate from the real sentences that people produce. Books may attempt to describe the system; academies may exist (as in France) to try to preserve its "purity." But the books and the academies have no independent measuring-rod of what is acceptable—they simply distill into abstract terms what the speakers of the language *deem* acceptable.

Structural linguistics began in the early part of the twentieth century with the work of the Swiss linguist, Ferdinand de Saussure,[4] and the issue just raised was expressed by him as an opposition between *parole,* the actual utterance, and *langue,* the mysterious underlying system.[5] A second key opposition in Saussure is that between two kinds of linguistics, two ways of studying language. *Synchronic* linguistics imagines *langue* as frozen at a particular moment in time, and consisting of all the relationships existing between elements of the language at that moment; *diachronic* linguistics study the change in language over time. Saussure demanded that linguistics be basically synchronic; the development of language over time he regarded as unimportant compared with its systemic character at a given moment.

A third fundamental aspect of Saussure's linguistics requires lengthier presentation, namely, that language is a system of *relationships* rather than of fixed terms. Words have a relationship to objective reality, but that does not mean that there is anything in objective reality that guarantees *the* meaning of any given word. Rather, the whole vocabulary of a language is available to come to terms with reality in complex and shifting ways. A given word is defined by what *differentiates* it from related words. The word "house" has a nice objective sound to it; but someone seeking specificity as to size or location might prefer, for the same object, "mansion" or "cottage," while someone thinking of function might prefer "home." The introduction into the language of some new word, like "condominium," may signal less a new reality than a reorganization of the words used for existing things. The most obvious way of making the point is to note that when we go to the dictionary to find the meaning of a word, all we find are other words (whose meanings can be expressed only in yet other words). Meaning lies entirely in relationship, in the unstable system of differences between related words. This does not deter us from consulting dictionaries, or from being satisfied, for practical purposes, with the "meanings" we find there; for we are used to working with language as a system of differences, rather than of fixed terms, even if we are not aware that this is what we are doing. But if we ask ourselves what the "meaning" of a word really is, we cannot do better than to say that it is "that for which the majority of the linguistic community does not prefer some other word"!

With this summary of structural linguistics, we return to our main concern, which is literary texts. Literary structuralism depends on the possibility of drawing an analogy between the text and the linguistic sentence. The analogy has to cover the three Saussurean emphases we have identified. First, by analogy with *parole/langue,* the text will have to be seen as a particular "utterance" generated out of a system of *possible* utterances that its producer, as a member of her group, has unconsciously internalized. Second, in terms of the synchronic/diachronic opposition, the text will have to be studied primarily not as the result of a process of development (which is how the historical-critical methods mostly look at biblical texts), but as part of a *system* that links it to other texts, and that links its own different parts to each other. Third, the text will have to be examined as having meaning not in itself, but in relation to other texts, in the structured *differences* between it and them.

THE MAIN TRADITION OF BIBLICAL STRUCTURALISM

After Saussure, the figures whose theories have most shaped biblical structuralism are Vladimir Propp, Claude Lévi-Strauss, and A. J. Greimas. In presenting the main features of their work, my intention is not to offer a history of great structuralists. These three names are merely foci for larger discussions of which they were a part. What is important is to identify the questions that, as a result of these discussions, we have learned to put to biblical texts.

Vladimir Propp and the Russian Fairy Tale

Propp was a Russian folklorist whose major work was *Morphology of the Folktale* (1928).[6] In it he examined a hundred Russian fairy tales to discover what they had in common at the levels of character and plot. His most productive suggestion had to do with plot structure; he claimed that all the stories could be reduced to thirty-one story elements, which he called "functions." The first of these are:

I.   One of the members of a family absents himself from home.
II.   An interdiction is addressed to the hero.
III.   The interdiction is violated.
IV.   The villain makes an attempt at reconnaissance.

And so on through:

XXIX.   The hero is given a new appearance.
XXX.   The villain is punished.
XXXI.   The hero is married and ascends the throne.

These functions can be grouped in a way that indicates the broad structure of the tale:

> Setting the stage for the main actions (I–VII)
> The "villainy" or lack that disturbs the status quo (VIII)
> The finding, equipping, and journey of the hero (IX–XV)
> The "combat" in which the hero overcomes the villain or the lack (XVI–XIX)
> Events of the hero's return journey (XX–XXII)
> The recognition and glorification of the hero (XXIII–XXXI)

Propp's major discovery was that although no one fairy tale contains (or could contain) all thirty-one functions, *the ones that a given tale does include are always in the given order.* This finding supports the analogy between the literary text and the linguistic sentence. At least in the case of Russian fairy tales, there seem to be rules of "syntax" for acceptable stories, analogous to rules for word order in English. The storytellers and hearers are applying these rules, unconsciously internalized, in their telling and hearing. The analyst can discover things about the underlying "system," the *langue* of Russian fairy tales; but this, like the system of language itself, has no other existence than in the individual stories, the *paroles*.

Propp implies that a large group of tales all tell, in different ways, the "same" story. For example, in the very common type of the "seeker" hero, the normal working of a society is in some way disrupted. To deal with the disruption, the hero must be separated from the society, part of whose resources must be diverted to equip him for what he must do.[7] The hero overcomes the villainy or lack, but this does not end the story. In order for the society to resume its normal working, the hero must be reintegrated into it, and this proves far from easy (for example, the returning hero often has difficulty being *recognized* by his own society). But reintegrated he eventually is, usually by his marriage. The social importance of this message is not hard to appreciate, and the society repeats it over and over in all its stories of this type.

The book of Judges provides a case unique in the Bible of a series of stories that have a common structure. This structure appears most concisely in 3:7-11, the account of the judge Othniel:

1. "The Israelites did what was evil in the sight of Yahweh" (3:7).
2. Yahweh in anger gave them into the power of an enemy (3:8).
3. "The Israelites cried out to Yahweh" (3:9a).
4. "Yahweh raised up a deliverer for the Israelites" (3:9b).
5. The deliverer with Yahweh's aid defeated the enemy (3:10).
6. "The land had rest" during the rest of the deliverer's life (3:11).

Immediately upon the death of Othniel, a new cycle begins, and the same pattern can be traced through the longer story of Ehud (3:12-30). Indeed, nearly all the material through Judges 16 can be fitted into the same pattern, and scholars refer to the "judge-cycles" of Othniel, Ehud, Deborah, Gideon, Jephthah, and Samson.[8] Is the point of the series to instill a single message by repetition, as Propp perceived his fairy tales to do?

An application to Judges of a method related to Propp's is found in Robert Culley's *Themes and Variations*.[9] Culley identifies in biblical narrative nine "action sequences" (having to do with rescue, prohibition, etc.) that could just as well be thought of as pairs of "functions" in Propp's sense.[10] In his section on Judges, Culley shows how each cycle is based on two obligatory action sequences; a WRONG → PUNISHED sequence, dealing with Israel's apostasy against God and the punishment, and a DIFFI-CULTY → RESCUED sequence, dealing with Israel's servitude to a foreign oppressor and the deliverance.[11] Within this necessary framework, the different stories make use of other sequences in various combinations, but only sequences of one of two types: TASK → ACCOMPLISHED (e.g., in Judges 4, Barak's commission to muster Israel's army) and ANNOUNCEMENT → HAPPENED (e.g., Deborah's prediction that a woman will get the glory from this campaign). Culley makes the further observation that, from the Gideon cycle onward, *all* of these elements get more and more incorporated into a quite different and more complex kind of sequence, which he calls the "life story." As his title suggests, Culley wants to strike a balance between what is common to the judge-cycles and how they differ. The differences are considerable; in particular, there is much tension between the "life-story" pattern and the action sequences. But in his desire to give adequate attention to the common pattern, Culley works in the spirit of Propp.

The best analogy to Propp is to be found, however, in the work of the biblical narrator (often called the Deuteronomist), for this narrator has provided, as a prelude to the judge-cycles, a "theoretical" statement of the meaning that all the stories will share! This statement is found in Judges 2:11-19, and refers not to *particular* events but to what would happen *repeatedly* in a series of situations involving different judges. The Deuteronomist thought of the stories of the judges, as Propp thought of his fairy tales, as repetitions of the "same" story

From Propp we have learned to ask, What constant patterns can we find in different stories, and what is the significance of these patterns?

Claude Lévi-Strauss and the Structural Analysis of Myth

The individual most responsible for the emergence of an interdisciplinary structuralist movement in the twentieth century is the French anthropologist Claude Lévi-Strauss, whose major work belongs to the period after World War II. He argues that each of the various activities of a society can be understood as a sort of language, and analyzed by techniques analogous to Saussure's linguistics. For example, kinship rules (which attain a fantastic complexity in societies termed "primitive") form a system in which permissible marriages are analogous to "proper" sentences in language, and forbidden marriages are like wrongly formed sentences.[12]

Much of Lévi-Strauss's anthropological work has no direct relation to our main concern, *literary* structuralism.[13] But his most important accomplishment *does* consist in reading texts, albeit texts of a very special kind, namely, transcriptions of Amerindian mythology. This work can perhaps best be introduced by referring to Lévi-Strauss's critique of Propp. When Propp's work was translated into French in the 1950s, Lévi-Strauss wrote one of the first reviews, in which (as well as expressing great admiration) he complained that Propp locates the meaning of his tales in what they have *in common* rather than in their differences.[14] He considers a group of story-fragments adduced by Propp (here slightly simplified):

1. A king gives the hero an eagle, which carries him away to another kingdom.
2. An old man gives the hero a horse, which carries him away to another kingdom.
3. A sorcerer gives the hero a little boat, which carries him away to another kingdom.[15]

The latter part of each sentence is the same, but the first parts differ. Propp's suggestion is that the roles played by the king/old man/sorcerer, on the one hand, or by the eagle/horse/boat, on the other, are empty categories ("donor," "magic agent") into which anything plausible can be put, so as to tell the "same" story over and over. Based on his work on myth, Lévi-Strauss suggests, on the contrary, that what a culture produces is *sets* of parallel stories in which the differences are as important as the parallels, because it is through these stories that the society comes to terms with its experience of similarity and difference in the world. He notes how, in the myths of the Americas, different birds—for example, eagle, owl, raven—appear in parallel stories. Propp would see these myths as equivalent, but Lévi-Strauss wants to probe the differences. Using a method based on Saussure's, he analyzes the differences into *binary oppositions*— eagle versus owl constitutes the opposition between the categories of "day" and "night," for example, while eagle/owl versus raven constitutes the opposition between "hunting" and "scavenging."[16] Applying this method to Propp's group of "magic agents" (eagle, horse, boat) suggests the oppositions animate versus inanimate, and, within the animate, earth versus air. The critical question would then be whether there is any linkage between the particular magic agent in a given tale and the corresponding "donor" (king, old man, sorcerer). Lévi-Strauss would claim that there are indeed such linkages, that within the mythic or folktale stock of a given culture, a change in one variable will be linked to changes in others (which may therefore be termed "covariable").

But to work out the system one needs a very large sample of stories. In his own major work on myth, Lévi-Strauss studies more than eight hundred Amerindian myths as they appear in around two thousand known transcriptions.[17] The extreme complexity of the oppositions that he finds operating in this vast corpus admits of no summary, but a small example, from near the beginning of the analysis, may be given.[18] Certain South American Indians have two theories about the origin of fire—that it was stolen from the jaguar, or that it was learned from the monkey. The first theory stresses the *difference* between the human and the nonhuman: the gaining of fire is part of a human conquest of the nonhuman world. The second theory stresses the *similarity* of the human to the nonhuman: the gaining of fire depends on human likeness to one kind of animals, monkeys. These theories generate (in Lévi-Strauss's analysis) two parallel sets of myths in which the protagonists are, respectively, jaguars and monkeys, and jaguars and humans. In these sets, "jaguars" is a constant, while "monkeys" or "humans" is a variable, and the choice of monkeys or humans entails a number of other choices between other pairs of variables (for example, in one myth a jaguar opens its mouth to swallow a monkey, while in a parallel myth a jaguar closes its mouth to avoid swallowing a human). One achievement of the parallel myths is to set monkeys and humans in extreme contrast, in order to counteract the uncomfortable sense of their closeness.

Some of the most stimulating biblical readings based on Lévi-Strauss's methods are those of the British anthropologist Edmund Leach. None of his major readings concentrates on Judges, but he does devote a few pages of a general theoretical lecture to Judges 19–21.[19] These chapters, according to Leach, function as a way to deal with an opposition between Gibeah and Bethlehem, the hometowns of Saul and David, Israel's first two kings, and by extension with the opposition between the two kings themselves. Judges 19, the story of the Levite's "concubine,"[20] moves from Bethlehem (the woman's home) to Gibeah (the scene of the outrage). This incident, notes Leach, leads to the rise of Saul: in Judges 21, all the men of Jabesh-Gilead are exterminated so that their virgin women can become wives to the male Benjaminite survivors of the war that followed the outrage, and it is presumably from one of these unions that Saul, a Benjaminite from Gibeah, emerges. Saul's first major act is to rescue the people of Jabesh-Gilead (who have somehow recovered from their extermination; 1 Sam 11). When Saul is killed (opening the way for David), it is the men of Jabesh-Gilead who rescue his body from Philistine outrage (1 Sam 31), and David commends them for this act (2 Sam 2:4-7). As soon as the remnants of Saul's house have been killed, David takes Saul's bones from Jabesh-Gilead and restores them to Gibeah (2 Sam 21:1-14), and this final incident in the saga is followed immediately by a reference to a Bethlehemite slayer of Goliath (21:19). Leach summarizes:

> Overall, the men of Jabesh-Gilead play a complementary role to the Levite's concubine. The latter takes the story away from Bethlehem in a context of fragmentation; the former brings [*sic*] it back again in a context of reunification.[21]

This analysis is, as Leach notes, much too brief and sketchy. Yet it is hard to doubt, however one feels about the particulars of the analysis, that he is onto something. The complex interplay in a series of passages in Judges and Samuel around the locations of Bethlehem, Gibeah, and Jabesh-Gilead demands some sort of explanation, and Leach has been able to pull the elements together. But his general attitude to the Bible is controversial, for he considers all biblical stories to be *myth,* and believes that they should be analyzed "without consideration of the order in which they appear," that is, like a jumble of mythic fragments.[22]

From Lévi-Strauss we have learned to ask: What is the significance of differences within similarities? Why are similar stories told with different protagonists? What are the fundamental (binary) oppositions with which the set of stories is working, and why are these oppositions so critical?

A.J. Greimas and Structural Narratology

Perhaps even more influential than Lévi-Strauss on the structural analysis of biblical narrative has been another French thinker, A. J. Greimas. Greimas continues and deepens Propp's impulse to formulate rules for how texts are structured. But he goes far beyond Propp's concentration on a particular class of texts, seeking to posit models that apply to narrative in general. Finding Propp very imprecise methodologically, he turns to Saussure, Lévi-Strauss, and others for rigor of method, and his approach is based on the linguistic paradigm. Here, I concentrate on two well-known models proposed by Greimas, to indicate their flexibility and breadth of application.

The first is the *actantial model.*[23] Anything that happens in a story, from the action of the story as a whole to some very tiny piece of action within it (even action that is contemplated or intended, without actually occurring) can be mapped onto the following grid:

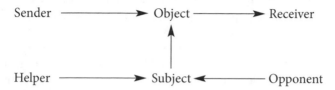

The *sender* is the one who initiates the action, with the purpose of transferring some *object* to a *receiver*. The action is to be carried out by the *subject*, who is aided and/or opposed in this by *helpers* and *opponents*, respectively. Thus, for "Little Red Riding Hood," we have the following pattern:

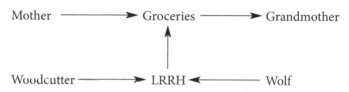

However, it is unusual for the characters in a story to line up so conveniently, one to each category. Sometimes more than one character can occupy the same slot, and a character can even occupy more than one slot. The roles of "helper" and "opponent" are not always filled. The pattern for "The Three Billy Goats Gruff," for example, is:

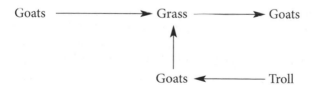

Such a model is of enormous generality, and may seem no more than a matter of common sense. Yet the roles in a story may be far from obvious to a superficial view, and deep insight can develop from trying to work out what they really are. I do not know of any creative application of the actantial model to a Judges text, but it has had an impact on the study of the book of Genesis. In one of the earliest of all structural analyses of the Bible, the French critic Roland Barthes applies the model to Jacob's wrestling with the angel in Genesis 32.[24] He concludes that a single actor, God, occupies in this story the roles of both sender and opponent. Barthes regards this situation as very rare, and suggests that the only type of story for which it is characteristic is stories about *blackmail!*[25] For biblical theology, this is a startling possibility, especially since the same pattern of divine activity has been posited in another major Genesis story, the account of the Garden of Eden in Genesis 2–3.[26]

Because of some theoretical problems, Greimas rejected the actantial model from his mature system.[27] It should be used only as a handy tool, and conclusions should not be based on it alone. It is included here because it exemplifies structuralist procedure in a particularly simple way. More important is another of his contributions, the *semiotic square:*[28]

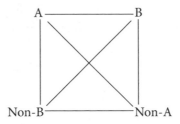

A and B are any two items felt to be opposites, for example, "hot" and "cold." Their relationship is called *contrary.* Non-A is "whatever is not hot," and its relation to A is called *contradictory* (likewise B and non-B). The vertical relations of non-A to B and of non-B to A are called relations of *implication.* That something is cold implies at least that it belongs to the class of things that are not hot. Hence B implies non-A (though the opposite is not necessarily the case), and likewise A implies non-B.

If the categories A and B cover all possibilities, then the square is trivial. For example, if we have a two-way switch and call "on" A and "off" B, then B and non-A, "off" and "not on," are exactly the same thing. But the example of hot and cold, trivial as it is, shows that things are not always so simple. The very existence of a term like "lukewarm" implies that when we talk of things being hot or cold, there are some things that are *both* not hot *and* not cold. If we knew exactly what we meant by "hot"—for example, "hot enough to burn skin"—everything would be hot or cold. But, as I have already indicated in discussing language, we *do* and *must* use words without knowing exactly what we mean by them!

Some of the binary oppositions identified by Lévi-Strauss in myths provide useful illustrations. For example, let A and B be "life" and "death." What would non-A, "non-life," be? It seems a very broad category, which might include both inanimate things and things that once were living but now are dead. But there are entirely different ways of thinking of the "non-life" category that lead to new possibilities of meaning. One possibility is to include in this category whatever is not *conducive* to life, and this is what seems to happen in certain mythic transformations in which "war" stands for non-life, and "agriculture" for non-death.[29]

The square becomes even more fruitful when we begin to define complex terms that combine more than one of the corner positions.[30] Combining the two right corners, for example, we ask, "What is both B and non-A?"; combining the bottom two, "What is both non-A and non-B?" Greimas offers an example concerning how we respond to propositions ("God is omniscient," or "It's a nice day").[31] A is "affirm"—we agree that the proposition is true; B is "refuse"—we deny its truth. Non-A is "doubt," which takes in the whole realm of things we do not specifically affirm, while non-B, similarly, is "admit," covering all the things we do not specifically refuse. The combination of A and B (affirm and refuse) implies a *legalistic* society, one that wants to be definite about everything, while the combination of non-A and non-B (doubt and admit) is *libertarian,* both skeptical and open. The combinations on the left and right axes suggest *optimism* (affirm and admit) and *pessimism* (refuse and doubt). This would open the possibility of analyzing real human societies as libertarian/pessimistic, or whatever. Greimas's square may be expanded to include the complex terms, as follows:

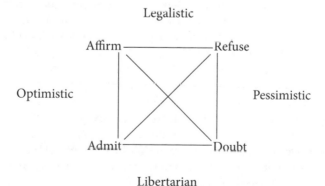

provide useful illustrations.

Greimas's influence on biblical studies is largely owing to the work of Daniel Patte, who is both a member of Greimas's circle and an American New Testament scholar. Patte has provided the most pedagogically helpful model, based on Greimas, for the structural analysis of biblical texts.[32]

From Greimas we have learned to ask: What general models are useful in analyzing the great variety of existing or possible literary texts? How general can we make the models before we encounter diminishing returns in the understanding of particular texts?

STRUCTURALISM AND CRITICISM

Structuralism has ceased to be a fashionable current in biblical or in general literary criticism. It is held by many to be passé, to have been overtaken by new currents, those of "poststructuralism." According to this account, some of the major figures who were active during the time that structuralism was in fashion were able to move in profitable new directions, while others, notably Greimas, continued to try to mine a spent deposit.[33]

Structuralism is criticized on many counts. Some of the criticisms are valid and necessary, but others are based on a stereotypical view of structuralism that needs to be challenged. My account will be based on that of Peter Caws, whose definition of structuralism I quoted at the outset. Caws argues that structuralism is well able to defend itself against its critics, but only on the condition that it become much more *self*-critical. If it does so, it will resume its place as an essential element in the current discussions out of which the other chapters of this book emerge.

One complaint against structuralism is that it tries to imitate the methods of the *natural sciences,* seeing its models for the analysis of texts as "natural laws" objectively valid for all texts, or at least all texts of a certain kind;[34] also that, in pursuit of this quest, it generates a mass of unnecessary quasi-scientific jargon. In this kind of structuralism, the text becomes just an example of general laws, leaving no place for subjectivity and the active role of the reader.[35] Another complaint is that, in its insistence on a synchronic view of the text, structuralism is *ahistorical and antimaterialist,* positing timeless structures that take no account of the text's belonging to a particular set of historical circumstances, and seeking to abstract from the text's material context patterns that have no material existence. Finally, structuralism is seen as *positivistic,* suggesting that there is a single "right" answer to the problems of the text, and as claiming that its view is *the* comprehensive one, able to account for all rival views and go beyond them.[36]

This is indeed a formidable catalog of alleged errors! Caws does not minimize the problems of structuralism, but claims nonetheless that it offers a major new option for understanding the human and social sciences, and that it has not been given anything like an adequate chance to show its potential. He sees the rejection of it as due more to the vagaries of academic fashion than to careful consideration of its claim to provide a new explanation of the fundamental fact that human beings find the world intelligible.

But structuralism must stop indulging in "megalomaniac pretensions" of being able to create models that are universally valid.[37] The mind's work of discovering patterns in experienced reality begins with what is immediately presented to it, with what is close at hand, and structuralism too should therefore concern itself first with small-scale and local intelligibility. Similarly, structuralism's concern is with the *material,* for the mind must begin with what is materially present to it. To understand this point, recall the difference between Propp and Lévi-Strauss. Where Propp wanted to turn things like eagles, horses, and boats into mere instances of general categories, Lévi-Strauss insists on their material differences, differences that exist in the mind's perception of the material world—in this case connections with air, earth, and water. It is true that abstract models are part of the mind's—and of structuralism's—way of working, but they have no reality in separation from the material world. For example, Greimas's actantial model consists of very general categories, but it should not be thought of as having any existence aside from particular cases where particular entities occupy the slots.[38]

Structuralism is likewise untrue to its basic impulse when it tries to bracket out subjectivity and the role of the *individual* mind in sense-making. The human subject cannot be treated objectively, as if it were merely a part of the intelligible world, because it itself *makes* the world intelligible.[39] The only place where the world's intelligibility can reside is in *individual* minds. Again, the analogy of language is helpful. Where is the "system" of English, English as a *langue,* to be found? It exists in a huge number of individual minds (Caws's word is "distributively"), and in no two identically. Its existence continues and changes through the endless interaction of all of these minds. One reason the claims of structuralism cannot be objectively true is that structuralism itself (like anything else) has only this kind of distributive existence. What it is for you will not be exactly the same as what it is for me, even if you accept my account of it. Even if you read the books I recommend, they will not say to you what they say to me. The reasons structuralism appeals, or not, to one person or another have to do with the individual characteristics of the people, not with the "truth" of structuralism.

Finally, to insist on this kind of critical view of structuralism is to break down the distinction between it and "poststructuralism." The latter is not a very satisfactory term. Along with "postmodernism," it is used to refer to the current intellectual climate, in which everything that has been regarded as stable, certain, and "natural"—from the nuclear family to the superiority of certain "classics" over other literature—is shown to be the result of historical developments that favor the political interests of specific human groups at the expense of others. Deconstruction, one of the main movements within poststructuralism (see chapter 6 of this volume), is for Caws simply structuralism in a critical mode. Structuralism implies a hermeneutic of suspicion: "The need for deconstruction arises when the externalization of knowledge [makes people] acquire ready-made structures . . . uncritically."[40]

The modes of literary structuralism—based on Propp, Lévi-Strauss, and Greimas—that I considered in the preceding section lay themselves open to the kinds of criticisms I have enumerated. But they also have potential for being put at the service of a radically critical structuralism. Consider, for example, the appropriation of Greimas by Fredric Jameson, an American Marxist critic who is at the center of current postmodern debate and has provided a major impulse toward the "ideological" reading of texts, including biblical ones.[41] Jameson wrote the foreword to the English translation of one of Greimas's major works.[42] Though Jameson has no use for any "orthodox" Greimasian system, he asserts the incomparable political value of Greimas's approach, provided it is used in a critical and flexible manner.

His main enthusiasm is reserved for the semiotic square. He insists that the square is *not symmetrical,* for example, that "white versus black" is not the same as "black versus white."[43] The square's greatest potential emerges at the non-B corner, which is generally the last to be occupied in analysis.[44] The white versus black example suggests why this is so. If we begin with A = white and B = black, then non-A will be a category that is familiar to us—the term "non-white" is common in our discourse. But no one ever says "non-black," which shows that the two initial terms are not symmetrical. "White" connotes "sharing in European culture," and "non-white" connotes not doing so. The white-black opposition is revealed as a shorthand, Eurocentric way of saying "us versus the rest." The square forces those of European background to ask what "non-black" might mean, and the fact that they are not able to answer this question shows that even when using the category "black," they never considered what might be specific to and valuable in black culture.[45]

The person who has most insisted on a critical structuralism in biblical studies is Mieke Bal, and it happens that the book of Judges has been the focus of her work on the Bible. Bal comes from a structuralist tradition different from Lévi-Strauss and Greimas, namely that of the French literary critic Gérard Genette. Genette's approach is more pragmatic and less philosophical, and more bound to the particular discipline of literary (especially narrative) studies. But it shares the structuralist impulse of trying to describe and organize the characteristics of narrative writing as such.[46]

Bal proposes "a model for narratological analysis,"[47] based on the functions in the text of speaking, seeing, and doing. How are these distributed, among the characters, and between the characters and the narrator? Are there characters who are only the objects, never the subjects, of these functions? Mere quantity is not the only issue; some characters may speak a lot, but may use only questions, while others use commands. What Bal means by speaking and doing is obvious; it is in seeing, or "focalization," that her special contribution lies. She shows the subtlety with which the point of view of the narrative shifts. (The one who sees at a given moment can be a character whom the text does not even name! For example, the birth scene in Genesis 25:25-26 is seen from the point of view of a midwife, though none is mentioned; a character in the story is here *created* by critical analysis.)

Bal applies the categories of action and focalization to the following speech in Judges 19. The old man who offered hospitality to the Levite is responding to the mob's demand that the Levite be handed over to them for sexual abuse:

> No, my brothers, do not act wickedly. Since this man has come to my house, do not do this wantonness. Behold my nubile daughter and his concubine; let me bring them out. Rape them and do to them what is good in your eyes; but against this man do not do this wanton thing.[48]

The man focalizes the actions (actual and intended) of the other characters, and tries to get the mob to share his point of view, to "see it his way" (he fails; cf. 19:25). He presents the Levite as an *acting subject*—"this man has come to my house" (the NRSV's "is my guest" misses this)—in contrast to his *objectification* of the women. He also focalizes the potential actions of the mob in a way that sharpens the contrast of male and female. Bal seizes on the difference between "act wickedly" and "do what is good" (a structuralist eye fixes automatically on this kind of opposition). For the mob's intended action toward the male Levite, the man uses only the language of wickedness; when referring to what they may do to the women, he uses the term "good." Bal is well aware that "do what is good in one's own eyes" is a conventional expression that usually refers to something *bad,* but this does not lessen the force of the verbal contrast. In order to get the mob to focalize outrages committed against a *man* as bad, the host invites them to focalize ("in your eyes") outrages committed against *women* as good.

In another book devoted to the accounts of Jael's killing of Sisera in Judges 4:17-22 and 5:24-27, Bal makes critical use of the semiotic square.[49] For example, she looks at how modern commentators treat the theological opposition between Yahweh and the gods of Canaan, and uses the square to work out the links by which these commentators arrive at ethical value judgments. As Bal analyzes the procedure, the commentators first transform the opposition "Yahweh versus the gods of Canaan" into two other oppositions, "high versus low" and "monotheism versus polytheism" (i.e., "singular versus plural"), resulting in the following squares (reduced to the four main terms):

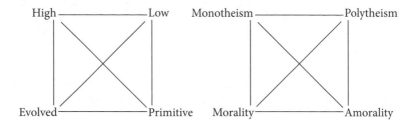

The high–low distinction has, first of all, a quite literal sense; Yahweh is a god of heaven, in contrast to the earth (agriculture) gods of the Canaanites. But this is transferred to "high" and "low" morality. The singular–plural distinction starts with monotheism and polytheism, but is transformed into the realm of sexual ethics via monogamy and polygamy, the latter being made to tie up with Canaanite sacred prostitution. These are semiotic processes going on not (at least not mainly) in the text, but in the guise of sophisticated "objective" scholarship.

To conclude this section, I ask the reader to observe how the discussion has touched on the subject area of almost every chapter in this book. Narrative and social-scientific criticism belong to the foundations of structuralism and all its subsequent development: feminism and gender analysis come to the fore in Bal, deconstruction in Caws, and ideological criticism in Jameson. I do not intend to imply by this that structuralism has the most comprehensive view of the current scene in biblical studies— it is for this sort or claim that it has been rightly criticized. But the discussion has shown that structuralism fully belongs to the interplay and conflict of methods that mark the current scene, and that the critical methods we use always impinge upon each other.

A READING OF
"FORDS OF THE JORDAN" INCIDENTS

Three times in the judge–cycles (Judg 3:27-29, 7:24—8:3, 12:1-6), there is recorded an incident in which the judge–deliverer's group occupies the crossing points of the River Jordan against another group, and inflicts great slaughter upon them as they try to cross. So similar are these incidents that one is at first tempted to count them among the elements that different judge–cycles have in common (compare my earlier discussion of Culley). However, on closer examination, one finds that the differences are even more compelling. Perhaps the most obvious difference is that, while the defeated enemies in the first two instances are foreigners, in the last case (12:1-6) they are fellow Israelites! The following reading will consist first of an analysis along the lines of Lévi-Strauss, whose method is well adapted to the treatment of such difference within similarity. Later, I shall employ Mieke Bal's model and the semiotic square to suggest how formal analysis may lead to broad-ranging critical conclusions.

The following presentation of the three incidents highlights both similarities and differences:

3:27-29	The judge (Ehud) summons the tribe of Ephraim to the war at the beginning of the war. Together they hold the fords of the Jordan, thus defeating the whole enemy (Moab). · There is no tension between Ehud and Ephraim.
7:24—8:3	The judge (Gideon) summons Ephraim to the war after the decisive battle. Ephraim alone holds "the waters . . . and also the Jordan,"[50] thus defeating a small part of the enemy (Midian). A quarrel ensues between Gideon and Ephraim; it is resolved.
12:1-6	The judge (Jephthah) fails to summon Ephraim to the war and defeats the enemy (the Ammonites) without them; Ephraim arrives after the war is over. An irresoluble quarrel ensues between Jephthah and Ephraim. Jephthah hold the fords of the Jordan, thus defeating Ephraim (who has become the enemy).

The common framework is the defeat by the judge of a foreign enemy. Also common to all three incidents is the theme of calling on Ephraim (the major tribe of the Israelite confederacy) to join the war. But this Ephraim theme is treated in very different ways, and represents the most obvious *variable*. The first and last passages present a complete contrast. In the first, Ephraim is summoned at the outset and takes a full part in the victory; in the last, Ephraim is not summoned and takes no part in the victory. In the first, the judge is in alliance with Ephraim; in the last, he is totally antagonistic to them. The two outer passages set up, therefore, two major oppositions:

1. Summon Ephraim (at the outset) *versus* Not summon Ephraim
2. Judge in alliance with Ephraim *versus* Judge antagonistic to Ephraim

The middle passage in the sequence seems, in an uncanny way, to occupy a middle position also in its meaning. In terms of the first opposition, Ephraim *is* summoned, but not at the outset, so that it takes only a small part in the victory. In terms of the second, antagonism *does* arise between the judge and Ephraim, but it gets resolved. In summary, something between a summons and no summons leads to something between full participation and nonparticipation in the war, and to something between alliance and antagonism! To use the language of Lévi-Strauss, the middle passage *mediates* the opposition between the other two.[51]

Our analysis cannot proceed any further along this line, because we have identified only one variable, the relationship of the judge to Ephraim (the other differences are simply consequences of this). We need to identify a *covariable,* something quite different that changes as the relationship of the judge to Ephraim changes. I suggest that the tribal geography of the judge provides such a covariable. Ehud belongs to Benjamin, a tribe located (like Ephraim) *west* of the Jordan. At the other extreme, Jephthah belongs to Gilead, a tribe located *east* of the Jordan. Again, the outer stories offer a simple opposition, east versus west. The middle story mediates this opposition too, for Gideon belongs to Manasseh, the only tribe whose territory spans *both* sides of the Jordan. These stories carry, it seems, a message about antagonism between the parts of Israel lying on the two sides of the Jordan, a message that can be carried only by a *group* of stories in their organized differences from one another and not by any one of the stories alone.[52]

Bal's model allows us to carry the discussion further. If I am right that the passages give insight into a deep-seated conflict, does the narrative remain neutral or take sides? One's first guess would be that stories of judges are told with a bias in favor of the judge. But does the treatment of action, speech, and focalization in the three stories support this?

In Judges 3:27-29, everything is harmonious. Only Ehud speaks, and the Ephraimites obey him. He and they act in unison. The two parties focalize the events in complete reciprocity; the Ephraimites see Ehud "at their head," while he sees them "following after" him.

Judges 7:24—8:3 begins in a way that is superficially similar to 3:27-29, with a summons to the Ephraimites and their successful seizing of the waters. But, aside from the fact that the decisive battle has already occurred before Gideon summons the Ephraimites, it may be significant that he does not summon them *personally.* The use of "messengers" seems to create distance, so that we are less surprised by the subsequent disharmony. In the conflict scene, 8:1-3, the Ephraimite view of the situation is given first (8:1), before Gideon's (8:2-3). And the reader who has been following the story carefully will agree with the Ephraimite version, for Ephraim is missing from the list of tribes summoned at the outset of the campaign (6:35). We may also see a contrast between the *speech* qualities of the two parties—the Ephraimites forceful, Gideon conciliatory and even wheedling. Thus this narrative seems to take the Ephraimites' side.

Most interesting is the final story in Judges 12:1-6. Jephthah and the Gileadites dominate the *action,* initiating the battle (12:4) and setting the Ephraimites a test, which they fail (12:5-6). The same dominance extends to a lesser extent to *speech.* Although the Ephraimites begin the dialogue with a strong speech (12:1, cf. 8:1), Jephthah responds with one just as strong (12:2-3; contrast Gideon's words in 8:2-3). And the test the Ephraimites fail is a speech test! Thus analysis of action and speech suggests a pro-judge bias. *Focalization,* however, yields a different picture. As in the case of Gideon, the reader agrees with the Ephraimite view, because the rest of the story confirms that Jephthah never summoned them. More important, verse 4 seems to give the Ephraimite view not only of this campaign, but of the fundamental relationship between Ephraimites and Gileadites. This verse is obscure, but taken literally (as in the NRSV) it suggests that the Gileadites formerly lived with the Ephraimites *west* of the Jordan, and that their migration to the east was blameworthy.

In all the passages, then, the Ephraimites seem to have the "right" view (that is, the narrator's view) of what is going on. It is jarring to read of the fall of forty-two thousand Ephraimites (12:6), but perhaps even this is to be seen as part of a powerful critique of Jephthah, a critique that begins with the tragic story of his daughter (11:30-31, 34-40) and ends with the note that he judged Israel only six years rather than the usual forty (12:7). The analysis suggests, then, that the message of the set of passages is pro-Ephraim, rather than pro-judge; or perhaps one had better say that there is tension in the book of Judges between these two perspectives. Bal's analytic approach is well adapted for identifying such tensions.

The semiotic square may take us even deeper. I suggest that the most profound opposition that emerges from this set of stories is between "inside" and "outside." The Ephraimites, who stand for those living in the land of Canaan, west of the Jordan, see themselves (and the narrator likely shares their perspective) as "insiders"—definitely members of Yahweh's community. Non-Israelites they see equally clearly as "outsiders." The status of people calling themselves Israelites but living outside the land of Canaan, east of the Jordan, is anomalous—are they inside or outside?[53] This suggests the following square:

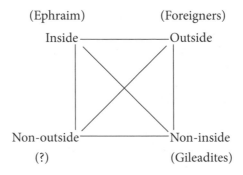

The Gileadites, who are geographically outside but who belong to Israel and ought to be inside, appropriately occupy the position of "Non-inside" in the workings of the semiotic square. But who, in that case, fit the "Non-outside" position? Presumably, those who are geographically inside but ought to be outside, that is, foreigners who live *in* the land.

This suggestion may help explain an odd feature of the structure of the book of Judges as a whole. I have referred to the "theoretical" statement about how judgeship works, which the Deuteronomist includes near the beginnings of the book (2:11-19). Instead of moving directly from this statement into the judge–cycles (which begin at 3:7), the editor interposes the section 2:20—3:6, which deals with the issue of why Canaanites were left in the land after Joshua. Given that this is not an issue that will receive particular attention in the judge–cycles, why is it included in the programmatic introduction to them? Perhaps, a structuralist would say, because, although it is not part of the surface agenda, it is part of the deep-structural problematic of the whole book. The possibility of *Israelites outside* the land, which I have argued to be an issue in the "fords of the Jordan" passages, implies, at the level of the mind's semiotic activity, the possibility of *non-Israelites inside* the land, and hence focuses attention on the problem of the Canaanites. The odd presence of 2:20—3:6 betrays an awareness (conscious or unconscious) of the importance of this problem.

CONCLUSION

Structuralists suggest that meaning comes to us only in patterns. Patterns are what the mind can perceive; indeed, minds create themselves through their perception of the patternedness in reality. In reading a text, the patterning activity of *my* mind responds to the patterning activity of other minds that produced the text. But there is every reason to expect that the structures will be immensely complex, and also, because so many minds have been at work, *unstable;* particularly so with an ancient text like the Bible, where these minds have worked in many languages (both in the normal sense of language and in the extended sense of cultural "languages," or sets of expectations). The mind's patterning activity is also an unpatterning activity—of seeing old patterning from a new perspective as problematic, of trying to unravel the bits of meaning and put them back together in more usable ways.

The most enduring and satisfying image of such activity is one suggested by Lévi-Strauss, that of the *bricoleur,* the "odd-job man."[54] The *bricoleur* uses whatever odds and ends he can find to fix things up, inventing tools if they are not available, always improvising to produce a workable world. This, according to Lévi-Strauss, is what primitive peoples do in creating myths—they take whatever bits the world offers and put them together in ways that seem to help to make sense, to make the world workable. But "advanced" minds do not do anything different in principle. Lévi-Strauss himself, in his myth-analyses, provides an excellent example. He does not take to his myth-analysis a set of structural techniques that he expects will clarify all the data. Rather, like the *bricoleur,* as he goes along he invents structural models that seem adequate to some of the data, and extends, modifies, or rejects them as further data demand. Jameson jokingly borrows this image of the *bricoleur* to describe his own approach to Greimas's system; he takes only what he finds useful for building his own models.[55]

It is as a *bricoleur* that you should approach this chapter and the analytical models that have been mentioned in it. These models are based on large numbers of texts, and have been found *satisfying,* in that they give at least to some minds a sense of seeing what is going on in texts, including biblical texts. They and other available models should be used for what prove to be worth, for their ability to satisfy us as we bring to the text our endless varieties of questions. But all models (whether their proponents admit it or not) have limits to their helpfulness. If your structural readings are limited to the wooden employment of other people's models, they will be impoverished and even boring. You have to make the work *your own*. If the structuralist account of the mind is correct, "structural analysis" is what you do all the time, as you look for significant patterning in the data you perceive, and create models that make the data workable for you. Formal structural analysis simply brings this process to greater self-consciousness. In fact, the formal models that have been found most useful, especially the semiotic square in the hands of a Bal or a Jameson, are the ones that provide the barest framework, and leave nearly everything to the people who employ them.

Your work as a structuralist is this: bringing your own questions as determined by your own setting, using other people's techniques only for help in devising your own, *to see what you can make* of the book of Judges.

FURTHER READING

General

Barthes, Roland. *The Semiotic Challenge.* Translated by Richard Howard. New York: Hill and Wang, 1988. See especially "Introduction to the Structural Analysis of Narratives" (95–135), a classic account of structuralist methodology, and "Wrestling with the Angel: Textual Analysis of Genesis 32:23-33" (246–60), one of the most influential structural readings of the Bible.

Caws, Peter. *Structuralism: The Art of the Intelligible.* Atlantic Highlands, N.J.: Humanities Press International, 1988. A philosophical statement of the claims of structuralism; also a defense against its critics that takes the criticisms seriously. The last part is for the philosophically trained, but the rest is reasonably accessible and of great importance.

Greimas, A. J. *Structural Semantics: An Attempt at a Method.* Translated by Daniele McDowell et al. Lincoln: University of Nebraska Press, 1983. A translation of the foundational work of a theoretician highly influential in the formation of biblical structuralism.

Greimas, A. J., and J. Courtés. *Semiotics and Language: An Analytical Dictionary.* Translated by Larry Crist et al. Bloomington: Indiana University Press, 1982. The standard reference work for all aspects of structuralism and its application to literary studies.

Harland, Richard. *Superstructuralism: The Philosophy of Structuralism and Post-Structuralism* (New York: Methuen, 1987). A bold and readable book that critiques structuralism from a poststructuralist perspective.

Lévi-Strauss, Claude. "The Structural Study of Myth." In *Structural Anthropology,* translated by Claire Jacobson and Brooke Grundfest Schoepf, 206–31. New York: Basic, 1963. Of enormous influence, and the best brief statement of Lévi-Strauss's approach to myth.

———. *The Raw and the Cooked.* Translated by John and Doreen Weightman. New York: Harper & Row, 1970. The first of a four-volume work on Amerindian mythology, this demonstrates (as "The Structural Study of Myth" does not) the scope and resourcefulness of the author's myth analysis.

Propp, Vladimir. *Morphology of the Folktale.* 2d ed. Translated by Laurence Scott. Austin: University of Texas Press, 1968. This first attempt to apply a recognizably structural method to the analysis of narrative (Russian fairy tales) has been very influential in biblical studies.

Saussure, Ferdinand de. *Course in General Linguistics.* Edited by Charles Bally et al., translated by Wade Baskin. New York: McGraw-Hill, 1959. The founding document of structuralism, introducing the linguistic categories with which later structuralists—and also poststructuralists—have continued to work.

Biblical

Bal, Mieke. *Death and Dissymmetry: The Politics of Coherence in the Book of Judges.* Chicago: University of Chicago Press, 1988. The most extended biblical work of an author who insistently brings biblical studies in touch with current critical theory. Bal's method, critical narratology, leads into a range of feminist, psychoanalytic, and ideological issues.

The Bible and Culture Collective. *The Postmodern Bible.* New Haven: Yale University Press, 1995. An extended, critical account of achievements and prospects in the application of new methods to biblical studies. See especially "Structuralist and Narratological Criticism."

Boer, Roland. "Fredric Jameson: The Contradictions of Form in the Psalms." Chapter 8 (pp. 180–203) of his *Marxist Criticism of the Bible.* London and New York: T. & T. Clark International, 2003. Summarizes the most important appropriation of Greimas in recent American scholarship, by the critic Fredric Jameson, and follows with an application of Greimas–Jameson to the book of Psalms.

Jobling, David. *The Sense of Biblical Narrative: Structural Analyses in the Hebrew Bible.* 2 vols. Sheffield: JSOT, 1988. Six structural analyses that use a method loosely based on Greimas and, especially, Lévi-Strauss, and stress the potential of structuralism for practical biblical exegesis.

Leach, Edmund. *Genesis as Myth and Other Essays.* London: Jonathan Cape, 1969. Brilliant and maddening structuralist interpretations of biblical themes by a leading anthropologist and an irreverent follower of Lévi-Strauss. Most successful is "The Legitimacy of Solomon."

Patte, Daniel. *The Religious Dimensions of Biblical Texts: Greimas's Structural Semiotics and Biblical Exegesis.* Atlanta: Scholars, 1990. A thorough presentation of Greimas's mature method by the most influential advocate of structuralism in North American biblical studies.

———. *Structural Exegesis for New Testament Critics.* Minneapolis: Fortress Press, 1990. Part of the Guides to Biblical Scholarship series, this book offers a simple practical method for the analysis of biblical texts. It is theoretically thin, and many readers will want to augment it with Patte's *The Religious Dimensions of Biblical Texts.*

6

DECONSTRUCTIVE CRITICISM

Achsah and the (E)razed City of Writing

DANNA NOLAN FEWELL

WHAT IS DECONSTRUCTION AND WHY SHOULD ANYBODY BOTHER WITH IT?

In the field of literary studies, deconstruction has received a lot of bad press.[1] Its theoreticians (most noted of whom in the West have been French philosopher Jacques Derrida and the late Belgian critic Paul de Man) have been attacked as being linguistic acrobats, unnecessarily obscure and all but unreadable.[2] As a reading process, deconstruction has been accused of being a nihilistic, apolitical, academic exercise that may have inspired some clever textual interpretations, even some radical theology (or atheology), but that has done little to change the ways in which most people read their texts and live their lives.

Deconstruction, with its radically different understandings of textuality and reading, has been particularly unwelcome to many in the field of biblical studies. Not only does deconstruction open biblical texts to nontraditional readings, thereby "decentering" the authority of traditional interpretations, but it also challenges the monopoly of what have come to be the authorized and acceptable methods of study, namely, those falling under the rubric of historical criticism and the more "established" kinds of literary and social-scientific criticisms.[3] Deconstruction threatens most where absolutism is dearest, whether the subject be "Truth," a firmly entrenched theory or method, or religious faith.

So, if you teach and write about the Bible, why should you promote deconstruction as a critical understanding if the end results are that you confuse your students, rankle your colleagues, and get yourself labeled a heretic by whatever religious constituency might be contributing to your salary? Or, if you are a student in biblical studies, either working on a liberal arts degree or preparing for some sort of leadership role in a synagogue or a church, why subject yourself to a view of language and culture that will only complicate the way you read, the way you write, the way you behave, and the way you view biblical authority and your own personal responsibility? Who needs the hassle?

Well, precisely those who thrive on hassle. Reading texts, after all, involves a lot of hassles. Any serious student of exegesis knows this. One passage can spawn a legion of interpretations. Sometimes an entire reading can stand or fall based on the translation of one little preposition. Simply identifying the beginning and end of the text to be studied can involve difficult and often arbitrary decisions. Even the most seemingly straightforward of texts have this uncanny habit of (to use the words of lyricist Paul Simon) "slip-sliding away" just when you think you have them all figured out.[4]

OTHER TRUTHS

For readers who recognize and who are not too bothered by how slippery texts are, deconstruction provides a helpful way of thinking and reading and writing. Deconstruction, as a theory of texts, allows that texts, like people, differ within themselves. No characterization, no matter how exhaustive, can completely capture the essence of who a person is. Our personality traits do not blend smoothly into one harmonious whole. If they did we would be stereotypes rather than real people. There is always something Other about us, something Else that differs from, something in excess of, the ways in which we are generally perceived. Likewise, a text does not manifest one uncontestable meaning.[5] There is always something Other, something Else, that falls through the cracks of any one interpretation. Moreover, just as we change through our encounters and relationships with other people, so textual meanings change as different readers read in different contexts with different goals in mind. A text's possible meanings and functions (like our own various roles in life) are not even necessarily compatible. More often, they are in tension with one another, competing, conflicting, and unsettling one another.

Let's try another image.[6] Imagine a large blue painting at the far end of the room—an abstract painting— nothing but blue. As you approach the work you realize that the blue is not uniform. Various shades shift back and forth from background to foreground depending on the angle of your perspective. You draw closer to examine the texture. You discover that the painting is not completely blue at all. There are red dots of various sizes, mostly around the margins, but a few scattered across the middle. You cannot tell if the red is emerging from beneath the blue or if the red has been applied on top of the blue. You first think that the red is an accidental spattering, perhaps not even intended by the artist. But then you begin to imagine that, if you scraped away the blue, you might find a whole field of red beneath. Then you wonder: What else might be beneath all that blue? What else is being eclipsed in order for blue to rule the canvas?

What does this painting mean? Is it a painting about blue? Or is it a painting about red? Is it a painting about dominance and submission, that is, the dominance of blue and the submission of red? Or is it a painting about subversion, that is, the subversion of blue by red? Or does the painting suggest that red lends blue its meaning? Or vice versa? How do you decide what this painting is about? The minute you settle on one interpretation, another claims your attention. What you discover is that the painting is not about *either* this *or* that. Rather, it is about *both* this *and* that. The meaning is undecidable, because, in fact, the meaning is unstable.

Texts are like this painting. There are obvious dominant subjects, subjects that both common and critical readings have recognized and accented. But even those subjects, accepted by consensus, do not elicit uniform interpretations. There are always various hues in the text, various dimensions of character, nuances of argument, ambiguities of imagery, vocabulary, and syntax that keep even the most commonly accepted subject from being decidable. And then there are elements that are often not considered to be subjects at all, seemingly incidental red dots scattered through the text that go unnoticed by many. Yet these supposedly incidental elements both define and are defined by whatever most readers consider to be of dominant concern. They may disturb, they may counter, they may discredit, they may dismantle, they may subvert, they may twist, they may draw attention away from the dominant meanings and subjects of the text. But whatever they do, they surely complicate and destabilize meaning.

Instability of meaning goes against the grain for most readers. Most readers want to know what a text says in order to categorize it, to file it away somewhere, and not to have to think about it again. We are trained to think in either/or categories and to regard learning as the accumulation of tidy facts and figures. We master texts. We decide what they are about. And once we have established the "truth" of the text, we move on to something else.

Our preoccupation with the "truth" of a text is grounded in a philosophical tradition (stemming from Plato) that posits that "reason can somehow dispense with language and arrive at a pure, self-authenticating truth or method."[7] The idea of an attainable, self-present truth compels most textual critics to look for *a* meaning, a "right" interpretation, and a method of reading that will allow us to reach that right (or at least "highly probable") interpretation. In biblical studies this usually takes the form of attempting to discover the original intention or the original situation or the original form of a text's inception. In other words, if we could just get back to the actual utterance, to that self-present truth, we could know what was meant.

Deconstruction, however, critiques this endeavor. As literary critic Christopher Norris writes,

> Language can fulfill the condition of self-present meaning only if it offers a *total and immediate* access to the thoughts that occasioned its utterance. But this is an impossible requirement. We simply cannot have what Derrida calls "a primordial intuition of the other's lived experience." In which case . . . it has to be admitted that language must always fail to achieve expressive self-presence, and must always partake of the indicative character which marks . . . the suspension of meaning.[8]

As with reading, so with writing: we cannot get beyond language. All systems of thought trying to arrive at truth are bound by their textuality. As texts they are subject to the disruptive effects of language, the suspension and the Otherness and the excess and the oscillation of meaning.[9] Despite every attempt to be direct, clear, and univocal, that is, singular in point and purpose, we cannot eradicate the Other from our discourse. There is always an excess of meaning. Traces of something Other inevitably remain.[10]

SPEAKING OF WRITING

Deconstruction is a reading event and cannot be appropriately separated from textual work.[11] The most famous example of a text's deconstruction, often cited and alluded to in discussions of deconstructive criticism, is Derrida's own analysis of a passage from Plato's *Phaedrus*.[12] In the passage, Socrates tells of an encounter in which the god Theuth divulges his "arts" to the Egyptian king Thamus, suggesting that these arts would be of benefit to human beings. Thamus, however, refuses the art of writing, remarking, "If men learn this, it will implant forgetfulness in their souls; they will cease to exercise memory because they rely on that which is written, calling things to remembrance no longer from within themselves, but by means of external marks. What you have discovered is a recipe not for memory, but for reminder." Agreeing with Thamus's negative pronouncement on writing, Socrates goes on to praise speech instead as the legitimate conveyor of meaning, of which writing is merely an inadequate copy.

Derrida deconstructs the text (or indicates how the text deconstructs itself) by pointing out the discrepancy between what the text says and what it does. What it says is that writing is to be condemned. What it does is to elevate writing by relying on writing as the medium to make the point that writing should be condemned. Hence the text is clearly at odds with itself.

Its language is slippery as well. The word translated "recipe" in Thamus's speech is the word *pharmakon,* which, as Derrida points out, can mean, among other things, both "cure" and "poison." Is writing a cure or is it poison? Whatever Plato's intention, the word stands—as does the entire text—with all its traces, contradicting itself and simultaneously preserving and discrediting the general gist of the passage as whole.

(EX)POSING POWER

So, what *is* deconstruction? Any specific definition would be reductionist and would fly in the face of what deconstruction is all about. Derrida himself claims that "there is no one single deconstruction"[13] and is more comfortable talking about what deconstruction is not than what it is.[14] Nevertheless, we must start somewhere. So, acknowledging the paradox of this endeavor, I offer Barbara Johnson's formulation (which is a distinctly literary one) as an accessible and helpful starting point:

> Deconstruction . . . is a careful teasing out of the conflicting forces of signification that are at work within the text itself. *If anything is destroyed in a deconstructive reading, it is not meaning per se but the claim to unequivocal domination of one mode of signifying over another.* This implies that a text signifies in more than one way, that it can signify something more, something less, or something other than it claims to, or that it signifies to different degrees of explicitness, effectiveness, or coherence. A deconstructive reading makes evident the ways in which a text works out its complex disagreements with itself.[15]

The presupposition here is that a text cannot be univocal. It has many voices, many meanings. What deconstructive reading does is to spell out these meanings and to disallow the "unequivocal domination" of one meaning over all the others. In the same vein, David Jobling writes, "What deconstruction deconstructs is the accumulation of power in discourse."[16]

Power? Domination? That's rather strong language to describe the rather simple process of communication, is it not? Do we not all speak and write in the interests of making plain sense, of conveying the truth as we understand it? What do power and domination have to do with it?

This is precisely where our customary thinking in "either/or" categories enters the picture. We are trained to think in binary oppositions: truth/error, presence/absence, serious/nonserious, theory/practice, literal/figurative, male/female, light/dark, positive/negative. Our oppositions, however, are rarely equal. Rather, we operate with a fairly value-laden hierarchy: truth is superior to error, presence to absence, theory to practice, and so forth. When texts argue "this" and "not that," or when we argue that a text means "this" and "not that," hierarchy is at work, and thus power and domination. Any claim to truth, whether blatant or subtle, is an exercise of power over any notion or person or social construction that does not fit that claim's definition of truth. And yet claims to truth cannot escape their linguistic packaging. Hence, they are subject to the slip-sliding effect: oppositions breaking down, hierarchies losing their footing. As hard as texts want to promote the "either/or" nature of their message, the "both/and" continues to manifest itself. Traces of other "truths," some completely incompatible with the dominant assertion of truth, flicker across the surface of the text, creating enough of a disturbance to keep a perfectly unified image from stabilizing.

Deconstruction seeks to uncover these disturbances. But deconstruction is far from being simply an academic enterprise. Rather, its ramifications address issues of power and domination both in the academy and in society at large. In "The Conflict of Faculties," Derrida writes:

> What is somewhat hastily called deconstruction is not, if it is of any consequence, a specialized set of discursive procedures, still less the rules of a new hermeneutic method that works on texts or utterances in the shelter of a given and stable institution. It is also, at the very least, a way of taking a position, in its work of analysis, concerning the political and institutional structures that make possible and govern our practices, our competencies, our performances. Precisely because it is never concerned only with signified content, deconstruction should not be separable from this politico-

institutional problematic and should seek a new investigation of responsibility, an investigation which questions the codes inherited from ethics and politics.[17]

What does this mean? It means (among other things—there are always other things!) that deconstruction is not simply an operation we perform on texts or something that texts do to themselves. Deconstruction is not just another method or theory of interpretation taking its place among other methods and theories in the academy. Rather, deconstruction's attention to Otherness leads readers "to stray into the margins and off the page"[18] into the surrounding culture and society. Attention to the Other leads to a critique of mainline scholarly traditions, canons, and institutions that have excluded the Other; it leads to a critique of social and political systems that marginalize the Other. In other words, how we read texts affects how we read the world. The opening of texts calls for the opening of politico-institutional structures. This is risky business in a world that encourages the status quo and rewards conformity.

Deconstruction does not, in and of itself, produce alternative (say, nonoppressive) structures. It is, after all, about opening up structures, not about bringing closure and security. Nevertheless, when coupled with ideological or political criticism, deconstruction can be used as an agent of change.[19] The moment we shift the question from "What truth is being claimed and what suppressed?" to "Whose truth is being claimed and whose suppressed?" we are in the business of politics. We are not only looking for traces, we are listening for marginal voices. We are discovering that the seldom-heard voices have truth to impart and that their truth is often at odds with a text's or an institution's "party line." To use Brenda Marshall's words, we are giving up "the luxury of absolute Truths, choosing instead to put to work local and provisional truths."[20]

UNSETTLING JUDGES

As a literary, religious, and political text, the Bible is certainly not immune to the kinds of conflicts, disturbances, and self-dismantling procedures we have been discussing. Nor is the field of biblical studies as a whole. As Jobling writes:

> The Bible needs to be read as a focus for fields of force—in the conditions both of its production and of its "reproduction" in historical and modern interpretation; as a battleground, over meaning,

over interpretation, over the right of interpretation. "Biblical stud-ies" is a discourse with no demilitarized boundaries in any direc-tion.[21]

In recent years the book of Judges has indeed become such a battleground. Historical and literary critics alike claim it as their territory, each camp insisting that their respective methods can recover "what the book is about." A deconstructionist might argue, however, that *re-cover* is indeed the operative word here, because in practice "uncovering" one meaning has resulted in "covering over" others.[22] The critical enterprise is one long exercise in re-covering.

All this re-covering does, nevertheless, point to the ways in which Judges deconstructs itself and can be deconstructed by readers. Ever since Martin Noth argued that the cyclical framework of Judges (sin, oppres-sion, repentance, deliverance) domesticated the obviously older stories in the book to fit the Deuteronomistic Historian's agenda, there has been a spate of readers working either on individual stories or on the cycle as a whole who have shown that, alas, Noth's description (however brilliant) is far too simple.[23] Even traditional readings that have taken the thematic approach, assuming, for example, that the book is about the "settlement" or about holy war have now been challenged by Mieke Bal's call for a coun-tercoherence: namely, that the book is about murder and, in particular, about the dissymmetry between the murder of men by women and the murder of women by men.[24]

What these newer readings have noticed are the incongruencies between the text's explicit assertions of meaning (which in and of them-selves are not univocal) and the stories used to illustrate those assertions. For example, the book of Judges asserts that it is about the settlement (2:6); the conquest (1:1-26); the reasons for the failure of the settlement and con-quest (1:27-36; 2:20-23); Israel's repeated faithlessness (2:11-19); and Israel's need for the monarchy (18:1; 19:1; 21:25). It employs an overarch-ing theodicy that asserts that Israel's suffering is a result of the people's infidelity to YHWH. The stories that supposedly illustrate these asserted structures of meaning, however, tend to be focused more on individuals and less on the nation's exploits. Moreover, in these stories of individuals we constantly find innocent people who are brutally oppressed in situa-tions that have little or nothing to do with religious fidelity. To return to our painting metaphor: the blue, with its varying hues, shouts out the interests of the nation as a whole, explaining the nation's successes and failures in terms of loyalty and betrayal to YHWH, while the red dots whisper unsettling questions about Other subjects—women, children, foreigners, murder, oppression, self-deception, divine and human self-interest, and so on—that disturb and disrupt blue Deuteronomistic meaning.

This incompatibility between assertion and illustration is but one of the ways in which the text is at odds with itself. Other possible sites of conflicting meanings might include ambiguous words or syntax, incompatibilities between what a text says and what it does, incompatibilities between literal understandings and figurative ones, and obscurity.[25] Such sites of conflict become apparent only in the act of reading—deconstruction is, we must remember, a reading event and not a particular method or procedure. Thus, we turn now to a specific text, Judges 1:11-15.

TEXTUAL INCITES: ACHSAH AND THE (E)RAZED CITY OF WRITING

Judges 1:11-15 offers a brief account of Caleb's offer of his daughter Achsah to the man who takes the Canaanite settlement Kiriath-sepher, and Achsah's subsequent request to her father for land and water. Although brief and seemingly straightforward, the story is not without its twists and turns and slips and excesses of meaning.

I offer four "authorized" translations of the text. By making concrete decisions concerning word choice and sentence structure, these translations have attempted to tame the text, to give a particular account of it. A quick comparison and contrast of the readings reveals how difficult a procedure this actually is. Different readers (in this case, readers who happen to be professional translators) find different meanings in the very same set of words. One might also note that, despite the differences, the translations are also quite similar. This is obviously owing, in part, to the common text. But it is also because of the similarity of readers. Despite the current calls for diversity in scholarly pursuits, the vast majority of Bible readers in the West are still at the mercy of scholars who, for the most part, are trained to read alike. Consequently, while the following discussion focuses on a particular biblical passage, we shouldn't forget, to use Derrida's words, "the political and institutional structures that make possible and govern our practices, our competencies, our performances." As we discuss this text, its readers, and some of its meanings, we might also remember that larger political issues are at stake, namely, how texts should be read and who should read them.

NRSV	REB
From there they went against the inhabitants of Debir (the name of Debir was formerly Kiriath-sepher). Then Caleb said, "Whoever attacks Kiriath-sepher and takes it, I will give him my daughter Achsah as wife." And Othniel son of Kenaz, Caleb's younger brother, took it; and he gave him his daughter Achsah as wife. When she came to him, she urged him to ask her father for a field. As she dismounted from her donkey, Caleb said to her, "What do you wish?" She said to him, "Give me a present; since you have set me in the land of the Negeb, give me also Gulloth-mayim." So Caleb gave her Upper Gulloth and Lower Gulloth.	*From there they marched against the inhabitants of Debir, formerly called Kiriath-sepher. Caleb said, "I shall give my daughter Achsah in marriage to the man who attacks and captures Kiriath-sepher." Othniel, son of Caleb's younger brother Kenaz, captured it, and Caleb gave him his daughter Achsah. When she became his wife, Othniel induced her to ask her father for a piece of land. She dismounted from her donkey, and Caleb asked her, "What do you want?" She replied, "Grant me this favour: you have put me in this arid Negeb; you must give me pools of water as well." So Caleb gave her the upper pool and the lower pool.*

What's in a Name?

The first bits of slippery language that we notice are the place-names. There is a tendency to transliterate rather than to translate the words. This produces a certain amount of obscurity for the non-Hebrew reader, because, as transliterations, the words merely designate place, providing the reader geographic information without contributing significantly to the meaning(s) of the story. The effect is misleading. The NRSV's use of *Gulloth-mayim* is a case in point. So Achsah wasn't happy with a place in the Negeb; she wanted a place called Gulloth-mayim. Some folks are never satisfied—always looking for a better neighborhood! If the meaning is limited to proper nouns, Achsah is portrayed as an ingrate. The words, as the other translations indicate, signify more: she's been settled on dry land; she needs a reliable water source to make the land arable. Within the names there are meanings, "traces," that constitute a reasonable request. But by obscuring the traces, translations such as the NRSV's keep the control of meaning in the hands of elite scholars who happen to know Hebrew.

A second case is that of the city itself. The Israelites—more specifically, the men of Judah—are to go up against the inhabitants of Debir. But, we are told, Debir was not always Debir, but was once known as Kiriath-sepher. Caleb even refers to it by its old name, thus indicating that the

Tanakh	*Boling, Anchor Bible*[26]
From there they marched against the inhabitants of Debir (the name of Debir was formerly Kiriath-sepher). And Caleb announced, "I will give my daughter Achsah in marriage to the man who attacks and captures Kiriath-sepher." His younger kinsman, Othniel the Kenizzite, captured it; and Caleb gave him his daughter Achsah in marriage. When she came [to him], she induced him to ask her father for some property. She dismounted from her donkey, and Caleb asked her, "What is the matter?" She replied, "Give me a present, for you have given me away as Negeb-land; give me springs of water." And Caleb gave her Upper and Lower Gulloth.	*From there they attacked the inhabitants of Debir. Debir used to be called Qiriath-sepher. Caleb had said, "Whoever devastates Qiriath-sepher and captures it, to him I'll give my daughter Achsah as wife." Othniel ben Qenaz, Caleb's "brother"— who was younger than he—captured it; and so he gave him his daughter Achsah as wife. When she arrived, he nagged her to ask tilled land from her father. But when she alighted from the donkey and Caleb said to her: "What's wrong?" she said to him: "Give me a blessing! The Negeb-land you have given me and you shall give me basins of water?" So Caleb gave her her heart's desire, The upper basins and the lower basins.*

Israelites themselves change the city's name to Debir. All this information is, of course, to provide a bit of historical and geographic orientation. It also functions, less benignly, to illustrate that words and s/words are both means of control. To the victors belongs the power to rename.

The power to rename is not absolute, however. Traces of meaning remain in these names so casually bandied about. Kiriath-sepher is, literally, "the city of writing" or "the city of books." But it is in the interests of the Israelites (and apologetic translators as well) to suppress that meaning. To spell out that the city to be destroyed is the city of books casts this conquest in a rather different light for any reader who respects learning and culture. Although the predominant tone in Joshua and Judges 1:1-18 foregrounds triumphalism, remnants of meaning undermine that attitude, suggesting that the place to be destroyed is a center of learning: where records are kept, where history and order are valued, a place where texts are produced. Information from outside this text further substantiates the city's pre-Israelite reputation: Joshua 15:49 identifies Debir as Kiriath-sannah, the city of instruction.[27] Even when one's allegiances lie with the Israelites, the loss of such culture may give the reader pause.[28] A city of writing is simply erased.

The Israelites erase and write over the city by word as well as sword. The new version of the city is called Debir. And what might "Debir" mean? An "inner sanctuary" (say the commentators). The root letters (*dbr*) support other traces, however: the verb "speak" and the nouns "speech" and "matter" and "plague." And so the new name stands struggling to contain its nuances. Religiosity, exclusion, privileged divine knowledge and presence, speech (as opposed to writing),[29] death, and just plain "stuff." The name Debir covers a culture with an ambiguous lot of stuff.[30]

The traces in Kiriath-sepher glimpse the loss of human life; for there to be a city of books, there must be a city of scribes. For there to be a center of learning, there must be a city of learners. But the text focuses its rhetoric elsewhere. The citizens of Kiriath-sepher are granted but one sign.[31] Only once are "inhabitants" mentioned. Then they are simply erased.[32] For these inhabitants, this is no longer a place of words. Nor is this a place where bodies are allowed to be their own signs.[33] No bodies in this story. Only the city and the land stand as subjects of value.

The Subject of Achsah

The national warfare is quickly reduced to personal matters: marriage and property. But even this keen observation of the obvious does not stand uncontested. Many commentators argue (or rather assume) that this story is not about individuals at all, but about whole clans or tribes and their settlement history. John Gray's description is a prime example of such thinking: "The tribal history here takes the form of popular saga, with charming personal touches. . . ." Achsah should be understood not as a woman, but as "a local or tribal dependent of the powerful Caleb clan of Hebron, which was affiliated with the kindred clan of Othniel after the occupation of Debir."[34] Such a figurative understanding turns the text into a quaint story, a folk-etiology whose sole, or at least main, function is to explain (although "with charming personal touches") how particular groups of people came to settle particular areas.

Displace "tribes" and "history" as the center of focus, however, and rather different meanings emerge. A father sets up his daughter as a military prize. Whoever takes the city can have his daughter. *Whoever,* he says. Luckily for her (we assume), that the whoever turns out to be an Othniel and not an Attila or, reading closer to home, an unnamed Levite from the hill country of Ephraim (see Judg 19). The "whoever" does raise questions about how we are to assess this kind of bargain. On the one hand, this is the stuff fairy tales and folktales are made of: princesses being married off to heroes. No doubt sexist, but consider the era. Besides, she could have done a lot worse.

On the other hand, what of Achsah herself? How is she perceived? Perhaps a clue is Achsah's name: "bangle" or "anklet." Is she a person? Or is she a trinket? Is she a subject in her own right? Or is she simply an ornament in the story, a "charming personal touch"? The name Achsah has other traces as well, as is borne out by its Arabic cognate, which means "to tether," or more specifically, "to hobble." This is something done to an animal or a captive. Suddenly we are invited to consider that ornaments and hobbles may indeed have something in common. Is Achsah another spoil of war? To her father, she is bait. To her future husband, she is his due reward. She is hobbled by her name and her ornamental role. Who needs to consider seriously a girl named Trinket? Like the land, Achsah is there to be taken. (And this won't be the last time we see the taking of a city associated with the taking of a woman, as we well know from the stories of David and Bathsheba [2 Sam 2] and Absalom and his father's concubines [2 Sam 16].) Does the text condone her use as a bargaining chip? Or does the fact that the bargaining chip turns bargainer render the original bargain somewhat ironic?

How does Achsah perceive herself and her circumstances? The text limits and renders ambiguous her subjectivity.[35] On the one hand, we see her obediently submitting to her father's arrangement; on the other, we hear the anklet rattling—we see her making demands that indicate she is less than satisfied with her lot. In the end, however, specific feelings are not voiced. Or are they? The Tanakh's reading grants her a self-awareness usually denied her. While other translations read her speech (in Judg 1:15) as something like, "Give me a blessing, for you have given me Negeb (or desert) land," the Tanakh has her insist, "Give me a present, for you have given *me* away as Negeb-land; give me springs of water." In the first instance she is the recipient of the gift of the land; in the second she is the gift, a gift equated with the land, and a cheap gift at that. These readings slip back and forth, both allowing her a critical sense of her circumstances and yet unable to agree on the precise nature of her self-understanding. Is she aware that she, like the land, is to be taken and owned by a victorious soldier? Or does she see herself as the landowner, attempting to improve her property? And in the end, we must recognize that Achsah's subjectivity, however it emerges, is at odds with how the text has told her story. For all her talk of gifts and giving, language that she has co-opted from her father (cf. Judg 1:12), we know that "gifts" and "giving" merely dress up the fact that she has been bought and the land has been taken by warfare. She has been used as the incentive for heroism and territorial expansion; she is the collateral for a piece of Canaanite real estate. Of course, the question remains, is this a prime piece of real estate or not? A city of books would suggest yes. Negeb (desert) land would suggest no. The reference to it as a "field" suggests maybe. And so the worth of the land, like the worth of Achsah, is up for grabs.

The biblical text both preserves and undermines Achsah's worth. What do commentators do with her? Alberto Soggin, for example, never even mentions her name in either of his commentaries (except in his translations, where her name is unavoidable).[36] But several interesting things happen in Soggin's translations that illustrate the ease with which subjectivity can be erased. In his 1972 translation of the Joshua passage, he reads 15:18 as follows: "When she came to him, she decided to ask her father for a field; and she alighted from her ass, and Caleb said to her, 'What do you wish?'" His 1981 translation of the Judges passage (1:14) reads, however, "When he came to her, he prompted her to ask her father for a field. She dismounted from the ass/She clapped her hands and Caleb asked her, 'What do you want?'" Who is arriving to meet whom? The grammar seems clear enough: a preposition plus a *qal* infinitive construct plus a feminine suffix, the natural reading being "Upon her arrival" or "When she came" (or some general equivalent). Yet Soggin would have us believe there to be some ambiguity of subject. Never mind that Achsah, mounted on her donkey, is the only one portrayed as traveling!

Soggin's renderings of the second clause ("she decided" [1972]/ "he prompted her" [1981]) pose not only the question of the subject but also the question of the verb. Someone is doing something to someone else, but who is doing what to whom? In terms of the subject, Soggin's change stands on somewhat stronger ground here. His emendation "he prompted her" (cf. REB and Boling's translation), while clearly not what the Masoretic text says, has the support of the LXX and the Vulgate. At least the move to remove the woman as subject has ancient tradition behind it. Ancient translators, too, were trained to read alike!

But let us detour to the verb itself, because how the verb is understood often governs how commentators identify the subject. Soggin translated this verb first as "decided" and then as "prompted." Other options include "moved" (J. Slotki), "persuaded" (H. Freedman), "nagged" (Boling), "urged" (M. H. Woudstra), and "induced" (REB; Tanakh) with commentators quick to explain that the word usually has the negative connotation of inciting or luring someone to do something evil.[37]

What is at stake here? As Paul Mosca unabashedly declares, it is the reputation of Othniel that is at stake. Not only does Othniel vie with Achsah to be the subject of the verb, he usurps her place as the subject of commentary. The critical question becomes, Is Othniel indeed heroic?[38]

Here is the dilemma: If Achsah is the subject of the verb, we get an Othniel who is easily manipulated by his wife (God forbid!). We are also left with the question, When does Othniel get around to asking for the land? If, reading with the LXX and the Vulgate (cf. REB and Boling), Othniel is the subject, we get a greedy hero who nags his wife to do something he is not willing to do himself. Some hero! In the end we see how interpreters are preoccupied with how the biblical text models men. Women are not considered to be subjects worthy of interest. Ideological investment incites (!), provokes yet other texts to deconstruct the texts originally under consideration.[39] And one should remember that the ideological investment has institutional sanction. Academic institutions decide who can offer critical readings. Consequently, scholars like Soggin are given permission to ignore, to erase, whatever is Other in the text.

However, no matter how hard commentators work to erase Achsah from the text, traces of her remain—more traces of her, we might say, than of Othniel! In fact, we might be wise to ask, Is Othniel even part of these negotiations at all? What if he, indeed, is absent?[40] In that case we would have to be willing to allow Achsah to remain the subject of her own action. The "him" in "she persuaded him" would then turn out to be none other than her father Caleb. Mosca argues that *lish'ôl* (usually translated "to ask") is "a perfectly good gerund construction, attested in preexilic as well as postexilic texts," consequently rendering the sentence, "When she arrived, she beguiled him, asking from her father arable land."[41] Achsah's request for water then becomes the actual request for a decent piece of land. If we have settled or unsettled the question of who persuaded whom, we might move on to the question of what Achsah does "from upon her ass" before making her request. The verb *tsanach* or *ṣanaḥ* is an elusive one, occurring only here (and in its Joshua parallel) and in Judges 4:21 in the context of Jael's murder of Sisera. What does the verb mean? Provided that we can bypass G. R. Driver's now-debunked argument that flatulence was involved, we are left with two contending readings (as is evidenced in Soggin's later translation). Either she dismounts from her ass before speaking to Caleb or she claps her hands from upon her ass before speaking to Caleb. Most translations and commentators read "dismount," inferring from the two contexts that the basic meaning must be "descend." My colleague David Gunn and I have argued[42] for the meaning "dismount" because we think it makes the most sense in both contexts: here Achsah dismounts from her animal; in Judges 4, where we understand the feminine subject of the verb to be Jael and not the tent peg, we see Jael dismounting Sisera after nailing his head to the floor.

Bal[43] has revived the reading "she clapped," a translation based on a similar Arabic word meaning "to strike." She contends that Achsah's action was a symbolic gesture designed to get her father's attention, because his immediate response is to ask literally, "What to you?" or, we might say, "What's the matter?" (cf. Tanakh and Boling) or "What do you want?" (cf. NRSV and REB). Simply dismounting from the ass would merely be a sign of submission and could hardly be what motivates Caleb's surprise. The meaning "to strike," she argues further, is also appropriate to both contexts since striking is indeed what is going on in the case of Jael and Sisera. Although Bal claims to make her argument on the grounds of philology, anthropology, and speech-act theory, we might also notice that she seems to have as much at stake in how the biblical text models women as many male commentators have in how the text models men.

If an assertive Achsah is the point of Bal's reading, however, she can surely find her without the linguistic strain.[44] An intertextual analysis would suggest that dismounting might indeed be the sort of emphatic gesture Bal thinks necessary to the episode. Read in connection with Genesis 24:64, where Rebekah alights unassisted from her camel to meet Isaac,[45] and in connection with Judges 19:28 (a natural closing frame for the book), where the Levite's wife lies across her donkey unable to move, Achsah's self-determined mobility need not be read as a mere sign of submission. She does, after all, dismount by herself, waiting for no man's help or permission. She refuses to be "hobbled," so to speak. By planting herself firmly on the ground, she communicates that she is willing to travel no further until she gets what she wants. And once on her feet, she can confront her father face-to-face. The action could easily carry with it the implicit message, "If you want this marriage to proceed without incident, you had better make it worth my while."

Or, read in a less assertive vein, we might see her dismount as overcoming the distance between herself and her father. She physically enacts the meeting of minds that she hopes to achieve. She might be using physical closeness as a tactic of persuasion, designed to signify to her father their familial intimacy and to remind him of familial obligation. His response, then, would not necessarily be surprise, but rather recognition of her strategy. He reads her body language to mean that she is about to initiate a conversation and to make a request.

Then there's always submission, that bugaboo we feminists hate so much. It stands, like the other alternatives, as a viable interpretation of her action.[46] When coupled with Boling's rendering of her speech as a question ("The Negeb-land you have given me and you shall give me basins of water?"), a respectful dismount merely sets the stage for a tentative request. Suddenly, our assertive Achsah dissolves into a deferential, unassuming young woman who would have never bothered her father with such an entreaty had she not been pushed into it by her husband. Boling caps off this warm familial interchange by having Caleb give her "her heart's desire," just as any loving father would do for his modest and respectful daughter.[47] And therein lies the lesson of how families ought to operate!

Contexts, Intertexts, and the Shifting of Meaning, or, What about the Others?

In addition to its internal instabilities, the entire story has a way of slipping and sliding in its production of meaning. What is the story saying? What is it doing? And is it saying and doing the same things?

The story sits in the book of Judges amid a catalog of military successes on the part of Judah (and, to a lesser degree, Simeon) and failures on the parts of the other tribes. It is placed as if to illustrate Judah's foregrounded triumph.[48] A superficial reading suggests that Caleb and, by extension, Othniel as his kinsman and Achsah as his daughter are all associated with Judah. This is not the first time such an association has been made. When chosen by Moses to spy out the land, Caleb goes as a representative of Judah (Num 13:6). The text never says explicitly, however, that Caleb is from the tribe of Judah. Rather, he and Othniel are called Kenizzites, and Kenizzites from early on are identified as foreigners. Of course, it should be noted that the translation of Kenaz as the personal name of an individual (cf. NRSV, REB, and Boling) obscures the problem of ethnic identity. In Genesis 36:11, 15, 42, Kenizzites are specifically classified as descendants of Edom. In Genesis 15:19, the Kenizzites are numbered among those to be dispossessed by the children of Abraham. Here is the question: Are Caleb, Achsah, and Othniel Israelites, or are they foreigners?[49]

The answer to this question affects how we see the story's function. Does the story illustrate the obedience and achievement of Judah, hinting that had the conquest been left to Judah it would have been more successful? We certainly do not get the impression that either Achsah or her kin would have been intimidated by a few iron chariots! Or does the story suggest that foreigners did what Judah was unable to do, that foreigners took what was allotted to Judah? In other words, does the story undermine Judah's, indeed all Israel's, supremacy? Does it applaud or does it mock Israel's attempt to take the land?

The story's placement complicates its meaning yet further. Because the story appears in two places, Judges 1 and Joshua 15, we can see how it interacts with its immediate contexts to produce different meanings. In Joshua, the episode appears in the midst of a long, detailed description of the tribal allotment of Judah. As part of the description it is anecdotal in its explanation of exactly how that portion of the land was taken. More precisely, however, it comes after Caleb approaches Joshua, reminding him of Moses' earlier promise. When Caleb and Joshua had returned with an encouraging report from the first espionage to Canaan, Moses had promised Caleb, "The land on which you have walked shall be an inheritance for you and your children forever because you have wholeheartedly followed YHWH my God" (Josh 14:9). Caleb's claim to the hill country around Hebron is confirmed. The capture of Kiriath-sepher, then, brings to conclusion Moses' promise. As the ending of Caleb's story, it completes his portrait as a man whose strength and determination shine even brighter in his later years, and it communicates that reward awaits those who are faithful to YHWH and his plans.

In the context of Judges, on the other hand, the taking of Kiriath-sepher is not an ending but a beginning. As such, it sets the tone for the remainder of the conquest and settlement—indeed, for the remainder of the book. It stands as a model of courage to the (other) tribes of Israel. It introduces the first judge of Israel as a great warrior. Of course, with its ethnically ambiguous characters and its erasure of a center of culture, it also undermines the us/them ideology that drives the conquest.

The inclusion of a female character also has multiple effects. In Joshua, where women are rarely mentioned and where the major concern is allotting patriarchs their patriarchal holdings, Achsah's request for fertile land is unusual indeed. Like the petition of the daughters of Zelophohad in Joshua 17:3-6, Achsah's bid for real estate stands as an exception to prove the rule, namely, that women do not usually own property and it is not likely that this Israelite policy is going to change. In Judges, where women appear more frequently, Achsah's story invites intertextual comparisons. Her status as a daughter sets the stage for all the other daughters of Judges whose fates will be decided by their fathers and husbands. Hence her story introduces the theme of female vulnerability, which will reach painful crescendos with the fates of Jephthah's daughter, Samson's bride, the Levite's wife, the women of Benjamin, Jabesh-Gilead, and Shiloh. And yet, Achsah's situation suggests that even in patriarchy women can sometimes have power, especially when they are treated with esteem by the men in their family. Unfortunately, Achsah's endogamous marriage and her demand for a home on cultivable soil also serve to accentuate all the daughters who are sold to foreigners (Judg 3:6), who are, in fact, dispossessed from the land-holdings of Israel. Consequently, as the story of a woman, Achsah's brief debut raises all sorts of unresolved issues about power, control, possession, personhood, and the social health of the Israelite nation.

We considered earlier the question of whether the story is literal or figurative: Does the story deal with individuals or does the story represent some sort of tribal settlement? In this same vein, we might also ask, Is the story some kind of theological allegory? We saw the slippery association of Achsah with the land. Might that not suggest an allegory at work? Does Caleb represent God, Othniel Israel, Achsah the land? Isn't God's promise of the land conditioned upon a successful conquest? Or perhaps Othniel and Achsah represent the ideal Israel that was meant to be courageous, determined, and undaunted by the obstacles to which the real Israel fell prey. Or is Achsah Israel's own self-perception: Having been given over to a situation not of her making, does she now find herself having to make additional demands of a God who has not carefully considered what all this story entails? Wasn't she promised milk and honey? And yet now she finds herself in a vastly overrated land having to insist on being blessed with the very basic necessity of life, water. And so we are left wondering, *Does* the story offer a model for all Israel? Or does the story subvert the divine promise? And is the subversion of the divine promise such a bad thing? The fact that the promised land of milk and honey is, like the garden of Eden,[50] imperfect might be its very attraction. An imperfect land, like an imperfect creation, may be what provides life its challenge. It may be what provides the plot for the ongoing story. It may be the very thing that will build Israel's (and God's) character.

WHAT'S THE MEANING OF THIS?

Such a simple story of the settlement has become unsettled and unsettling. Not only have individual words and narrative elements revealed themselves to be undecidable, the entire story as a cultural construct has shown that it, too, can change its stripes depending on its contexts, its intertexts, and its readers. Like Achsah, we have asked for water and have received more than we bargained for—two springs instead of one. Or, to turn the metaphor, we are perhaps more like Caleb, who is pushed into seeing that there is something more to be done with Achsah and Achsah's story than simply to surrender her and it to the possession of Whoever happens to be master in the City of Books.

What is really at stake here in all this reading and counterreading of Achsah and company? And what is the point of reading if the point of what you are reading is not forthcoming? Reflections on these questions are not easily separated. To begin with, the point is that there is no one point to a text. There are many points, and deconstruction refuses to allow any one point to prod the others into submission. This does *not* mean that a text can say anything the reader wants it to say. Texts have rights, too. Texts have constraints.[51] Deconstruction does not give the reader permission to violate those constraints. Nevertheless, within those constraints, a text can mean a lot of things. Within those constraints, a text can always be read Otherwise. And deconstruction would suggest that we have an ethical responsibility to read Otherwise.

How do deconstruction and reading and ethics relate? First of all, deconstruction insists that readers be up front about the limitations of their reading method(s). Don't pretend that your particular critical method will answer satisfactorily all the "important" questions about a text. Method plus text always equals a surplus of text. Don't even pretend you know what all the "important" questions are. Other readers will tell you otherwise—if, of course, academic institutions allow those other readers to speak. After all, who should be allowed to read is a question that has all of academia in turmoil. We find ourselves back with the scribes in the City of Books dealing with the threat of erasure, suppression, (ex)termination. The issue of academic honesty has turned into one of academic freedom.

Deconstruction also asks, Who, what is allowed to be the subject of a reading? What has recognizing subjectivity to do with ethics? Why should we care whether or not a literary figure gets a hearing? Perhaps because the way we read literary texts has the power to shape our attitudes and values. Why anyone should care what happens to a girl named Achsah has as much to do with the crime reports in our newspapers as it does with the biblical text. What happened to the inhabitants of the City of Writing challenges our own military policies and our own educational practices and our own ethnic prejudices as much as it does those policies, practices, and prejudices of ancient Israel. Attending to the Other in our reading is a step toward attending to justice in our own neighborhood.

Why bother with deconstruction? What difference does it make how we read?

It may make all the difference in the world.

FURTHER READING

General

Places to Start

Atkins, G. Douglas. *Reading Deconstruction: Deconstructive Reading.* Lexington: University Press of Kentucky, 1983. Includes discussions of the works of Derrida, Hartman, and Miller as well as interpretive essays employing deconstructive criticism.

Caputo, John D., ed. *Deconstruction in a Nutshell: A Conversation with Jacques Derrida/Edited and with a Commentary by John D. Caputo.* New York: Fordham University Press, 1997. An accessible and engaging introduction to the thought of Derrida and deconstruction.

Norris, Christopher. *Deconstruction: Theory and Practice.* Rev. ed. New York and London: Routledge, 1991. Traces deconstruction from its roots in structuralism and New Criticism through to its current critics. Devotes much attention to Derrida, Nietzsche, Marx, and the Yale School. Good bibliography.

For Teachers

Atkins, G. Douglas, and Michael L. Johnson, eds. *Writing and Reading Differently: Deconstruction and the Teaching of Composition and Literature.* Lawrence: University of Kansas Press, 1985. Collection of accessible essays by well-known critics on the topics of pedagogy, reading, writing, and criticism.

Marshall, Brenda K. *Teaching the Postmodern: Fiction and Theory.* New York and London: Routledge, 1992. Contains a helpful introduction to postmodern thought. Offers postmodern readings of current literary works, including Toni Morrison's *Beloved.*

For More Advanced Readers

Culler, Jonathan. *On Deconstruction: Theory and Criticism after Structuralism.* London/Melbourne/Henley: Routledge & Kegan Paul, 1983. This has become a classic introduction to deconstruction and its critical consequences.

Derrida, Jacques. *Of Grammatology.* Translated by Gayatri Chakravorty Spivak. Baltimore and London: Johns Hopkins University Press, 1974, 1976. Derrida's classic discussion of the problematic status of writing in the Western philosophical tradition. Translator's preface is one of the better introductions to Derrida's thought.

Deconstruction and Biblical Studies

Adam, A. K. M., ed. *Handbook of Postmodern Biblical Interpretation*. St. Louis: Chalice, 2000. A collection of brief explanations and discussions of subjects, methods, concepts, and theorists commonly found in postmodern critical discourse.

———. *Postmodern Interpretations of the Bible—A Reader*. St. Louis: Chalice, 2001. A collection of exegetical essays employing deconstruction, intertextual readings, and various kinds of political criticisms.

Aichele, George, and Gary A. Phillips, eds. *Intertextuality and the Bible. Semeia* 69/70 (1995). Intertextual readings on a range of biblical texts as well as contemporary cultural texts illustrating a variety of theoretical perspectives.

Beardslee, William A. "Poststructuralist Criticism," in *To Each It's Own Meaning: An Introduction to Biblical Criticisms and Their Applications*. Edited by Steven L. McKenzie and Stephen Haynes, 253–67. Louisville: Westminster John Knox, 1999, rev. ed. Situates deconstruction in the Western philosophical discussion, explains key terms, and offers a deconstructive reading of the first of Luke's Beatitudes.

The Bible and Culture Collective. *The Postmodern Bible*. New Haven: Yale University Press, 1995. Collaborative work on different, mostly postmodern, forms of criticism. Covers both Testaments.

Culley, Robert C., and Robert B. Robinson, eds. *Textual Determinacy,* Part One and Part Two. *Semeia* 62 (1993) and *Semeia* 71 (1995). Essays focus on how meaning is determined by the interplay of texts and the reading process.

Detweiler, Robert, ed. *Derrida and Biblical Studies. Semeia* 23 (1982). Contains three essays that move toward "a critical approximation of Derrida's style and tactic" plus an example of Derrida himself engaging in the interpretation of (among other things) biblical texts.

Fewell, Danna Nolan, ed. *Reading between Texts: Intertextuality and the Hebrew Bible*. Louisville: Westminster John Knox, 1992. Essays focus on how meanings are created as texts overrun their borders to connect with other texts and contexts.

Jobling, David, and Stephen D. Moore, eds. *Poststructuralism as Exegesis. Semeia* 54 (1992). Essays engaged in postmodern exegesis.

Jobling, David, Tina Pippin, and Ronald Schleifer, eds. *The Postmodern Bible Reader*. Oxford: Blackwell, 2001. A theoretical companion to the Bible and Culture Collective's *The Postmodern Bible* consisting of a collection of essays on biblical texts by well-known postmodern literary critics, philosophers, and social theorists. Helpful commentary and contextualization by the editors.

Moore, Stephen D. *Poststructuralism and the New Testament: Derrida and Foucault at the Foot of the Cross.* Minneapolis: Fortress Press, 1994. A highly accessible, personal, and inviting introduction to poststructuralism and its impact on New Testament studies. Excellent glossary and list for further reading.

Phillips, Gary A., ed. *Poststructural Criticism and the Bible: Text/History/Discourse. Semeia* 51 (1990). Essays devoted to critical method, theory, and exegesis.

Sherwood, Yvonne, ed. *Derrida's Bible: Reading a Page of Scripture with a Little Help from Derrida.* New York: Palgrave Macmillan, 2004. A collection of conference presentations employing Derridean theory and concepts to the reading of biblical texts.

7

IDEOLOGICAL CRITICISM

Judges 17–21 and the Dismembered Body

GALE A. YEE

INTRODUCTION

One of the latest approaches to the interpretation of the Hebrew Bible is ideological criticism. The publication of Norman K. Gottwald's *The Hebrew Bible: A Socio-Literary Introduction* in 1985 can be seen as a major step toward this approach.[1] In 1990, the Society of Biblical Literature Consultation on Ideological Criticism of Biblical Texts conducted its first session.[2] In 1992, a special volume featuring ideological criticism appeared in *Semeia,* an experimental journal exploring new methods of biblical interpretation. In addition to articles applying ideological criticism to biblical texts, this volume includes a fine introductory bibliography on ideological criticism.

Ideological criticism uses literary methods within a historical and social-scientific frame in a comprehensive strategy for reading biblical texts. (See chapter 1 for a discussion of these critical approaches.) On the one hand, the social sciences and historical analyses help to reconstruct or "unmask" the material and ideological conditions under which the biblical text is *produced.*[3] On the other hand, literary-critical methods address how the biblical text assimilates or "encodes" these conditions in *reproducing* a particular ideology.[4]

For example, in Catholic high school religion classes in the late 1950s and early 1960s, female students read and discussed a book titled *Charm.* The book cover was bright pink and pictured an elegant, gloved woman in a full-skirted dress and a pillbox hat. The book offered instruction on such matters as makeup and clothes (which were very modest), posture, "charming" social skills, and etiquette in dating "boys." Concerning sexuality (although the word was never used), advice to a chaste young woman was never to venture beyond a goodnight kiss, and always to "save herself" for her future husband. Today, instruction has changed dramatically. Magazines such as *Glamour* and *Seventeen* targeted at adolescent girls feature very thin young women in various stages of undress and provocative sexual poses. The articles describe in detail "how to please your man in bed" and "how to convince your man to use a condom."

An ideological critic has a twofold task in analyzing the radically different messages encoded in these diverse texts. First, in an *extrinsic analysis*, the critic investigates the social and historical worlds in which these texts were produced: attitudes of the time regarding gender relationships, body image, sexuality, economic and social ideals, with particular reference to women, and so forth. The critic tries to determine which group produced the text and whose socioeconomic interests it serves. Then, in an *intrinsic* analysis, the critic focuses on what the text actually says (content) and how it says it (rhetoric). The critic's concern is to determine how the texts incorporate or "encode" the particular ideologies of their time regarding gender, class, race, and so forth, and thereby reproduce these ideologies.

To facilitate this twofold reading strategy, ideological critics of the Bible often appropriate the models developed by Marxist literary critics. (See entries under *General* in Further Reading.) However these literary critics redefine Marx's relationship between *base* (socioeconomic relations) and *superstructure* (culture, ideology, politics, and legal system), the core insight remains that literature is grounded in historical, real-life power relations. Literature is regarded as an ideological production of social practices.

WHAT IS IDEOLOGY?

To comprehend what ideological criticism does, one must understand what ideology is.[5] This is no simple task. "Ideology" has taken on popular connotations that give it a negative meaning. The term routinely appears in newspapers and television broadcasts. For example, presidential candidate Michael Dukakis's acceptance speech at the Democratic convention on July 21, 1988, included this sound bite: "This election is not about ideology; it's about competence." Here, the word suggests some abstract system of extremist ideas at both ends of the liberal–conservative spectrum. Radical leftists or ultra right-wingers "have" ideologies; the mainstream or majority—typically assumed to be "people like me"—do not. Ideology in this context is what "other people" have. This negative identification of ideology with extremist views is definitely *not* what is understood as "ideology" in critical theory.

Ideology is not simply a set of doctrines or ideas, although it certainly contains these. As a complex system of values, ideas, pictures, images, and perceptions, ideology motivates men and women to "see" their particular place in the social order as natural, inevitable, and necessary. According to the Marxist theorist Louis Althusser, "ideology is a 'representation' of the imaginary relationship of individuals to their real conditions of existence."[6] Ideology encourages people to internalize an "unreal" relationship to the "real" world. For example, slave owners made ideological use of biblical texts such as Ephesians 6:5—"Slaves, be obedient to your earthly masters . . . as to Christ"—to keep African-American slaves from rebelling. Although many slaves resisted this message, many others internalized it. Ideology *constructs* a reality for people, making the oftentimes perplexing world intelligible; it is not, however, the actual state of affairs in its entirety. While it helps people to understand or make sense of the world, ideology concurrently masks or represses their real situation or standing in the world. All people have an ideology or, more correctly, ideologies that organize and direct their lives. These ideologies "resolve" the contradictions and struggles in daily existence.

Marxist theory is primarily concerned with the network of economic class relations. It examines how ideology "explains" any unequal distribution of wealth, prestige, and control over the means of production—land, natural resources, factories, and so forth—in a given population. Dominant ideologies are produced primarily by the class in power (and internalized by the subordinate class) in order to reproduce particular sets of class relations. Yet ideology governs other social relations as well. Differences among genders, races, ethnicities, educational levels, and religion also exist and interconnect in complex ways.[7] Hence, there are ruling-class ideologies and lower-class ideologies, sexist ideologies and feminist ideologies, racist ideologies and Afrocentric ideologies, and so forth. These ideologies cooperate, confront, and often clash with one another in the "real" world. They articulate "reasons" for these differences and provide a basis for social control or social resistance when conflict erupts because of them. For example, in the antebellum South, racist, classist, and sexist ideologies cooperated in providing an excuse for the rape of black female slaves by their owners.

IDEOLOGICAL STRATEGIES

Ideologies operate through a number of strategies to produce their desired social effects. They *unify* social groups. By linking the abstract level of ideas with the concrete level of social practices, ideologies are *action-oriented*. They *rationalize* certain interests, beliefs, or behaviors by providing credible explanations for them. Moreover, they *legitimate* these beliefs or interests by sanctioning them, by having people accept their authority. They *universalize* historically specific values, ways of acting, and so forth as the only valid ideals for everyone for all time. They *naturalize* them by identifying them with the "common sense" of a society, so that they become seemingly self-evident and "natural." Thus the Marxist literary critic Fredric Jameson regards ideologies as "strategies of containment," because they close off any critical questioning of the actual historical situation and repress both its contradictions and evidence of power struggles.[8]

WHAT IS IDEOLOGICAL CRITICISM?

Ideological criticism presumes that the *text* (1) is a *production* of a specific, ideologically charged historical world that (2) *reproduces* a particular ideology with an internal logic of its own. One can understand the relationship among text, ideology, and history by comparing these relationships in a dramatic production. A staging of *Hamlet* does not mechanically "reflect," "mirror," or "express" Shakespeare's dramatic text of *Hamlet*. The staging manipulates the text of this play and performs it interpretively; it generates a unique production. Ideology, like the dramatic script, is a production of sociohistorical realities; the literary text, like the dramatic production, orchestrates and reworks this ideology to "re-produce" it in its own way:

history/ideology ⟶ dramatic text ⟶ dramatic production

history ⟶ ideology ⟶ literary text[9]

Ideological criticism entails, then, an extrinsic analysis that uncovers the circumstances under which the text was produced and an intrinsic analysis that investigates the text's reproduction of ideology in the text's rhetoric.[10] Because of the complex interrelation between production and reproduction, extrinsic and intrinsic analyses should be regarded as two sides of the same coin. A preliminary intrinsic analysis observes ideological gaps, contradictions, and competing voices in the text. Critics then read the text backward, so to speak, to determine the nature of the material-ideological power struggles that the text's ideology tries to resolve. They then return to a more complete intrinsic analysis to ascertain precisely how the text encodes and reworks the ideological conditions of its production.

Extrinsic Analysis

Extrinsic analysis makes use of the social sciences and historical criticism to understand the complex social structures of specific historical groups and their interrelationships with other parts of the society. Its major focus is the *mode of production* dominant in the society producing the text. The term refers to the complete operation of social relations (family organization, status, class, gender, etc.) and forces (technological, political, juridical, etc.) of a society's material production. Three dominant modes of production can be distinguished during the course of ancient Israelite history: a *familial* mode, a *tributary* (or tribute/tax-based) mode, and a *slave* mode. Each mode is undergirded by its own political economies, social structures and relations, power groups, and dominant ideologies.[11] These aspects of a society in their specific historical manifestations are what the ideological critic must uncover.

Certain explicit questions interest the ideological critic. What are the major social, political, and economic structures in a society at a particular time? Where are the sites of power located in these structures, and what kind of power do they exhibit? How do these groups break down according to class, race, gender, ethnicity, region, religion, occupation, and so forth? What control do they exert over the means of production? What are the conflicts, struggles, and contradictions among these various social arrangements? What are the ideologies produced by these groups? Which one is dominant? On whose behalf do these ideologies speak? Whose voices, what groups, do they exclude or distort? What is the social location of the author of the text? What ideology does this author hold in relation to the dominant ideology?[12]

Intrinsic Analysis

Intrinsic analysis determines how the text encodes in its rhetoric the oftentimes conflicting circumstances of its material-ideological production. It makes use of literary-critical methods such as narrative criticism, structuralism, and deconstruction to accomplish this. The text is presumed to be a symbolic resolution of real social contradictions, inventing and adapting "solutions" to unresolved ideological dilemmas. For example, racist texts published by white supremacy groups such as the Ku Klux Klan present "solutions" to the real-life conflicts between the races. One such "solution" is shipping all blacks to Africa. The Final Solution, as the Nazis called it, to the "problem" of the Jews was the extermination of six million of them. Just as the dramatic production does not merely "express" the dramatic script, the literary text does not simply "express" the ideology of its time. The text can also confront and challenge this ideology in reproducing its own ideology. Intrinsic analysis therefore attempts to determine the precise relationship of the text to the ideology of its production.

Intrinsic analysis pays special heed to particular *absences* in the text. As Marxist literary critic Pierre Macherey states, "In order to say anything, there are other things *which must not be said*."[13] In trying to articulate what it regards as the "truth," the text cannot express things that will contradict that "truth." In these silences, in the text's gaps and absences, the presence of ideology is most tangibly perceived. Already determined through extrinsic analysis are the social locations of power, their conflicts and their ideologies. Taking an opposing perspective, intrinsic analysis asks about those voices that are excluded: perhaps those of women, of other tribal groups, or of the poor.[14] Intrinsic analysis uncovers competing voices, marginalized by the society's power structures that are encoded in the text by their very absence. The text conceals and represses these voices in its attempt to resolve the contradictory opinions they pose.

Moreover, intrinsic analysis requires an in-depth investigation of *rhetoric*: that is, a text's artful ability to persuade its audience to accept a particular ideology. Because it is a means of persuasion, a text's rhetoric is thus a form of power. The social strategies of ideology—how they universalize, rationalize, and legitimate certain values, behaviors, and so forth—have already been discussed. The text reorganizes ideology and reinscribes its strategies in written form through the rhetorical features of persuasion. An important part of these features is the commonly recognized elements of structure, such as characterization, plot, repetition, point of view, symbolism, irony, foreshadowing, and framing. Hence, the various and often contradictory ways in which a text portrays individual characters, involves them in specific plots, presents the story from a certain point of view, makes ironic comments or dogmatic statements, and so forth, reveal its particular ideology.

JUDGES 17–21: AN EXTRINSIC ANALYSIS
OF THE DISMEMBERED BODY

The provocative conclusion to the book of Judges, Judges 17–21, provides an excellent occasion for illustrating ideological criticism. As stated earlier, an ideological critique begins with a preliminary intrinsic analysis by noting ideological absences, contradictions, and competing voices. The critic then reads "backward" in an extrinsic analysis to unmask the power struggles the text tries to resolve. To simplify the steps, however, I will assume the results of a standard intrinsic analysis. The most obvious ideological comment of Judges 17–21 is that the violence and anarchy of Israel's tribal period are explained by the absence of a king (17:6; 18:1; 19:1; 21:25). Determining when such an ideology could have been produced, then, is one of the first steps in an extrinsic analysis.

The dating and editing of these chapters have been disputed. (See chapter 1 of this volume regarding theories on the editing of Judges and the Deuteronomistic History.) Commentators usually regard these chapters as an "appendix" added during the exilic/postexilic period, years after the main body of the book took shape.[15] My thesis poses a challenge to this late dating. A strong case can be made for assigning Judges 17–21 to the preexilic Deuteronomist in the seventh century, the producer of the first edition of the Deuteronomistic History (Joshua—2 Kings). The prestate or tribal period (c. 1250–1020 B.C.E.), which the Deuteronomist describes in Joshua and Judges, operated under a *familial* mode of production. The Deuteronomist himself lived several centuries later. He worked in a society that functioned under a *native tributary* mode of production, in its specific historical configuration during or just after Josiah's reform (c. 627–609 B.C.E.). The conflicts between these two modes of production are quite evident in the Deuteronomist's editorial statement: "There was no king in Israel; every man did what was right in his own eyes."

As its name implies, the familial mode of production in Israel's tribal period was characterized by strong patrilineal, kinship- and village-based social groupings wherein the family was the basic socioeconomic unit. These family households collected into clans, which formed themselves into the largest social units, the tribes. (See chapter 3 in this volume.) The economy was based on highland agricultural and pastoral production. The tribal lineages owned and administered the land, which was the principal means of production. The tribes were self-sufficient, self-protecting entities, having mutual, family-based relations with one another, on the whole. Because "in those days there was no king in Israel," the tribes were tributary-free, that is, they paid no tribute or taxes to a king or ruling elite who appropriated their surplus wealth. Instead, this wealth went directly back into the tribe. Women were materially and ideologically subordinate to men. Nevertheless, they wielded considerable informal power and authority in family household management. Dividing lines between the so-called domestic sphere and the public sphere were blurred in such a family/kinship-based society.[16]

Because of a number of internal and external factors, Israel moved to a native tributary mode of production (c. 1020–587 B.C.E.).[17] Tribal government became centralized under a king. In contrast to the tribal period, the community was now characterized by the "haves" and the "have-nots."[18] The king and his ruling elite would make up a small percentage of the population at the top of the social pyramid, with the peasants, the bulk of the population, at the bottom.[19] Peasant life was difficult under a tributary mode of production, because it was the peasant who bore the heaviest tax burden of the state. In order to finance a centralized bureaucracy, costly war efforts, ambitious building projects, and a luxurious lifestyle at court, the king and the ruling class extracted surpluses from the peasants, in both human and natural resources. After a generation, this heavy taxation would lead to the impoverishment and decline of the lower classes.

The changes in political system and mode of production had a negative effect on prestate Israel's tribal structure. In order to maintain his centralized political control, the king had to subvert and ultimately destroy the social solidarity and authority of the tribal "body": the family and lineage groups that had the potential for conspiracy and revolt. For example, in the politics of state centralization, Solomon tried to "dismember" tribal organization and kin group loyalties when he redivided his kingdom, cutting across tribal boundaries to create twelve tax districts (1 Kgs 4:7-19).[20] Moreover, a number of studies demonstrate how the sex and family laws of the Deuteronomic code slowly eroded the authority of the male head of the household in favor of the state.[21]

State formation would also have an adverse effect on the status of women in Israel. As power shifted from the family household to the state, with its male king and male political and religious bureaucracies, female power and prestige receded. When the family household became progressively more impoverished by the state, women would bear the greater burden. Hierarchical relationships among male and female family members intensified as society itself became more economically and politically stratified by the state.[22]

Although the monarchy with its tributary mode of production supplanted the tribal structure with its familial mode of production, it never completely erased popular tribal kinship loyalties and household economies and ideals. The familial mode persisted in rural areas, since the state did not have the technical and administrative apparatus to oversee the kingdom totally.

In its present form, edited by the Deuteronomist, Judges 17–21 tried to resolve ideologically the conflicts between the two modes of production (one dominant, the other subordinate but still stubbornly present) in their specific historical forms during King Josiah's time in the seventh century (c. 640–609 B.C.E.). Scholars usually regard the Deuteronomist's edition of the Deuteronomistic History as propaganda for Josiah's reform policies.[23] The Deuteronomist had only high praise for the ruler of the southern kingdom of Judah. Josiah was depicted as the ideal by which all the other kings were judged. Under his rule, the Book of the Law was discovered in the temple (2 Kgs 22:3-20). His first public response to the find was a covenant renewal ceremony, where he read this law to the people (2 Kgs 23:1-3). He then purified and centralized the cult by destroying what he considered "idolatrous" (2 Kgs 23:4-20, 24). Finally, he commanded the Passover to be celebrated in Jerusalem (2 Kgs 23:21-23).

Nevertheless, by examining the subtext of the narrative critically, one realizes that Josiah's cultic reform involved the ruthless destruction in God's name of all high places and local shrines except the Jerusalem temple. These native Israelite sanctuaries were licit under older laws, and ministered to a substantial portion of the population. The Deuteronomist glosses over the class conflicts Josiah's "religious" reform entailed. However, when the reform is viewed from an economic standpoint, these class conflicts are strongly foregrounded.[24]

For seventy-five years prior to Josiah's reform in 640 B.C.E., Judah was reduced to Assyrian vassalage. Its ruling classes squeezed all they could from their peasant economic base to pay the tribute to Assyria, while still preserving their privileged lifestyle. However, the balance of power shifted with the decline of Assyrian power during Josiah's time, especially after the death of Ashurbanipal in 627 B.C.E. Josiah saw an opportunity to intensify his hold on Judah and extend his control into the former northern kingdom of Israel. This expansion would considerably enlarge his tax base and stimulate the faltering economy of his state.

Josiah could not, however, finance this expansion by raising taxes on a peasantry already strained under current tariffs. Nor could he raise taxes on the wealthy, because his own political hold had been rather shaky since his controversial rise to power (2 Kgs 21:23-24). He could not afford to alienate either of these two groups.[25] He therefore initiated a "religious" reform that made his appropriation of peasant surpluses more efficient. He reorganized the collection of taxes, tributes, and fees *that were already assessed* so that they flowed directly into Jerusalem's coffers. He thus bypassed the local leaders, who had been collecting these revenues for him, but who also had been taking their cut.

Significant for understanding Judges 17–21 is that the local class, which was pocketing its share of peasant funds in the rural and remote areas of the kingdom, was largely composed of country *Levites* of the priestly house often called the Mushite.[26] These Levites ministered in the high places and sanctuaries in Judah and in the former northern kingdom, and they competed with Jerusalem and its Zadokite priesthood for cultic revenues. They prospered from their tax collection, as well as from tithes on peasant sacrifices and pilgrimages to shrines. Rallying Judah under an ideology of cultic "reform," Josiah tore down the religious sanctuaries of the Levites in the areas surrounding Jerusalem and in Judah (2 Kgs 23:4-14). He then turned northward and destroyed their major shrine at Bethel and other holy places in the former kingdom of Israel (2 Kgs 23:15-20).

By destroying competing cult centers, neutralizing their priests, and promoting a religious ideology that made Jerusalem the only legitimate place to worship YHWH, Josiah sought to ensure that an enormous flow of cash would come into his capital city. The desire for this influx of funds lay behind the following law regarding pilgrimage festivals:

> Three times a year all your males shall appear before the Lord your God at the place that he will choose: at the festival of unleavened bread, at the festival of weeks, and at the festival of booths. *They shall not appear before the Lord empty-handed; all shall give as they are able,* according to the blessing of the Lord your God that he has given you. (Deut 16:16)

The command to celebrate Passover in Jerusalem illustrates another site of struggle between the tribal and tributary modes of production. In tribal Israel, Passover was a family-oriented feast celebrated in the local household (Exod 12). The feast promoted the communal values and kinship relations typical in the familial mode of production. The religious, social, and economic shift from the family to the state is evident in the directive to make a pilgrimage to Jerusalem to observe Passover. The religious (ideological) means that promoted the family values of the tribal mode of production were thus co-opted by the Jerusalem elite to exercise its social, economic, and ideological power over the people.[27]

The socioeconomic and ideological conflicts between the tribal body and the tributary mode of production, the competition between the Jerusalem priesthood and the rural Levitical priesthood, the fiscal ambitions of King Josiah, the destruction of regional sanctuaries, and the centralization of worship in Jerusalem all provided the material and ideological circumstances that produced Judges 17–21. It is these power struggles, ideological dilemmas, and social contradictions that the text tries to "resolve." We can move on to an intrinsic analysis of Judges 17–21 to determine how the text encodes these struggles in its reproduction of the deuteronomic ideology.

INTRINSIC ANALYSIS OF THE
DISMEMBERED BODY

Fascinated by absences and contradictions, an intrinsic analysis uncovers very significant ones in Judges 17–21. In a book devoted primarily to judges and heroes, no such individuals inhabit the concluding chapters. Instead one encounters a ragtag bunch of questionable virtue: a son who embezzles from his own mother; a corrupt Levite on the lookout for a fat buck; another Levite who sacrifices his wife to save his own hide; an assortment of idolatrous, inhospitable, and warmongering tribes. The notion of absence and contradiction can be extended to biblical scholarship—the *consumption* of the text by the academic guild—on Judges 17–21. As was pointed out, scholars often regard these chapters as an exilic or postexilic "appendix" added after most of the book was formed. Mieke Bal likely is correct in arguing that the elimination of Judges 17–21 from the so-called authentic material depends on a politics of coherence that privileges a reading focused on male heroes, political nationalism, and military accomplishments.[28]

The most striking absence is textually explicit: "In those days, there was *no king* in Israel." This editorial comment is strategically repeated throughout these chapters (17:6; 18:1; 19:1; 21:25). Accompanying the first and last of these statements is the deliberately ironic note, "Every man did what was right in his own eyes."[29] What is "right" in men's eyes are a woman's rape and torture at the hands of a predatory mob, her ghastly dismemberment, an intertribal war that almost extinguishes one of Israel's members, the seizure and rape of more women to replenish this tribe. The orderly framework of apostasy, oppression, crying out, and deliverance that shapes much of Judges disintegrates by the end. Indeed, the complete absence of order in these final chapters culminates in the most brutal events in the book.[30]

The ideological thrust of the editorial remarks is straightforward: the absence of a king accounts for the chaos and cruelty of Israel's tribal period. Nevertheless, this explicit absence masks an imperceptible one. In order to extol the monarchy, the text must conceal the social hardships and contradictions of a society actually governed by a king and his ruling elite. Embedded ideologically in the text are the conflicts between familial and tributary modes of production. The text implies a positive appraisal of the latter at the expense of the former. Although diminished by the state, tribal and lineage loyalties were still evident during Josiah's time and were potential sources for rebellion. Judges 17–21 provides an ideological means of "dismembering" such allegiances and suppressing revolt.

Characterizing the tribal period as anarchic and violent at the end of Judges, the Deuteronomist at the same time foreshadows the establishment of the Davidic monarchy in the next two books of his history (1 and 2 Sam). He ultimately paves the way for his ideal king, Josiah (2 Kgs 22-23). Keeping these absences and contradictions in mind, we can proceed to an investigation of the text's rhetoric.

Judges 17–18: Cultic Chaos

The stories in Judges 17–18 underscore the disintegration of Israel's cult during the tribal period. Each chapter is filled with irony, humor, and ambiguity that ridicule this decline. Judges 17:1-6 introduces Micah, a resident of the northern hill country of Ephraim. He is just returning the eleven hundred pieces of silver he had filched from his unnamed mother. Possibly, she is Delilah, who, according to the preceding chapter, betrays Samson to the Philistines for precisely the same amount (16:5). No reason for Micah's confession is given; it may have been prompted by genuine contrition, a guilty conscience, or fear of his mother's curse upon the thief. The ambiguity highlights the cavalier attitudes these characters have toward the cult. The mother calls a blessing down upon the wayward but seemingly repentant son. Apparently forgetting the second commandment (Exod 20:4), she announces that she is consecrating the silver to YHWH to make an idol of cast metal for her son. She contributes, however, only two hundred pieces toward it. Evidently she pockets the rest, although the text is unclear. Along with this idol, Micah also boasts of a shrine. He installs one of his sons as its priest and has more cult objects made—an ephod and a teraphim.[31]

Homemade idols of stolen silver, private shrines, personal priests, self-made sacerdotal gear: these are hardly the proper trappings of one whose name means "Who is like YHWH?" The repeated references to cult objects throughout Judges 17–18 emphasize an idolatrous worship practiced by sacrilegious men.[32] They highlight a wicked age when "there was no king in Israel; every man did what was right in his own eyes" (17:6). The Deuteronomist implies that a king like Josiah would rid the country of such cultic abuses.

In the next scene (17:7-13), a young Levite traveling from Bethlehem in Judah finds his way northward to Micah's house. He seeks a place in which to settle and make a living. Micah hires him on the spot, without asking for references: "Stay with me, and be to me a father and a priest, and I will give you ten pieces of silver a year, a set of clothes, and your living" (17:10). The freelancing Levite agrees to Micah's offer, but, ironically, he does not become a "father" to Micah. Instead, he becomes like one of Micah's sons in his house. The father–son relationship becomes empty because it is reversible. With the Levite's coming, Micah's glee is palpable: "Now I know that the Lord will prosper me, because the Levite has become my priest" (17:13). Not only does Micah obtain a priest, but his very own *Levite* at that, who guarantees God's favor—or so Micah thinks.

Poor Micah discovers otherwise in Judges 18, when he and his Levite encounter the tribe of Dan. Just as the peripatetic Levite journeys northward in search of a place to settle, so too the landless tribe of Dan migrates north to find an "inheritance" to colonize.[33] Five Danites scouting potential territory accept hospitality in Micah's house (18:2). Once they recognize the Levite, they inquire about his circumstances. The Levite's broad hints to the Danites—"he hired me/I have become his priest" (18:4)—do not go unnoticed. However, unlike Micah, who requested no references, the Danites test the Levite's priestly skills: they want to know if their mission will succeed (18:5). The Levite's ambiguous reply reveals his shrewdness: "Go in peace. The mission you are on is *nokaḥ* YHWH." The rare Hebrew word *nokaḥ* apparently can signify both "in front of" and "opposite," so that the Danite's mission can be either "favorable" or "unfavorable" to God.

The Danites evidently understand their instant oracle in the former sense, because they continue their journey northward. Reporting to their comrades in the south, they urge the capture of Laish, a city inhabited by a peaceful, unsuspecting, and defenseless people (18:7-8). Six hundred fully armed warriors then set out. Along the way, they loot Micah's shrine, taking its idol, ephod, and teraphim; they are completely oblivious to his earlier hospitality toward them. Witnessing this raid, the Levite makes a halfhearted attempt at protest (18:18). The Danites basically tell him to shut up and offer him the post of tribal priest. Thus, an idol of stolen silver gets stolen; a bought priest gets bought again, for an even bigger price (18:19-20). Micah pursues the Danites to recover his possessions, but his whining is rather pathetic: "You take my gods that I made, and the priest, and go away, and what have I left?" (18:24). Homemade gods and a callous priest. Indeed, Micah had nothing in the first place! And thugs that they are, the Danites threaten to set their "hot-tempered fellows" on Micah and his household.[34] Seeing himself hopelessly outnumbered, Micah returns home. The "mighty warriors" continue on to Laish and destroy the helpless town. They rename it Dan after their eponymous ancestor, and there they enshrine their purloined idol.

Finally, the narrative provides more information about the money-grubbing Levite who will service this idol. He is the grandson of Moses himself and his name is Jonathan! He and his sons will minister to the Danite shrine and Micah's idol "until the time the land went into captivity" (18:30).

The underlying grotesquerie of Judges 17–18 can be contextualized in the Deuteronomist's propaganda for Josiah's so-called religious reform. His ideological production legitimates Josiah's brutal demolition of the northern sanctuaries. A recurring theme in his edition of 1 and 2 Kings is a polemic against the ostensibly illicit cult and priesthood Jeroboam I established at Dan and Bethel. These northern shrines rivaled the royal cult in Jerusalem. The Deuteronomist reproaches Jeroboam for setting up the "two calves of gold" at these shrines (1 Kgs 12:25-33). In his opinion, Jeroboam's "idolatry" led to the fall of the North in 721 B.C.E. (2 Kgs 17:20-23). His reference to "the captivity" in Judges 18:30 most likely refers to this event.

Judges 17–18 anticipates this condemnation through a rehearsal of Dan's dubious beginnings. Although its partner in cultic crime, Bethel, is not explicitly named, it is certainly included in the censure.[35] The ideological critic needs to ask, "Why Dan and not Bethel?" in Judges 17–18. Assuming that he wanted to disparage the tribal system, the Deuteronomist focuses on Dan, thus reproaching the tribal name and therefore the tribal affiliation.

Furthermore, the portrayal of the Levite is significant. Tracing his origins to Moses encodes the priestly rivalry between the Mushite and Zadokite families. The Deuteronomist represents the Levitical competitors of the Jerusalem priesthood as unscrupulous opportunists. Both Micah and the tribe of Dan pay impressive fees for the Levite's "services," and so they guarantee his financial security. However, within the overall thrust of the Deuteronomist's propaganda, any hint of Josiah's own economic ambitions in neutralizing the country Levites and redirecting their revenues to Jerusalem is absent in this narrative. The centralization associated with a tributary mode of production is repressed in the text.

Tribal Israel certainly does not escape caricature either. It is depicted as uncivilized; no king ruled and cultic disorder was rampant. Furthermore, because this was a time when kinship relations were highly prized, the breakdown of these relations in the text is quite remarkable. A son betrays his mother. A "son" (the Levite) abandons his "father" (Micah). A shameless tribe violates the laws of hospitality and the host–guest relationship. These themes will carry over into Judges 19–21, where another tribe ignores hospitality codes, a Levite delivers his wife to rapists, and tribal lineages nearly wipe each other out. The Deuteronomist shifts the history of tribal collapse back two generations to the prestate period itself. He completely suppresses the fact that the monarchy deliberately broke up the "tribal body" in order to establish and preserve a tributary mode of production.

Judges 19–21: Social Chaos

Significant issues of gender intersect with those of class in an ideological critique of Judges 19.[36] Class and gender interests are most apparent at the beginning of the chapter in the unequal power relations between the Levite and his wife. The Levite, as the extrinsic analysis observes, is one of the local cult leaders, who obtains his wealth from the revenues peasants offer at regional shrines. His woman is described as a *pilegesh,* wife of secondary rank, usually translated "concubine" (19:1). For a man who already has children by his primary wife, one of her main roles is to provide sexual pleasure.[37] A *pilegesh* can also be taken in order to provide children when the primary wife is barren (cf. Gen 16, 20). While a primary wife is already subordinate to her husband, the *pilegesh* endures a double subordination in her position as secondary wife.[38] The inferior status of the woman in our story is particularly foregrounded after her rape, when the text describes her husband as her "master" (*'adon;* 19:26-27).

Intrinsic analysis, acutely aware of absences in the text, notices furthermore that there is no textual mention of a primary wife. Her absence provides the first clue to the Levite's character. In contrast to Israel's patrilineal ideology, where men typically marry and have sons to carry on the family name, the Levite apparently eschews a primary wife and uses his secondary wife for sexual gratification.

Whereas the Levite of Judges 17–18 came from Bethlehem in Judah to settle in the northern hill country of Ephraim (17:7-8), this Levite leaves Ephraim to pursue his wife, who had left him and returned to her father's house in Bethlehem. The Levite seemingly does not care for his wife, because he waits four months before going after her.[39] The reason the Hebrew text gives for the wife's departure is that she "fornicated" against her husband.[40] The literal sense of her action, that she actually had illicit sex with other men, presents interpretive problems. Why would her father accept such a shameless daughter and allow her to remain with him for four months? Why would her husband expend the time and effort to bringing her back? Under the law she must be put to death (Lev 20:10; Deut 22:22).

A stronger case can be made for considering her act figuratively. It is her very abandonment of her husband that the Deuteronomist describes as "fornicating" against her husband. Anthropological studies of women's resistance to male authority provide a helpful model. For example, disrupting the household by vacating it abruptly is one of a number of strategies women adopt to exercise autonomy in androcentric societies.[41] In a society that so rigorously supervises the sexuality of its women, the daring act of leaving a husband would be judged, as the Deuteronomist does in this case, as a metaphoric act of "fornication."[42]

Besides bringing dishonor upon herself, the woman brings dishonor upon her husband, for it becomes publicly apparent that he cannot control her actions. Moreover, the extent of a man's disgrace correlates inversely with the status of the one who shames him: the lower the status, the greater the shame. That the deserting woman is a *pilegesh* therefore compounds the Levite's humiliation.

Feminist scholars have already pointed out that the biblical text primarily encodes male-male power relations. Women's voices are usually absent, muzzled, or mediated by the male narrator. Stories ostensibly about male–female relations are more often about the struggles among men for honor and status. Men frequently manipulate their relations with women in order to achieve certain goals in their relations with other men.[43]

And so it is in Judges 19. The story shifts in verses 3-9 from the Levite and his wife to the Levite and his father-in-law. Although it has been suggested that this narrative is about male bonding,[44] cross-cultural studies point out that the host-guest relationship is essentially one of unequal power relations. The flamboyant display of generosity by the father-in-law toward the Levite symbolizes the moral and conceptual subordination of the guest to the host.[45] Through this subordination, the Deuteronomist contributes to his carefully constructed portrayal of the Levite. Against the male ideology of his own time, an upper-class Levite seems to bypass a primary wife (and his procreative duties) and takes for himself a secondary wife just for sex. He is doubly dishonored when his *pilegesh* abandons him, and he is taken down a few more social notches by his father-in-law's shrewd hospitality.

Following the pattern of Judges 17–18 (Levite–tribe), after his caricature of the Levite, the Deuteronomist launches into a negative portrayal of the tribes. The Levite finally resolves to quit his father-in-law's house and return north to Ephraim with his wife. It is significant that he refuses to spend the night in Jebus, which he scorns as a "city of foreigners who do not belong to the people of Israel" (19:12). Jebus, the author emphasizes in an editorial note, is in fact Jerusalem (19:10), the favored capital of the future monarchy, of King Josiah, and of the Deuteronomist. In an ideological plug for his royal city, the Deuteronomist implies that had the Levite overcome his prejudice and chosen Jebus for his night's stay, he would have found safety and security. Certainly, the story would have been different for his wife. However, at sundown the Levite and his company reach the town of Gibeah, "which belongs to Benjamin" (19:14). Instead of a welcome from extended tribal kin, "no one took them in to spend the night" (19:15).

Eventually, the Levite is offered hospitality by an old man living in Gibeah as a resident alien (19:16-21). A gang of town thugs during their merrymaking encircles the house. They are not very subtle about their intentions toward the Levite: "Bring out the man who came into your house, that we may have intercourse with him" (19:22).

Male-male rape should be understood in the context of male-male power relations.[46] The phallus serves as a weapon of aggression that establishes a relation of dominance and submission. A man who is raped by other men figuratively becomes emasculated and "feminized." The Deuteronomist progressively disgraces the Levite in this way. The shame caused by his wife's abandonment and the subordination by his father-in-law intersect here and become sexualized by this threat of gang rape. As already noted, the extent of a man's disgrace correlates inversely with the status of the ones who shame him. The rapists are described as a "perverse lot" (19:22).[47] Shamed and feminized by his secondary wife and her father, the Levite is in danger of becoming even more humiliated and emasculated by degenerate men.

The old man leaves his house to reason with the hooligans. Ironically, he addresses them as kin: "No, *my brothers,* do not act so wickedly. Since this man is my guest, do not do this vile thing" (19:23, emphasis added). He offers the would-be rapists his own virgin daughter and the Levite's wife as a substitute for his male guest (19:24). The rape of women—indeed, of his own daughter—is less repugnant for the old man than the rape of the Levite, which he describes as a "wicked act," a "vile outrage" (*nebalah*). The old man enjoins the mob to "Ravish them. Do to them *what is good in your eyes*" (19:24, emphasis added).[48] The violation echoes the Deuteronomist's censure of the whole tribal period, when "there was no king in Israel and every man did *what was right in his own eyes.*"

The negative portrayal of the Levite becomes exacerbated. In a callous act of self-preservation, he seizes his wife and shoves her out to the mob. She is raped and abused the whole night. Released in the morning, she falls down at the door of the house where her "master" was safely ensconced (the text for the first time identifies the Levite as her *"ʾadon,"* 19:25-26). He leaves the house to continue his journey, and behold, his fallen wife blocks his passage. Oblivious to her pathetic, tragic, horrific condition, he orders her to "'Get up, we are going.' But there was no answer" (19:28).

The cultic chaos that the Deuteronomist lampoons in Judges 17–18 resurfaces in 19–20. The Levite dumps the woman on his donkey and heads back to Ephraim. Upon entering his house, he takes *the* knife (i.e., a knife that is reserved for ritual purposes)[49] and "seizes" his wife again, just as he had "seized" his wife to throw her out to the crowd.[50] In a perversion of sacrificial ritual, he severs her body into twelve pieces (19:29-30). The possibility that the woman may still have been alive during her dismemberment—the Hebrew text does not say that she has died[51]— makes the Levite's brutal gesture even more harrowing. Undoubtedly, the Deuteronomist intends that the Levite's act be contrasted with 1 Samuel 11, where Saul, under the power of God's spirit, hacks a yoke of oxen to pieces. The first king of Israel then sends the pieces throughout the territory to summon the tribes to war against the Ammonites. As ideological propaganda for the monarchy, the depiction of Saul is positive in 1 Samuel 11. He heroically delivers the people of Jabesh-Gilead, who are besieged by the Ammonites. The Levite, however, whose profession should guarantee that the ritual is legitimate, becomes the agent of a grotesque anti sacrifice that desecrates rather than consecrates. A woman's raped and battered body replaces the sacrificial animal.

Responding to the Levite's grisly communication, the tribes assemble at Mizpah, their members numbering four hundred thousand strong (Judg 20:2). By noting that they gather "as one man" and act "as one man" (20:1, 8, 11), the Deuteronomist highlights a corporate entity that will soon incur his reproach: "Every man did what was right in his own eyes."

The tribes ask of the Levite, "Tell us, how did this criminal act come about?" (20:3). But the Levite blatantly suppresses the truth of the matter. He states that the "lords of Gibeah" (20:5) rose up against him. "They intended to kill me," he declares. In fact, those who demanded the Levite were not "lords" but a "perverse lot." In the ideology of male prestige, it is infinitely preferable to be attacked by lords than by the local louts. It is certainly more compatible with the Levite's own upper-class station and his perceived importance. Furthermore, it was not the plan of these ruffians to kill the Levite. They intended what could be regarded among males as a fate worse than death; they wanted to rape him.

Brazenly glossing over the fact that he delivered his wife into the mob, the Levite then recounts that "they raped my concubine until [literally, "and"] she died." But, as noted earlier, the text allows for the disturbing possibility that the Levite killed her himself. The only truthful statement the Levite makes is that he took his wife and cut her into pieces and sent her throughout Israel's territory (20:6). And the truth is not honorable: instead of providing a decent burial—the least he could have done for his wife—the Levite hacks her up and sends her out in a clearly self-serving act. He thus prolongs the villainy against her. The tribes supposedly gather to hear *her* story, the one behind the bloodied arm, hacked leg, and battered head that they received. Her limbs cry out her agony, only to be censored and silenced by her husband's rhetoric.

The Levite concludes his speech by referring to the "vile outrage" the town of Gibeah has committed against Israel, and he enjoins the tribes, "Give your advice and counsel here" (20:6b-7). Commentators normally refer to this episode as the "outrage of Gibeah," but the object of the "outrage" is ambiguous. The Hebrew word for "outrage" is *nebalah*, which the Levite uses here to refer to his wife's rape. However, in 19:23-24, the word is used by the old man to depict the gang-rape attempt on the Levite. The Levite manipulates the *real* outrage against his wife (which he himself caused) to exact retribution for the *attempted* outrage against himself. He could not reveal to the tribes that he was almost raped by dissolute men. He would have incurred dishonor and loss of prestige. Instead, he manipulates his relationship with a woman in order to maneuver his male relations to accomplish his personal vendetta against Gibeah.

Having completed his humiliation and censure of the Levitical class, the Deuteronomist removes the Levite from the scene. He goes after the tribal body next. The social chaos in Judges 20–21 parallels the cultic chaos described in Judges 17–18. Having been duped by the Levite, the tribes wage war against Benjamin. Noteworthy is the kinship language used to describe these intertribal relations (20:13, 23, 28; 21:6). In order to break down kin-group relations among the tribes, the Deuteronomist depicts these "brothers" as engaged in a senseless internecine war. Four hundred thousand Israelites advance against twenty-six thousand Benjaminites. The Deuteronomist describes their confrontations in a slapstick manner. Despite their remarkable numerical advantage, the Israelite tribes are initially decimated by Benjamin. On day one, they lose twenty-two thousand men, almost the number of their opponents themselves (20:21); on day two, eighteen thousand (20:25). But by day three, only thirty men are lost (20:31, 39), and the momentum turns in Israel's favor. They wipe out the tribe of Benjamin, leaving it only six hundred men (20:46-48).

Having intended the extinction of Benjamin, and thus having sworn not to give their daughters to its survivors (21:1), the tribes inexplicably have "compassion for Benjamin their kin" (21:6, 15). But where to get women to replenish Benjamin? The cycle of violence then continues, and the rape of one woman becomes the rape of six hundred. In contrast to 1 Samuel 11, where King Saul protects Jabesh-Gilead, tribal governance and familial allegiance destroy the citizens of that city. Four hundred virgins from Jabesh-Gilead are seized (21:8-12). Two hundred more are taken from the city of Shiloh, a local shrine where a deity cannot protect the people (21:19-23). To explain the anarchy of this period, the Deuteronomist concludes, "In those days there was no king in Israel; every man did what was right in his own eyes" (21:25).

CONCLUSION

An ideological analysis reveals that Judges 17–21 should be contextualized during the time of King Josiah as a literary production of the preexilic Deuteronomist. To support Josiah's so-called religious reform, which demolished popular cult centers that competed with Jerusalem, the Deuteronomist conducts a propaganda war against their clergy, the country Levites. According to Judges 17–18, they are corrupt opportunists intent on financial gain. In Judges 19–21, they become heartless individuals who foment civil war to avenge attempts to dishonor them. But repressed in the text are Josiah's own fiscal ambitions for the state and his redirection of the enormous revenues collected by the Levites into the Jerusalem treasury.

Moreover, Judges 17–21 is a systematic attempt by the Deuteronomist to break up the tribal body in service to the monarchy. It encodes the conflicts between the familial and tributary modes of production. It shifts the history of tribal collapse two centuries back to tribal Israel itself. It subverts prestate kin-group connections in order to centralize and stabilize monarchic sovereignty. The woman's fractured body becomes an ideological symbol of tribal disintegration.[52] As the Levite literally mutilates the body of his wife, the Deuteronomist narratively dis-members the "body" of the tribes.

FURTHER READING

General

Acker, Joan. *Class Questions: Feminist Answers*. Gender Lens Series. Lanham: Rowman and Littlefield, 2006. A materialist-feminist study that integrates the concept of class with those of gender and race for a more comprehensive understanding of social inequalities.

Eagleton, Terry. *Criticism and Ideology: A Study in Marxist Literary Theory.* New ed. London: Verso, 2006. Seeks to develop a more sophisticated relationship between Marxism and literary criticism. Particularly helpful are the chapters on the different modes of production (chapter 2), and the various ways they interrelate, and the significant relations between history, ideology, and the text (chapter 3).

———. *Ideology: An Introduction.* London and New York: Verso, 1991. A lucid, often witty, introduction to the complexities of ideology. Includes chapters on the definition and strategies of ideology, the major thinkers, and the intricate relations among ideology, discourse, and power.

———. *Marxism and Literary Criticism.* Berkeley: University of California Press, 1976. Repr. London: Routledge, 2003, with new preface by the author. A brief look at four central topics of Marxist literary criticism and relevant theorists: literature and history (Marx and Engels); form and content (Lukács, Goldmann, Macherey); the writer and political commitment (Marx and Engels); the author as producer (Benjamin and Brecht).

Eagleton, Terry, and Drew Milne, eds. *Marxist Literary Theory: A Reader.* Oxford and Cambridge, Mass.: Blackwell, 1996. Contains excerpts from the works of twenty-four representative Marxist literary critics, with introductions by the editors.

Homer, Sean. *Fredric Jameson: Marxism, Hermeneutics, Postmodernism.* New York: Routledge, 1998. Provides an entrée into the work of one of the most significant and influential Marxist literary theorists, particularly Jameson's *The Political Unconscious: Narrative as a Socially Symbolic Act* (Ithaca, N.Y.: Cornell University Press, 1981) and *Postmodernism, or, the Cultural Logic of Late Capitalism* (Durham, N.C.: Duke University Press, 1991).

Selden, Raman, et al. "Marxist Theories." In *A Reader's Guide to Contemporary Literary Theory.* 5th ed., 82–114. Harlow, U.K.: Pearson Education, 2005. A short, accessible introduction to Marxist literary theory, including recent scholars (Williams, Eagleton, and Jameson), with bibliography.

Biblical

Boer, Roland. *Marxist Criticism of the Bible.* New York: Sheffield Academic Press and T. & T. Clark International, 2003. Reads selected biblical texts from the Hebrew Bible through the lens of Marxist literary theorists, such as Althusser, Gramsci, Eagleton, and Jameson.

———, ed. *Tracking* The Tribes of Yahweh: *On the Trail of a Classic.* JSOT Sup 351. Sheffield: Sheffield Academic Press, 2002. Assembles a number of biblical scholars to discuss the impact of Gottwald's *Tribes of Yahweh* more than twenty years later. Several comment on Gottwald's application of Marx in analyzing ancient Israel, particularly Boer's own contribution, "Marx, Method and Gottwald."

Ceresko, Anthony R., OSFS. *Introduction to the Old Testament: A Liberation Perspective.* Rev. and updated ed. Maryknoll, N.Y.: Orbis, 2001. An accessible introduction to the Hebrew Bible that applies Gottwald's theory of Israel's social origins, emphasizing the dynamics of social power and conflict that are embedded in the texts and highlighting the political engagement of the reader who interprets them.

Clevenot, Michel. *Materialist Approaches to the Bible.* Maryknoll, N.Y.: Orbis, 1985. A helpful presentation of the "materialist" school of reading the Bible. The first half of the book deals with the Hebrew Bible.

Coote, Robert B., and Mary P. Coote. *Power, Politics, and the Making of the Bible: An Introduction.* Minneapolis: Fortress Press, 1990. A brief survey of formation of the biblical tradition, canons, and ancient commentaries from the tribal period of Israel's history (c. 1250 B.C.E.) to the time of the Babylonian Talmud (c. 530 B.C.E.). Emphasis on the power struggles and conflicts among the elites who produced the Bible.

Gottwald, Norman K. *The Hebrew Bible in Its Social World and in Ours.* Atlanta: Scholars, 1993. A convenient anthology of essays revealing the emergence and development of Gottwald's socioliterary thinking.

————. *The Politics of Ancient Israel.* Louisville: Westminster John Knox, 2001. Employing a critical use of the social sciences, Gottwald attempts to reconstruct the governing structures of Israel, particularly in its ancient Near Eastern context.

————. *Tribes of Yahweh: A Sociology of the Religion of Liberated Israel.* 25th anniversary ed. Biblical Seminar 66. Sheffield: Sheffield Academic Press, 1999. Originally published in 1979, a monumental study of the origins of Israel, perhaps the first of its kind to incorporate a socioliterary method. The 1999 edition has a new preface in which Gottwald reflects on the impact of *Tribes* over the years.

Jobling, David, Peggy L. Day, and Gerald T. Sheppard, eds. *The Bible and the Politics of Exegesis.* Cleveland: Pilgrim, 1991. A fine collection of essays in honor of Norman K. Gottwald, incorporating his socioliterary approach to the Hebrew Bible.

Jobling, David, and Tina Pippin, eds. *Ideological Criticism of Biblical Texts. Semeia* 59 (1992). A collection of essays arising from the Society of Biblical Literature Consultation on Ideological Criticism of Biblical Texts. A talk by Fredric Jameson is reprinted in the collection. Includes a good bibliography on ideological criticism.

Mosala, Itumeleng J. *Biblical Hermeneutics and Black Theology in South Africa.* Grand Rapids: Eerdmans, 1989. A materialist reading of biblical texts from a South African perspective.

Pixley, Jorge. *Biblical Israel: A People's History.* Minneapolis: Fortress Press, 1992. A brief survey of Israelite history from a socioeconomic perspective. Convenient charts on the modes of production and power relations in each period.

Segovia, Fernando F. "Reading the Bible Ideologically: Socioeconomic Criticism." In *To Each Its Own Meaning: An Introduction to Biblical Criticisms and Their Application.* Edited by Steven L. McKenzie and Stephen Haynes. Rev. and expanded, 283–306. Louisville: Westminster John Knox, 1999. Applies a liberationist hermeneutics to a reading of the historical Jesus.

Yee, Gale A. *Poor Banished Children of Eve: Woman as Evil in the Hebrew Bible.* Minneapolis: Fortress Press, 2003. Employs ideological criticism to Genesis 2–3, Hosea 1–2, Ezekiel 23, and Proverbs 7. Argues that a study of gender must be accompanied by an investigation of class, race/ethnicity, and colonial history for a comprehensive understanding of the ideological production of biblical texts.

8

POSTCOLONIAL CRITICISM

Who Is the Other in the Book of Judges?

URIAH Y. KIM

It is difficult for those who have never experienced being treated or rep-resented as an "Other" in relation to the Western subject to understand all the fuss postcolonialism has stirred. Why can't the Rest of the world just follow the program outlined by the well-meaning folks from the West?[1] Well, for a start, the Rest of the world has suffered greatly in the last five hundred years or so at the hand of the West, justifying its con-quest, domination, and exploitation of the Rest as an effort to bring civi-lization to the Rest—to transform the Rest into the likeness of the West. Unfortunately, the Rest is still suffering from the continuing legacy of colo-nialism, which has not been adequately addressed.[2] New modes of colo-nialism (neocolonialism) are forming to maintain the great divide between the West and the Rest. Moreover, knowledge about non-Western peoples and their worlds has been shaped by an epistemological system formed by the West's desire to narrate its own identity—to put itself as the subject of world history—and to represent and manage non-Western folk as the Other.

Postcolonialism as a critical theory emerged in the academy about three decades ago to address the continuing legacy of colonialism in today's world. As a critical theory it questions Western epistemology sim-ilar to the way feminism has critiqued androcentric knowledge. For cen-turies, women were viewed as inferior to men and their knowledge trivial in comparison to the knowledge produced by men, which is accepted as objective and scientific. Similarly, non-Western peoples were viewed as inferior and their knowledge as primitive, superstitious, nonscientific vis-à-vis the knowledge produced by the West. Just as feminism has exposed the all-encompassing system of knowledge that favors men, postcolonial-ism uncovers the wide-ranging system of knowledge that is biased in favor of the West. Feminism's project is not simply for the well-being of women but for all humanity, and thus men as well as women have the ethical responsibility to work toward creating a more equitable world along

gender lines. Similarly, postcolonialism's project is not only for the benefit of non-Western peoples but for all humanity, and the peoples of the
West along with the Rest have the ethical burden to shape a more equitable world.

Modern biblical scholarship claims to study the Bible from an objective perspective, but it emerged within the context of colonialism and continues to favor the history, experience, and aspirations of the West.
Interpreting the Bible from such a context remains problematic and
underexamined. Postcolonial criticism investigates and critiques Western
hermeneutical practices of interpreting the Bible, the most important cultural and religious artifact of the West. One of the unfortunate outcomes
of historical criticism is the marginalization of contextual interpretations
of non-Western readers of the Bible as illegitimate, primitive, superstitious, or nonscientific. Increasingly, however, people who are represented
as the Other are refusing to read the Bible through the eyes of the West.
Postcolonial criticism offers a way for these folks to read the Bible on their
own terms and challenges those who insist on interpreting the Bible from
the perspective of the West, which invariably benefits the West at the
expense of the Rest. This essay will introduce postcolonial criticism by
summarizing briefly the emergence of postcolonialism in the world and
in the academy, discussing the basic features and concerns of postcolonial
criticism, and applying it to the book of Judges.

THE EMERGENCE OF POSTCOLONIALISM IN
THE WORLD AND IN THE ACADEMY

Postcolonialism examines and questions every artifact of Western "mon-
uments" of knowledge and every *iota* of Western "documents" of power.
Even the term "postcolonialism" itself is contested. Some prefer to use the
term with the hyphen ("post-colonialism") to indicate a chronological
moment when many of the West's formerly colonized "nations" became
politically independent shortly after World War II. This term signifies a
beginning of new relations between the West and the Rest. However, if
"post-colonial" nations are understood simply as now independent
nations that were once colonies of Europe, then the term would include
the United States, Australia, and Canada, which became independent
prior to World War II. The use of the term in this way can overlook the
fact that many native peoples and ethnic and racial minorities in these
nations continue to remain in unequal relation to the descendants of the
European settlers. The term without the hyphen ("postcolonialism") indi-

cates continuity with the anticolonial movement, which helped colonized peoples to achieve political independence from the West and equal rights for minorities and natives in the West. It signifies an allegiance to struggles among non-Western peoples who are still dependent on the West politically, economically, and culturally. The use of the term in this way reflects a critical stance against colonialism in the past and its ideological rhetoric (colonial discourse) that is still operative in the present. It also acknowledges the unequal power relation between the West and the Rest in present forms of neocolonialism and is committed to developing a more equitable relation between them. In this essay I will use the term without the hyphen ("postcolonialism") to reflect such understanding.

It should be clear that postcolonialism emerged out of the struggle and experience of the colonized peoples. Unfortunately, the theoretical articulation of postcolonialism by many fine scholars, like postmodernism, has gained a reputation for obscurity and academic jargon that ordinary people and scholars outside the field find difficult to understand.[3] Different peoples in different locations struggled with various problems imposed by colonialism. Different groups have developed different narratives and histories about their struggles with the problems they had to confront. In my case, I see myself as part of the Asian-American community in the United States. This community has its own history of struggle against an American nationalism, rooted in racism since its inception. Asian Americans have been viewed as permanent strangers, foreigners, aliens in the United States owing, in part, to the politics of race and identity based on a discourse of nationalism that equates "real" Americans with being white. As a result, Asian Americans have experienced the danger of being viewed as others rather than as subjects in American history.

The struggle of Asian Americans can be seen as part of the civil rights movement in the United States, but it can also be viewed as part of a larger, global movement for liberation among the colonized peoples. Postcolonialism follows the well-traveled path covered by the footsteps of millions who participated in anticolonial movements in the twentieth century. Anticolonialists tried to restore self-rule by overthrowing the colonial rule of the West. There were those who were not only active in the political arena but who also contributed in the intellectual arena. They exposed the problems and consequences of not only losing control of their land and its resources but also of losing control of their right to produce knowledge on their own terms vis-à-vis the West. Franz Fanon and Albert Memmi were among intellectuals who raised devastating critiques against colonialism and analyzed the effects of colonialism on both the colonizer and the colonized.[4] Colonialism harms the very soul of an individual, both the colonizer and the colonized. Fanon in particular passionately articulated the problem of colonialism and voiced an uncompromising condemnation of it that has inspired and influenced the subsequent generations of postcolonial thinkers.

Even after the independence of former colonies, many have argued that colonialism has not gone away but has morphed into a more subtle form that is still devastating humanity in general, but especially the Rest. Many point to Edward Said's book *Orientalism* as paving the way for a new discipline called postcolonial studies, which examines the effects of colonialism on the world and on cultural texts in particular.[5] It marked a turning point in the study of colonialism and its continuing effects on the world. Said argued that without understanding the enormous influence cultural texts have on the mind-set of the people of the West and the Rest, one could not begin to access the damage caused by colonialism. His most influential argument was that there was a connection between the production of knowledge and the colonization of the Rest by the West. He challenged the chronic habit in the West to deny and distort the cultures and histories of the Orient/Other. Orientalism was a science of understanding that represented non-Western peoples and cultures as different from the West, as the Other, for the purpose of constructing and advancing the identity and interest of the West. Through the lens of Orientalism the West represented the Orient as a place and its inhabitants as inferior, feminine, irrational, and weak in comparison with the West. The works of politicians, writers, historians, biblical scholars, and many others shaped and spread Orientalism in the service of Western interests.[6] To put it simply, Orientalism made racism, the superiority of the West over and against the Other, legitimate. Postcolonialism is a critical theory that tries to draw attention to this connection, to critique knowledge acquired and influenced by this connection, and to retrieve and construct the knowledge of the Other that has been distorted, neglected, or suppressed in the West.

Said tried to do away with the dichotomy of Orient–West by regarding the Orient as merely an ideological construct of the West in the service of Western identity discourse. But because it did not dismantle the dichotomy itself, his effort did not satisfy many scholars. After all, knowledge produced by Orientalism continued to have enormous influence on the way people thought about the Rest. Among the next generation of scholars, Homi Bhabha and Gayatri Spivak are consistently noted as important proponents of postcolonialism.[7] They focused more on the subjectivity of the colonized than on what had been done to the colonized by the colonizer. Bhabha advocates moving away from seeing the nation as the center of history and exploring new spaces from which to write histories of peoples. He argues that the nation is not a fixed social formation. Its instability to unite the people/culture with the state/land shows up in the space of liminality, the inbetween space, where people and culture do not simply comply with the script of the national discourse and "a process of hybridity" occurs.[8] Bhabha wishes to break away from the dualistic thinking that lies behind Orientalism, the "us and them" attitude that sees the people and culture within the imagined community as "us," and any people or culture outside of it as the Other.

Hybridity in culture and people is reality at the local level that constantly questions, disrupts, ruptures, and discontinues the nation's effort to construct a coherent identity through cultural texts, including history writing. Spivak, on the other hand, problematizes the notion that in order to write a history from a location other than the nation (the space of liminality for Bhabha), one simply has to make subalterns (those marginalized) the subjects of their own history. She frames this question by asking whether the subalterns can speak for themselves. She argues that the subalterns cannot speak for themselves because they are in a position where they can only be known, represented, and spoken for by others. By ascribing a voice to the subaltern or representing the subaltern, postcolonial scholars, who themselves have been trained and located in the West, are in actuality speaking for and representing the subaltern, and, as a result, they have replaced Western scholars as the centered subject/agent in respect to marginalized groups. Both Bhabha and Spivak are trying to dismantle Orientalism by complicating and problematizing the representation of the Other and by articulating theoretically what happens when different cultures and peoples engage each other.

BASIC CHARACTERISTICS AND CONCERNS
OF POSTCOLONIAL CRITICISM

It was not until a decade after postcolonialism emerged as an analytic tool in academia in the 1980s that some biblical critics began to employ critical tools and insights from postcolonial studies to interpret the Bible.[9] A simple definition of postcolonial criticism would be an investigation that employs analytic tools and insights from postcolonialism to interpret the Bible. But it is not limited to tools or insights associated with or derived from postcolonialism. In fact, postcolonial criticism uses all types of tools that are available to biblical scholars but is committed to drawing its interpretive energy from postcolonialism. Postcolonial interpreters use notions such as hybridity, liminality, and other terms that are not new but have been redefined and reconfigured by postcolonial theorists to articulate the complex relationship that occurs when the West and the Rest encounter each another.

Postcolonial interpreters use the tools of biblical studies as counter-tools to expose the effects of colonialism on the text and on its interpreters. This can be most clearly seen in the reading strategy of postcolonial criticism. It is a reading against the grain in the sense that it critiques and questions the reading of the Bible from the West's perspective; it is a disobedient reading or oppositional reading that refuses to accept the reading of the text by the West as the norm, as the only reading.[10] It is and must be confrontational at times. It refuses to acknowledge the superiority of the reading strategies developed by the West; it treats scholarship from the West and the Rest equally. This way of reading, both confrontational and complementary to that of the West, characterizes the postcolonial. Ultimately, it seeks a third way of reading the Bible—the first can be described as the reading from the perspective of the West and the second can be characterized as oppositional to the West—that is an alternative to the first and second readings.

Biblical scholars who use postcolonial criticism start with the condition and experience of the Rest rather than with the text. They make intellectual use of the experiences of those who have been colonized by the West in the past and of those who are marginalized by neocolonialism in the present. This is not to say that postcolonial criticism ignores the experiences of those who are of the West. In many ways, the Rest has no choice but to learn about the history and experience of the West, since its history, experience, and aspirations are already built into the Western academic system of knowledge and cultural texts of various kinds. It understands that the West–Rest dichotomy is an ideological construct that needs to be dismantled; yet it utilizes this dyad in order to address the unequal power relation between the West and the Rest that has been shaped by colonialism. Failure to investigate the connection between Western imperialism and the plight of the Rest takes a position that leaves the status quo intact.

Postcolonial interpreters appreciate historical criticism for its contribution to the knowledge of the Bible and the world "behind" the text. However, they insist that biblical scholars must acknowledge that historical criticism emerged in the context of Western imperialism and, therefore, biblical scholarship accumulated through historical criticism must be used critically.[11] It can be argued that interpretations based on historical-critical methods were basically contextual interpretations of the West, that is, interpretation and investigation were driven by Western experiences and interests. Although biblical scholars conducting historical-critical research claimed that they were not influenced by the interests and concerns of their context, Kwok argues that "the political interests of Europe determined the questions to be asked, the gathering of data, the framework of interpretation, and the final outcome."[12] Questions and concerns of historical criticism were different from those that emerged from contexts outside of the West and situations faced by racial minorities in the West. Thus, postcolonial interpreters are not apologetic in raising problems and interests that stem from different locations around the world.

Postcolonial interpreters scrutinize the role of the Bible and its interpreters in colonialism. The colonizers used the Bible to justify their claim to the land, the destruction of native peoples and cultures, and the colonization of the mind and soul of the colonized.[13] The Bible was an integral part of colonial discourse, which facilitated the exploitation and management of the colonized. Biblical scholars, as Said has argued, were also complicit in the machinations of colonialism. Failure to examine the connection between biblical scholarship and colonialism is to become complicit, wittingly or unwittingly, in maintaining the inequitable relationship between the West and the Rest. Therefore, postcolonial interpreters provide a critical focus on how colonialism has influenced and shaped the contours of biblical scholarship and try to put colonialism at the center of biblical scholarship. They take into account the continuing legacy of colonialism in the very fabric of the discipline of biblical studies and colonial habits in the practice of biblical scholars, including non-Western scholars. To disconnect biblical scholarship from current affairs is to treat the Bible primarily as an ancient text that matters only to a small number of specialists and to hide its direct impact on today's world. Postcolonial interpreters insist that interpretation of the Bible must address issues and concerns that matter to the world at large, rather than only to the guild of biblical scholars.

THE QUESTIONS POSED BY POSTCOLONIAL CRITICISM

The questions postcolonial criticism asks can be divided into three levels.[14] The first level engages with *the biblical text*:

- Who were the Israelites? Who were included and excluded in this group identity? How are they portrayed in the text?

- Who were the non-Israelites? What assumptions about them lie behind the text? How are they depicted in the text? Are there stereotypes about them?
- Do the non-Israelites speak? Who speaks for them? Are we given access to their point of view?
- How does the text construct difference among people? Is the difference real, ideological, or imaginary?
- Who commissioned the text? Is there an empire behind the text? Does this text have a clear stance for or against the political imperialism of its time? What unequal power relations are evident in the text?
- Are there suppressed and neglected voices in the text?
- Who are the marginalized or the Other in the text?

The second level engages with *modern biblical scholarship* and raises the following questions:

- What questions and concerns does the scholar bring to the text?
- Whose history, experience, and interests are being inscribed in the scholarship? From whose perspective or context is the text being interpreted?
- Does the accepted scholarship on the biblical text advance the interests of the West at the expense of the Rest?
- Does biblical scholarship appeal to nationalism, Orientalism, and other ideological discourses to express the superiority of the West over the Rest?
- How do biblical scholars portray the non-Israelites and the Israelites? Do they speak for the Israelites or the Other?

The third level engages with *contemporary interpreters:*

- Who see themselves as the Israelites in our time and why? Who are designated as non-Israelites in our time and why?
- How can the contemporary interpreter read the Bible without perpetuating the "us and them" paradigm that constructs one group as superior to another?
- How is the text unsafe (oppressive) as well as safe (liberative) for the interpreter's context?
- What questions and concerns arise from one's context when interpreting the text?

- What ethical responsibility does the contemporary reader have in light of the fact that the Bible and its interpreters had a role in forming unequal relations between the West and the Rest in the past that are still sustained by contemporary readers today?

A POSTCOLONIAL EXEGESIS OF THE BOOK OF JUDGES

A Politics of Identity and Violence against the Other

Since his formulation of the "Deuteronomistic History (DH)" hypothesis, Martin Noth reinforced the practice of reading the book of Judges as a historical book by including it within the DH.[15] One of the more enduring legacies of Noth is the notion that the DH was a history written in the likeness of modern historiography. This view resonated well at the time with biblical historians who, for the most part, were using the methods that have been used by modern historians since the emergence of the discipline of history under the tutelage of Leopold von Ranke in the nineteenth century. Ranke's famous declaration, that he wanted not to pass judgment on the past but simply to report *"wie es eigentlich gewesen ist"* (as it actually happened), has been used as the principle of the modern discipline of history. But, in practice, modern historiography was limited to a political history that described great deeds by great men of the West. It eventually developed into a discourse of nationalism, which narrated a successful story of how the West developed into the nation seen as the pinnacle of civilization. The Rest was forced to imitate the development of the West and relegated to tell its histories through the story of the nation. To put it bluntly, the West was the subject of history, and its identity, experiences, aspirations, and destinies were asserted as the history of the world. Histories of the Rest were subsumed under the "world" history in which the West was the subject.

Historical investigations in biblical scholarship were not immune from appealing to the discourse of nationalism in its effort to write the history of ancient Israel. In doing so, biblical scholars, wittingly or unwittingly, inscribed Western experiences, aspirations, and destinies into the history of ancient Israel. They viewed the DH as a narration of the development of Israel as a nation-state, a model the West imitated and fulfilled when it developed into one.[16] In the process, they infused the identity of the West into the history of ancient Israel; the West replaced Israel as the subject of ancient Israel history. An understanding of the book of Judges as part of a history that relates the development of the nation remains in biblical scholarship as a dominant assumption. Such an understanding is complicit in the politics of identity that legitimates the identity of the West but not that of others. One must keep in mind such politics of identity in interpreting the book of Judges.

Interpreters need to recognize that whenever they appeal to the discourse of nationalism to interpret the book of Judges, they are predisposed to framing their interpretation within the identity discourse of the West. They must use it critically, keeping in mind that other cultures have their own methods of narrating history and their own assumptions about the past. Furthermore, whenever one places oneself in the identity of the West through the discourse of nationalism ("who we are"), one is also susceptible to using the lens of Orientalism to accept (mis)representation of the Other ("who we are not"). David M. Gunn notes that often biblical commentators equate the ancient culture with Oriental culture, "said to be unchanging from ancient until modern times."[17] In commenting on ancient tribal organization, Robert Boling observes that the Westerners have experienced such tribal organization in recent history, "where popular preconceptions of tribes and tribesmen are formed by the American experiences with its 'Wild West' and the European experience with colonies."[18] The practice of commentators comparing the behavior or the deficiency in moral and cultural character of Israel's neighbors (or the ancient time in general) with that of Israel's superior moral and religious character (or the modern time in general) goes unquestioned. Critics continue to find "primitive" behaviors comparable to the behaviors of non-Israelites in cultures from the Rest of the world. Thus, it does not take much to equate an inferiority in Israel's neighbors with the Rest and to equate the superiority of Israel with the West.

At the beginning of her book *Death & Dissymmetry*, Mieke Bal wonders why biblical scholars insist on seeing Judges as a historical book: "In spite of the acknowledged impossibility to establish a chronology of the events narrated in Judges, not a single commentary refrains from attempting to do so, or at least bringing up the problem of chronology."[19] She argues that such a strong commitment to keep a coherent military-political history for reading Judges is motivated by the desire to connect maleness and nationalism, and reflects a modern interest in maintaining a world that is represented in the book, namely, that of gender-bound violence. Another reality narrated in Judges that needs to be examined from a postcolonial perspective is the existence of violence against those who are constructed as the Other. The desire to employ the discourse of nationalism in reading Judges as a coherent historical work keeps the West as the subject of the narrative with the Rest relegated to play the role of the Other. Regina Schwartz also notices biblical scholarship's preoccupation with history and its easy projection of nationalism into the Bible.[20] Such a habit, she argues, is dangerous, because the West's interests are read "into the Bible through the backdoor of something as seemingly innocent as historical-critical scholarship" but it ends up offering interpreters "evidence" for justifying the oppression of other people.[21]

Using the Bible to rationalize the subjection of other people has been all too common in the history of engagement between the West and the Rest. J. Clinton McCann provides an example of the (mis)use of the book of Judges by Christian interpreters to legitimate violence against others: "Puritan preachers in colonial North America suggested that the indigenous peoples were to be viewed as Canaanites while the Christian English settlers were the successors of the Israelites—God's New Israel."[22] McCann proposes that the book of Judges cannot be used to sanction mistreatment of others if one believes that God loves all people and not just the chosen ones. He argues that "the references to Canaanites and other peoples named in the book of Judges as enemies of Israel must be understood symbolically."[23] This move leads to his conclusion that

> when references to "the Canaanites" are heard symbolically as references to ways of organizing social life that perpetuate injustice and ultimately produce oppressive inequalities that threaten human life, then the book of Judges will not be heard as justification for any "chosen" group to take the land and/or resources of others.[24]

This sounds innocent enough. However, Schwartz locates the origin of violence against others in the very act of representing the Other, whether symbolic or real: "Violence is not only what we do to the Other. It is prior to that. Violence is the very construction of the Other."[25] One cannot simply blame the interpreters for their (mis)use of Judges to justify violence against others. To understand the Other in Judges symbolically will only lead to slotting some group into that symbolic Other. In order to make it improper to appropriate Judges to oppress the Other, we first need to examine the very process of constructing the Other in Judges.

The book of Judges is filled with violent stories involving the Israelites and other peoples who lived in the same land. In contrast to the book of Joshua, which describes the Israelites as having conquered the whole land and achieving peaceful settlement, what we find in Judges is an ongoing conflict between them and other folks because not all the natives in fact were eliminated (see Judges 1). Israelites were living side by side with other inhabitants. Judges describes them living among the local population (1:31-33). But, in some cases, it also notes the indigenes living among them (1:21, 27, 29, 30). It depicts the land as a "contact zone," to use a postcolonial term, where "people of different geographical and historical backgrounds are brought into contact with each other, usually shaped by inequality and conflictual relations."[26] Israel was in a space of cultural and geographic liminality. It was primarily located in the central highlands between areas along the coast and lowlands controlled by the Canaanites and the Philistines (newcomers to the land, like the Israelites) and areas controlled by emerging Transjordan kingdoms such as Midian, Moab, and Ammon on the eastern front. What we see in Canaan is a competition between the Israelites and other peoples fighting over the land once populated by the local Canaanites. Israel's neighbors wanted to settle in Canaan just as much as the Israelites did. Different parts of the land experienced different patterns of occupation—a combination of the conquest, the migration, and the revolt models is needed to draw the complex picture of Canaan at the time of Israel's settlement adequately. At some sites, the Israelites, depicted as outsiders displaced the local Canaanites. At other sites, foreigners such as the Philistines, Sea Peoples from the Aegean area, displaced the Canaanites. The Israelites and the Philistines were among several groups of people who competed over the land.

The hostility among these neighbors was real and fierce. Depicting Israel's neighbors as enemies in Judges, however, made the situation worse. The Canaanites and other neighbors were presented as Israel's antagonists in Judges without much qualification. Once their neighbors were portrayed as foes, it did not make a difference who the opposition was at the time of a given crisis. Judges ignores the fact that some of these inhabitants were related to the Israelites—for example, the Ammonites and the Moabites were related through Abraham's nephew Lot (Gen 19:30-38) and the Midianites were related through Abraham's second wife, Keturah (Gen 25:1-4). In fact, according to more recent theories, the Israelites were not outsiders to Canaan at all. They were in fact Canaanites. But the various groups of people were all the same to the Israelites in the reality of representation. The others were constructed as adversaries who were sources of their infidelity and oppression.

In order to formulate their own identity as a group, it seems that humans have a habit of constructing the Other negatively: they are who we are not. This demarcation justifies acts of violence against the Other. Sam Keen calls human beings "the enemy-making animals" that need to create villains to bear the burden of their insecurity and suppressed hatred.[27] He argues that if humans leave this habit unchecked and unexamined, then they will continue to make hostile relations with each other worse than they are and find excuses to rationalize aggression against each other. The Rest in particular has suffered greatly as a result of the habit of the West to represent the Rest as its Other. From a postcolonial perspective, the habit of equating the Rest with Israel's opposition, and thereby vindicating the taking and exploiting of the land and its resources and the acts of hostility against the Rest, needs to be stopped.

A Narrative of Struggle for Identity

In its very first verse, the book of Judges opens with the "us versus them" mentality: "Who will go up first for us against the Canaanites, to fight against them?" Then the Deuteronomistic prologue (2:6—3:6) sets the stage for the conflict between the Israelites and their neighbors. The coinhabitants of the land are introduced as antagonists who are to be eliminated or at least put under control, and definitely not to be intermingled with. The prologue claims that the Israelites were surrounded by rivals and were forewarned that they would be turned over into the hand of "their enemies all around" if they did not stay faithful to God and followed the gods of their neighbors (2:11-15). This warning is carried out throughout chapters 2–16, where each crisis begins with the formulaic saying that the Israelites had done "evil in the sight of the Lord" (3:7; 3:12; 4:1; 6:1; 10:6; 13:1), which results in the Israelites being handed over to their foes with God's authorization (3:8; 3:12; 4:2; 6:1; 10:7; 13:1).[28] Who were their neighbors who persecuted them? The prologue states that the Israelites lived among "the Canaanites, the Hittites, the Amorites, the Perizzites, the Hivites, and the Jebusites" (3:5), the stock peoples of Canaan according to the Exodus tradition. Thus, one expects the Israelites to be struggling with these peoples. But what we read are their conflicts with the Arameans (3:7-11), the Moabites (3:12-30), northern Canaanites (chapters 4 and 5), the Midianites (chapters 6–8), the Ammonites (chapters 10–12), and the Philistines (chapters 13–16). It makes no difference which ethnic group the Israelites were in dispute with. The narrative fixes the role of Israel's Other as the antagonist in the construction of Israel's identity. The representation of the Other as the villain who always schemes to plunder and oppress the Israelites is the common threat that would unite different tribes into one Israel and help to forge a coherent community of Israel.

Judges uses the word *goy* (often translated as "nation") to refer to Israel's coinhabitants of the land (2:21, 2:23, 3:1),[29] but the most common word

Judges uses to designate the Other is the *ᵓoyev* ("enemy"; 2:14, 2:18, 3:28, 5:31, 8:34, 11:36). Israel's others are united in their enmity against Israel. On the other hand, the narrative uses *beney yisraᵓel* ("the sons of Israel" but translated as "the Israelites" in the NRSV; this term is used more than seventy times, 1:1, 2:4, 3:2, 4:1, etc.) and *ᵓaḥim* ("brothers," but also translated as "kinsfolk" in the NRSV; 9:1, 18:8, 20:13, etc.) to construct Israel's identity as a kinship group. The claim is that the Israelites are united by blood relations and, therefore, Israel's identity is "natural."[30] The Other can never be included in Israel, according to such ideological construct. There is a "natural" separation that can never be crossed.

The narrative paints the Other in very broad strokes and is not interested in providing their specific characteristics, although there are rare instances of this. In referring to the Midianites, it says, "For they had golden earrings, because they were Ishmaelites" (8:24), and "the crescents" were on the neck of the camels of the kings of Midian (8:21, 8:26). According to Genesis, the Ishmaelites were "children" of Ishmael, son of Abraham and Hagar (Gen 16) and the Midianites were "children" of Midian, son of Abraham and Keturah (Gen 25:1-4). It is surprising that Judges lumps these two distinctive peoples together as one. However, this is a common strategy in identity politics. From Israel's perspective, Ishmaelites and Midianites were interchangeable; there was no difference between these two different ethnic groups. When Samson wanted a Philistine woman for his wife, his parents asked him, "Is there not a woman among your kin (*ᵓaḥim*), or among all our people, that you must go to take a wife from the uncircumcised Philistines?" (14:3). The Philistines were labeled "the uncircumcised" (14:3; 15:18) and they were the only ones to be branded as such in the DH (1 Sam 14:6, 17:26, 36, 31:4; 2 Sam 1:20). The practice of circumcision had a special importance to the Israelites. It was a sign of the "everlasting covenant" between God and Abraham's children (Gen 17:9-14). God warns that whoever does not practice circumcision will be "cut off" from the people (Gen 17:14). The practice of circumcision functions as an identity marker, a cultural practice that distinguishes Israelites from the Philistines, their archenemies during the period of Judges, in the days of Saul and David, and during Josiah's time when the first edition of the DH was most likely edited.

The leaders of the other peoples are also portrayed through broad strokes. They either have no description from the narrator or are comical and incompetent. King Cushan-rishathaim (3:7-11) has no description and says no word. King Eglon (3:12-30) is described as "a very fat man" (3:17) and the only word attributed to him is "silence" (3:19), which ironically is an apt description of the silencing of the Other. King Jabin of Hazor does not speak. He lets his commander do the fighting (chapters 4–5). Sisera ignominiously runs away on foot, only to be slain by a woman, whose husband's clan was at peace with King Jabin. Oreb and Zeeb were two captains of Midian who were killed without saying a word; they couldn't say a word because their heads were severed (7:25). Zebah and Zalmunna were the kings of Midian whose words only hastened their death (8:18-21). The king of the Ammonites demanded that the Israelites return "his land" (11:13); the narrator gives Jephthah thirteen verses to make a case that the land belongs to Israel (11:15-27). But the king of the Ammonites does not get a chance to make a rebuttal (11:28). Finally, the leaders of the Philistines need the help of a woman, Delilah, to capture Samson (chapter 16). One wonders how these leaders were able to oppress the Israelites in the first place. Nevertheless, they had one common goal—to oppress the Israelites.[31]

What was the purpose of constructing the Other negatively? Perhaps it was to justify the conquest and ownership of the land. Because the Israelites did not have the "natural" link to the land (the biblical narrative depicts them as coming from outside of the land, as foreigners), did they feel that they had to make a connection to the land through their theology? The land belonged to them because God promised the land to their ancestors. Constructing Israel's Other as the adversary who wanted to destroy its very existence by denying its ownership of the land helped Israel's various groups to unite as one people who were collectively threatened by the common enemy. This strategy is a characteristic of "anticonquest" ideology in colonial discourse, which describes "the literary strategies that allow colonizers to claim foreign lands while securing their innocence."[32] Some of the characteristics of this ideology are that: (a) it authorizes traveling to the targeted land which is defined as a God-promised land; (b) it constructs the image of the targeted land and its people; and (c) the "conquest" is authorized by God. According to Musa Dube, "Basically, the narrative casts the people of the targeted land negatively in order to validate the annihilation of all the inhabitants."[33] But it is important to establish the superiority of the colonizing people against the colonized so that "the anticonquest ideology can posit that it is acceptable to dispossess, depopulate, resettle, enslave, or annihilate those who are supposedly less deserving."[34] The larger narrative from Genesis to 2 Kings reveals these elements: (a) God has given the authority to the Israelites to travel to Canaan which is described as a promised land (Genesis to Exodus); (b) the land is described as a land "flowing with milk and honey" but its people are constructed negatively (Exodus to Deuteronomy); and (c) God has commanded the Israelites to conquer the land (Joshua and

Judges). In Judges, no justification is needed for the conquest of the land because it has been established in the previous books. In the story of the migration of Dan (Judg 18), one can see all three characteristics of the anticonquest ideology: (a) the tribe of Dan is looking for a territory to live in, sends spies to look for a place to settle, and receives a confirmation from Micah's priest that the mission will go well; (b) the spies come to Laish and observes that the people live securely, "lacking nothing on earth, possessing wealth" (18:7); and (c) God gives them permission to conquer the city, "The land is broad—God has indeed given it into your hands—a place where there is no lack of anything on earth" (18:10). The Danites burn down the city and put its inhabitants to the sword and then they rename the city Dan (18:27-29).

An interesting dialogue occurs between Jephthah and the king of Ammonites over the ownership of a territory east of Jordan (11:12). The Ammonites waged war against Israel over this piece of land. Jephthah, as the newly selected leader of the Gileadites, sent couriers with this message: "What is there between you and me, that you have come to me to fight against *my land?*" (11:12, emphasis added). The king of the Ammonites replied: "Because Israel, on coming from Egypt, took away *my land* from the Arnon to the Jabbok and to the Jordan; now therefore restore it peaceably" (11:13, emphasis added). Both Jephthah and the Ammonite king claim that the territory is "my land." Jephthah delivers a long argument that God has given the land to the Israelites; therefore, the Ammonites have no claim to it. Jephthah concludes his long speech with a challenge: "Let the Lord, who is judge, decide today for the Israelites or for the Ammonites" (11:27). The passage ends without a word from the Ammonite king (11:28), implying that the claim made by Jephthah (and the Israelites) was correct, leaving the Ammonite king speechless. The Ammonite king perhaps did not respond because Jephthah's arguments were heavy on rhetoric but light on facts.[35]

This story reminds us that every piece of land can be contested. Every site has a history of its own, full of "inscriptions" left by diverse groups of people who inhabited it over a long period of time. In its effort to write a national history, colonial discourse erases the prior history of the territory and sees it as an empty space for its own history to unfold in time. The land is seen as empty, ready to accept new people and their narratives. From a postcolonial perspective, however, it is viewed as a palimpsest, written and overwritten by successive inscriptions, where there are always traces of previous inscriptions, other histories, and other memories. Jerusalem, the cultic center and capital of Judah, was once called Jebus, inhabited by the Jebusites (1:8, 21; 19:10-12). The narrative is not clear as to when Jebus was conquered and who conquered it: Judah took Jerusalem and set the city on fire (1:8); the Jebusites continued to live in Jerusalem among the Benjaminites "to this day" (1:21); a Levite decides to bypass Jebus (with the parenthetical note that it is Jerusalem) because it is "a city of foreigners, who do not belong to the people of Israel" (19:12).[36] Bethel and Dan were two cultic centers of the Northern Kingdom, which once belonged to the Other. Bethel was formerly called Luz (1:22-27). A man and his family were spared from the sword of the house of Joseph because he cooperated with them and showed them the way into the city. Then "the man went to the land of the Hittites and built a city, and named it Luz" (1:26). Dan was formerly called Laish (18:27). Hebron was formerly called Kiriath-arba, inhabited by the Canaanites (1:10). Debir was formerly called Kiriath-sepher (1:11; see the insightful essay by Danna Nolan Fewell in this volume). These traces of those who traveled the territory prior to the arrival of the Israelites remind us that no inscription on the land is permanent and every overwritten inscription on it can be recovered.

Who belongs to Israel? In the book of Judges, clear boundaries as to who belonged to Israel had to be drawn, in order to construct its identity as a people set apart from the Other, as a people "exceptionally different" from the Other.[37] This was not an easy task. The book of Judges indicates an ongoing questioning of Israel's identity without coming to a definite answer. Which people are inside the boundaries of the community of Israel? This is not clear or certain. There is some arbitrariness regarding which group belongs to Israel and which group doesn't. In the list of clans that participated in the battle against Sisera (5:12-23), Machir (5:14), who participated in the battle, and Meroz (5:23), who did not, are listed among the tribes of Israel. But they are not usually mentioned as one of the tribes. What happens when a group belonging to Israel behaves like the Other? The Benjaminites in Gibeah betray the trust of a fellow Israelite (19:22-30) who decides to bypass Jebus/Jerusalem because it is "a city of foreigners, who do not belong to the people of Israel" (19:12) but comes to a violent encounter with the men of Gibeah. Then there are cases where a group or a person is situated in a liminal position, blurring a neat division. An unnamed man of Luz helped the house of Joseph to conquer his own city (1:22-26). Is he Israel's enemy even though he helped Israel accomplish its mission? A Midianite has a dream of God giving victory to Gideon (7:13-14). Is one who dreams of Israel's victory an enemy of Israel? Heber the Kenite had a peace agreement with King Jabin of Hazor (4:17), with whom the Israelites were at war. Nevertheless, his wife Jael helps the Israelites by killing King Jabin's captain. Where does she belong? How about Delilah?

Is she an Israelite or a Philistine? Those who are characterized by hybridity and liminality pose a threat to Israel by blurring and disrupting the boundaries that are needed to forge a coherent identity for it.

However, the narrative of Judges tries to maintain one clear boundary throughout: the Israelites are not to marry the Other. More specifically, the sons of Israel must stay away from other women of the land. This prohibition was tied to God's command not to prostitute themselves with other gods. Sexual fidelity was inherently tied to divine fidelity. But, the sons of Israel had a weakness for other women and other gods. The narrative warns that for the sons of Israel to marry women from outside inevitably leads to worshipping their gods. The prologue ends on the ominous note that the Israelites "took their daughters as wives for themselves, and their own daughters they gave to their sons; and they worshiped their gods" (3:6). The book of Judges concludes with the story of the abduction of four hundred women from Jabesh-gilead and an unspecified number of women from Shiloh in order to restock the Benjamin tribe after the war between it and the rest of the Israelites left only six hundred men of its own (21:8-24). This was done in order for the Israelites to remain faithful to God (for they swore not to give their daughters to the rebellious tribe) and to maintain the purity of the Benjaminites (by not marrying women outside of Israel). Sexual fidelity and divine fidelity are connected and work together to confirm Israel's distinct identity.

The book of Judges sees non-Israelite women as a threat to the purity or divine fidelity of the sons of Israel. Another way to look at this is to understand that the identity of Israel is constructed along the lines of gender: Israel as man and the Other as woman. Israel's identity is connected to maleness. Not only foreign women but women in general pose a threat to this Israeliteness or maleness. Women have the capacity to neuter the sons of Israel. The strongman Samson twice surrendered his secrets to other women (14:1-17; 16:4-20). It was a woman, Delilah, who neutralized his strength, his manliness. He used to "ravage" (from the verb *harav,* "to lay waste, make desolate") the Philistines, but now he "performed" (from the verb *sahaq,* "to laugh, sport, play") for them. This reversal of gender role undermines the relationship between Israel and the Other, Israel as man and the Other as woman. It is not just foreign women who deconstruct Israel's identity. An Israelite woman humiliated Abimelech when she killed him with a millstone (9:53-54). Jephthah lamented that his daughter caused him to "bow down" (11:35; *kara*ᶜ). Furthermore, the Israeliteness was inscribed on the body of women. Jephthah sacrificed his daughter in order to keep his fidelity to God (11:34-40). The Levite's concubine was cut-up into twelve pieces to symbolize the severed disunity of

Israel (19:29-30; 20:6). Attempting to preserve his masculinity, the Levite tells the other Israelites that the men of Gibeah wanted to kill him (20:5) when they actually wanted to have sexual intercourse with him. To prevent being placed in the sexual position of women, he pushed his concubine to the men of Gibeah and lied to his people to save his male honor, his identity as a son of Israel.

"Who is an Israelite?" is a question that is left unanswered when the construction of identity disintegrates at the end of the book. The internal dissension that had been in the background to this point comes to the fore in the last episode of the book. The Levite's concubine was dismembered into twelve sections to symbolize the disunity of Israel and to challenge the Israelites to reconfirm what it means to be an Israelite. A civil war broke out between Benjamin, who refused to turn over the men of Gibeah for punishment, and the other tribes of Israel. The narrative claims that "all the men of Israel" (*kol 'ish yisra'el*) were "united as one man" (*'ish 'ehad haberim*) against the city (20:11). The war ended in complete destruction of Benjamin, save six hundred men who were able to escape to the wilderness (20:47-48). Then the sons of Israel lament that one tribe was "cut off" from Israel, because the other tribes vowed not to give their daughters to the Benjaminites (21:1-7), who were not permitted to marry outside of Israel if they wanted to stay within its boundaries. In order to reconnect them to Israel, the leaders propose to supply women to the surviving men from two sources. They destroy Jabesh-gilead but spare four hundred virgins to give to the six hundred Benjaminites (21:8-14). They then instruct the men to abduct untold number of young women from Shiloh for their wives (21:20-24). Benjamin is reunited with the other tribes through acts of violence, concluding the book of Judges on an ominous note: "every man did what was right in his own eyes" (22:25). The identity of Israel is not as cohesive as the narrative tries to portray; it needs acts of aggression to barely maintain its form. The narrative struggles to sustain its unity, as it is cut and recut like the Levite's concubine, always in danger of fragmenting again and again.

CONCLUSION

The identity of Israel, united as one people threatened by the Other, is constructed through acts of violence. The Other is represented as an enemy who wants to destroy and oppress Israel, and as a woman who threatens the divine and sexual fidelity of its men. But who is the Other? The book of Judges is unable to clearly define and sustain who the Other is. It shows that there are too many ruptures and discontinuities to draw a unified identity. The narrative is unsure who is an Israelite and who is an Other. Identifying a group as Israelite and another as belonging to the Other thus becomes dangerous. The fact that Israel's identity was questioned throughout the narrative should warn us against using the narrative to support any ideological discourse, but especially colonial discourse, which was used to justify colonizing the Other. In the post-9/11 world, such an identity discourse only makes hostility between peoples of different nationalities, cultures, religions, and ideologies worse than it already is. It can be easily used to rationalize violence against each other. Who see themselves as the Israelites and who are relegated into playing the role of the Other in the post-9/11 world? Who is the Other? This should not be an easy question to answer. Unless we see ourselves in the Other and see the Other in ourselves, we are in danger of repeating the habit of making enemies of our neighbors, representing the Other negatively in order to sanction our use of violence against them.

FURTHER READING

General

Ashcroft, Bill, Gareth Griffiths, and Helen Tiffin. *Post-Colonial Studies: The Key Concepts*. London: Routledge, 2000. A helpful collection of key terms in postcolonialism.

Bhabha, Homi K. *The Location of Culture*. London: Routledge, 1994. A collection of essays by one of the foremost theorists of postcolonialism. Terms like "hybridity," "liminality," among others, developed and expounded by Bhabha, have become a requisite part of the postcolonial vocabulary.

Fanon, Frantz. *The Wretched of the Earth*. New York: Grove, 1966. A significant work by one of the most influential anticolonial voices articulating forcefully the need for the formerly colonized peoples to move beyond (to decolonize) their colonial condition and mind-set.

Memmi, Albert. *The Colonizer and the Colonized*. Boston: Beacon, 1965. An important analysis of the relationship between the colonizer and the colonized that condemns colonial relations to be detrimental to both parties but more so to the colonized than to the colonizer.

Said, Edward. *Orientalism*. New York: Random House, 1978. Many point to this work as a seminal work that started postcolonial studies as an academic discipline. It analyzed and critiqued the connection between the production of knowledge about the Orient and colonialism.

Spivak, Gayatri Chakravorty. *The Post-Colonial Critic: Interviews, Strategies,*

Dialogues. Edited by Sarah Harsym. New York: Routledge, 1990. This is a collection of interviews with one of the leading postcolonial theorists. Discusses various postcolonial issues in a more accessible manner.

———. "Can the Subaltern Speak?" In *Colonial Discourse and Post-colonial Theory*. Edited by Patrick Williams and Laura Chrisman, 66–111. New York: Columbia University Press, 1994. Spivak questions whether the subalterns (especially the women) can speak for themselves and problematizes the intellectual's role in constructing the marginalized and speaking for them.

Young, Robert J. C. *White Mythologies: Writing History and the West*. London: Routledge, 1990. This work critiques the way the West wrote history. It argues that the West made itself the subject of a single "world" history, leaving the Rest of the world as no more than "surplus" to its narrative. It has generated much debate on writing history and postcolonial theory.

———. *Postcolonialism: A Very Short Introduction*. Oxford: Oxford University Press, 2003. This short book introduces postcolonialism from the ground level, presenting the central issues and concerns of postcolonialism through actual events, situations, and stories of people rather than examining the abstract theory of postcolonialism. This is a compelling introduction that speaks to the heart as well as the mind of the reader.

Biblical

Donaldson, Laura E., ed. *Postcolonialism and Scripture Reading. Semeia*, 75. Atlanta: Society of Biblical Literature, 1996. One of the first collections of essays by biblical scholars on postcolonialism's impact on interpreting the Bible. It focuses critically on imperialism, neocolonialism, and Eurocentrism.

Dube, Musa W. *Postcolonial Feminist Interpretation of the Bible*. St. Louis: Chalice, 2000. Examines the connection between patriarchy and imperialism in interpreting the Bible. It is a good resource for understanding methods and assumptions behind postcolonial criticism.

Kim, Uriah Y. *Decolonizing Josiah: Toward a Postcolonial Reading of the Deuteronomistic History*. Sheffield: Sheffield Phoenix Press, 2005. Examines the Deuteronomistic History from a postcolonial perspective.

Kwok, Pui-lan. *Discovering the Bible in the Non-Biblical World*. Maryknoll, N.Y.: Orbis, 1995. In order for the Bible to be relevant to the people of Asia, Kwok suggests that postcolonial scholars need to use methods other than historical criticism and put Asian cultural texts in a dialogue with the Bible.

———. *Postcolonial Imagination & Feminist Theology*. Louisville: Westminster John Knox, 2005. Encourages feminist theologians to expand their theological imagination by engaging with postcolonialism and postcolonial theologians to include issues of gender in their work. For biblical scholars, chapters 3 and 4 are of particular interest, where she discusses the connection between postcolonialism and feminist biblical interpretation.

Segovia, Fernando. *Decolonizing Biblical Studies: A View from the Margin.* Maryknoll, N.Y.: Orbis, 2000. A collection of essays by a noted biblical scholar in North America advocating a postcolonial reading strategy.

Sugirtharajah, R.S. *Postcolonial Criticism and Biblical Interpretation.* Oxford: Oxford University Press, 2002. An excellent introduction and argument by a prolific biblical scholar for readers of the Bible to engage with postcolonial criticism.

———. ed. *The Postcolonial Biblical Reader.* Oxford: Blackwell, 2006. A collection of important essays that shaped postcolonial criticism in biblical studies, including works by R. S. Sugirtharajah, Fernando Segovia, Kwok Pui-lan, Laura Donaldson, Stephen Moore, Tat-siong Benny Liew, and Musa Dube, among others.

Whitelam, Keith W. *The Invention of Ancient Israel: The Silencing of Palestinian History.* London: Routledge, 1996. A controversial book that examines the relation between biblical scholars and their representation of ancient Israel in the image of the West, which, Whitelam claims, has obscured the history of ancient Palestine. This work follows the spirit of Said's *Orientalism.*

9

GENDER CRITICISM

The Un-Manning of Abimelech

KEN STONE

"Gender criticism" is not a phrase that one encounters very often in biblical studies. Even outside of biblical scholarship, in fact, the phrase is considered ambiguous. Thus the literary theorist Eve Kosofsky Sedgwick opens a methodological essay on the subject with the statement that "'Gender criticism' sounds like a euphemism for something."[1] The phrase's ambiguity is partly owing to the fact that, as Sedgwick goes on to observe, the analytic questions associated with any useful notion of gender criticism are derived in part from, and closely related to, several other fields of study, including, in particular, feminist criticism and lesbian and gay studies. Like several of the "criticisms" outlined in other chapters of this volume, gender criticism is most often practiced as an interdisciplinary enterprise. Its practitioners utilize a range of methods when those methods shed light on the issues explored by gender criticism.

How, then, might we grasp the particular angles of vision from which gender criticism approaches its objects of study? Wrestling with this question, Sedgwick chooses to emphasize the analytic link between gender and sexuality while suggesting that gender criticism can usefully be understood as "not criticism *through* the categories of gender analysis but criticism *of* them."[2] That is to say, concepts associated with gender—including man and woman, male and female, masculinity and femininity—are used by gender criticism, but they are not taken for granted or assumed to have stable referents. It would therefore not be quite right to say, for example, that gender criticism simply combines "women's studies" with the study of "men" or "manhood." Representations of men and cultural notions of manhood are indeed studied by gender criticism, as are representations of women and cultural notions of womanhood. However, instead of studying "men" or "women" as such, gender criticism analyzes critically the cultural notions and social processes that function not only to differentiate "men" from "women," but also to differentiate some men or male characters from other men or male characters, and some women or female characters from other women or female characters. It also highlights instances in which gender takes unexpected forms or fails to conform to dominant assumptions, including the widespread assumption that gender can always be understood in strictly binary terms (e.g., male versus female, or masculine versus feminine). Refusing to be confined by this assumption, gender criticism even explores such gender-related topics as "female masculinity" or intersexed bodies—hardly conventional objects of analysis for either "men's studies" or "women's studies" as traditionally practiced.[3]

Gender criticism therefore involves the interpreter simultaneously in at least two analytic moves. On the one hand, it underscores the significance of gender throughout society and culture, analyzing the role of gender in a range of cultural products, including biblical texts. On the other hand, it does not simply adopt gender notions as tools for analysis, but also problematizes those same notions as objects of analysis. In the process, those notions, including the very distinction between "man" and "woman," are potentially destabilized, especially under the influence of such recent developments as queer theory. Although in practice these interpretive moves are not separable, they will be considered here in turn for purposes of convenience.

ANALYZING (WITH) GENDER

An important point of departure for much gender criticism has been the modern distinction between sex and gender. This sex/gender distinction was initially developed as an analytic tool by English-speaking psychiatrists, who wished to differentiate biological sex, on the one hand, from socialized gender identity, on the other.[4] According to the terms of this psychiatric distinction, "sex" refers to the biological difference between male and female, whereas "gender" refers to the social or psychological differences between "masculine" and "feminine."[5] Using this distinction, psychiatrists hoped to understand how, for example, a transsexual might have a male biological sex while identifying psychologically with a feminine gender.

However, the distinction between sex and gender has been most influential in English-speaking feminism.[6] For many feminists, the sex/gender distinction has provided a tool for analyzing the subordination of women to men that, it has been hoped, will avoid naturalizing such subordination. One common form of naturalization takes place when women's oppression is justified by appeals to supposed biological facts. Most feminists who make use of the sex/gender distinction acknowledge that biological differences between men and women exist and refer to these biological differences as matters of "sex." However, culture and society organize and give meaning and significance to biological sex differences. The construction and organization of such differences are therefore analyzed under the rubric of "gender." Thus, historian Joan Scott calls gender "a social category imposed on a sexed body";[7] film theorist Teresa de Lauretis refers to it as "a symbolic system or system of meanings, that correlates sex to cultural contents according to social values and hierarchies."[8] The distinction between sex and gender therefore corresponds roughly to a distinction between nature and biology, on the one side, and culture and society, on the other side.

One influential exploration of the sex/gender distinction, which has some relevance for both gender criticism and biblical interpretation, can be found in Gayle Rubin's 1975 essay "The Traffic in Women." Rubin calls for analysis of the "sex/gender system," which she defines as "the set of arrangements by which a society transforms biological sexuality into products of human activity, and in which these transformed sexual needs are satisfied."[9] If human economic systems transform raw materials into goods and property, often in ways that result in economic inequality, so also "sex/gender systems" transform biological elements, "the biological raw material of human sex and procreation," into social relations of gender, usually in ways that result in inequality between the sexes.[10]

Rubin examines the mechanisms of this transformation through a reading of, among other bodies of theory, structuralist kinship accounts. Such accounts argue that incest taboos function to enforce exchanges of women between groups of men.[11] By prohibiting certain sexual partners, incest taboos cause men to seek out other sexual partners. Consequently, men exchange their own daughters and sisters for daughters and sisters from other kinship groups. These exchanges result in a network of social alliances that hold traditional kinship societies together. While Rubin criticizes the tendency to universalize such exchanges, she also notes that structuralist kinship theory provides a way of understanding the symbolic logic of many societies that do subordinate women to men. Functioning as agents of sexual exchange, men establish and negotiate their relations with one another through their relations with women. Women, reduced to the status of objects, serve as the "conduit of a relationship" between men.[12] Thus, men and women are differentiated from one another by being assigned specific roles in relation to kinship, society, and the quest for sexual partners.

The potential relevance for biblical interpretation of this gendered conception of women as "conduits" for relations between the men who
exchange them can be seen in, among other biblical texts, Judges 3:5-6.
Here we read that the Israelites lived among peoples of Canaan "and they
took their daughters as wives for themselves, and their own daughters they
gave to their sons; and they worshiped their gods."[13] As in Rubin's
"sex/gender system," male characters are here the subjects, and female
characters the objects, of exchange. Although Judges 3 takes a dim view
of the social relations that developed between the Israelites and other peoples living in Canaan as a result of these exchanges of daughters, other biblical texts make clear that such exchanges of women were understood in
ancient Israel to solidify social relations between groups of men (e.g., Gen
34:8-12). Although structuralist kinship accounts, even as reworked by
Rubin, are probably insufficient for a complete understanding of biblical
texts dealing with incest,[14] it seems clear that exchanges of women are
understood to function in certain biblical texts, including texts from
Judges, as ways of establishing or strengthening alliances between men.

However, not only relations of alliance, but also relations of conflict, can
be forged in terms of the "traffic in women." As Regina Schwartz points out
in a discussion of biblical narrative, "when women are stolen, rather than
peaceably exchanged, the relational directions reverse, from friendship
toward fear, from alliance toward hostility."[15] The potential importance of
this point for readers of Judges may begin to emerge when we recall that
the book includes quite vivid representations of women being "stolen,
rather than peaceably exchanged," for example, in chapters 19–21. Exploring such representations in terms of the sex/gender distinction, gender criticism insists that there is nothing inherent in women that makes them
naturally more suited to being exchanged or stolen, and nothing inherent
in men that requires them by nature to exchange or steal women. The
assumption that men are properly subjects of exchange, and women properly objects, is a matter of gender and society rather than sex and biology.

To say that these assumptions are a matter of gender and society is not
to imply, however, that such assumptions are easily changed. As sociolo-
gist Pierre Bourdieu observes, gender assumptions gain much of their
force or symbolic weight from the "insertion" of the opposition between
women and men "into a system of homologous oppositions," including
oppositions between outside and inside, public and private, dry and wet,
up and down, active and passive, and so forth.[16] Because these oppositions
shape our social world, our perceptions of that world, and the bodily dis-
positions produced by our interaction with that world, the system that
they form seems natural and legitimate even though it is produced by

ongoing social practice. Both Rubin and Bourdieu suggest that the cultural notion that men are properly subjects of exchange, and women properly objects, is one of the core assumptions grounding the subordination
of women to men.[17] However, from Bourdieu's perspective, this assumption may prove especially difficult to dislodge partly because the distinction between subject and object is one of those oppositions that often
stands in homologous relation to the division between men and women.

Gender criticism utilizes such gender theorizing to generate analytic
questions that can be used in the interpretation of literary, including biblical, texts. For example, if men often negotiate their relations with one
another through their dealings with women (as Rubin, Schwartz, Sedgwick
and others suggest),[18] then readers might ask whether any given biblical
representation of relations between male characters and female characters
has some significance also for relations among male characters; and, if so,
what that significance might be.[19] So too, if the opposition between women
and men takes on cultural significance partly from its insertion into a system of "homologous oppositions" (as Bourdieu and others suggest), then
readers might ask whether a biblical text that includes male and female
characters also refers to, or is structured on the basis of, other oppositions
that help to shape the gendered significance of the text in question. We shall
return to a possible instance of this from Judges.

Moreover, as these examples indicate, gender criticism does not separate its questions about women and constructs of womanhood and femininity from questions about men, manhood, and masculinity. Although
the emergence of "masculinity studies" in academia has led to concerns
about reinscribing male dominance or supplanting feminist politics under
the guise of gender studies, feminist scholars such as Naomi Schor also note
the potential value of "apply[ing] the insights of gender study to decon-
structing masculinity."[20] Unfortunately, there are still surprisingly few studies of the Hebrew Bible that attempt to examine its assumptions about
manhood critically as cultural gender notions, in spite of the fact that most
biblical characters are male characters.[21] However, the book of Judges itself
seems to recognize on some level that manhood is something that one must
demonstrate in culturally appropriate ways, and not something that one
naturally displays by virtue of being biologically male. In Judges 8:21, for
example, after Gideon's son refrains from killing two captive kings out of
fear, those kings goad Gideon into killing them with the taunt, "As the man
is, so is his strength." This taunt implies a cultural association between
manhood and warrior strength, while simultaneously indicating that men
are not understood to embody or display such gendered strength simply
by virtue of being biologically male. Gideon, a "mighty warrior" (Judg

6:12), is able to demonstrate his manly strength, whereas his son does not.[22] As one commentary rightly puts it, Gideon's son is represented by Gideon's enemies as "not man enough to carry out" the task at hand.[23]

The ideas that manliness must be achieved or demonstrated to others, and that only some men will pass the tests of manhood and then not always to the same degree, seem to be very widespread cross-culturally.[24] However, the specific content of assumptions about manly performance can also vary significantly. Moreover, such assumptions are not always spelled out explicitly in texts but rather remain implicit.

In order to tease out assumptions about gender in general, and manhood in particular, that may have shaped biblical texts, some scholars therefore find it useful to read those texts in relation to a cluster of assumptions about gender known from what anthropologists call the "Circum-Mediterranean" world (which includes parts of what is often referred to today as the "Middle East").[25] Although there are many local differences among such societies, anthropologists point out that many traits related to gender are and have been widespread throughout the Circum-Mediterranean world. These traits include a gendered division of labor; patriarchal household, and patrilineal kinship structures; an assumption that male prestige, reputation, and honor depend not simply on being a "good" man, but also on being visibly and publicly "*good at* being a man,"[26] especially in contests or conflicts with other men; a corresponding fear, on the part of men, of feminization as a source of shame; a valorization of female chastity; and the belief that manly vigilance is required to guard the chastity of those women on whose sexual purity a man's personal, familial or tribal honor are thought to depend. Although all of these traits may or may not be relevant for the interpretation of any given biblical text, knowledge of such traits and the ways in which they shape social dynamics often allows the biblical critic to produce an interpretation of gender dynamics, including dynamics of manhood, in the Bible.[27] One might, for example, appeal to such dynamics in order to argue that Judges 8 uses assumptions about manly display and warrior strength to demonstrate that Gideon's son is not "good at being a man," even if Gideon is. Thus, the reader may be prepared to doubt whether Gideon's sons, in the verses that follow, will be able to demonstrate their manliness in culturally expected ways, and so to be subjects of Israelite manhood.

DESTABILIZING (WITH) GENDER

If Gideon can be represented in Judges 8:21 as more "manly" than his son, at least with respect to warrior strength, then "manliness" appears not to be a state that a male biblical character either inhabits or fails to inhabit by virtue of that character's sex. Members of the "same" sex can display, or in the case of literary characters can be represented as displaying, gender traits such as "manliness" to varying degrees. But to the extent that a male fails to display traits, or act in ways, that a particular culture or society understands as "manly," that male runs the risk of appearing to be the opposite of "manly." That is to say, he runs the risk of being "feminized." Within cultures and societies that are characterized by rigid gender differentiation and hierarchy (as ancient Israel was), such feminization is, for males, often considered a source of shame or loss of prestige. Texts produced in such a society, including biblical texts, can make use of such dynamics for purposes of plot development, characterization, or imagery. Indeed, texts from both the Bible and the ancient Near East speak negatively about men who, by failing to demonstrate manly capabilities (e.g., in battle), "become women" (Jer 51:30).[28]

Such dynamics underscore the important point that gender difference is not simply a matter of distinguishing, in culture-specific ways, between two sexes. Gender difference also involves ways of making distinctions among members of the "same" sex. Biblical scholars have long recognized, in fact, that "conventional sex symbols" were used, in Israel as well as other parts of the ancient world, to separate out "the ideal 'man's man' and 'woman's woman'" from their peers.[29] Such distinctions can be made on the basis of many different criteria, including not only strength (as in Judges 8) but also "prowess in battle";[30] the ability to sire children if a man, or bear children if a woman; dress (cf. Deut 22:5); the use of a spindle (cf. 2 Sam 3:29; Prov 31:19); or—significantly, in most cultures—sexual practice. But however such intrasex gender distinctions are made, in a world (real or literary) where "feminine men" or "manly women" are thinkable (even if such persons are considered frightening or stigmatized), we have moved outside of stable, binary notions of gender into something more fluid and ambiguous.

By underscoring such ambiguities, gender criticism moves (as Sedgwick's discussion of gender criticism notes, and as the research trajectories of Sedgwick and Rubin indicate), in the direction of contemporary lesbian and gay studies and queer theory.[31] Queer theory grew out of lesbian and gay studies during the 1990s, but it does not restrict its attention to questions of homosexuality. Situated at the point of overlap between gender studies and sexuality studies, queer theory highlights instead not simply the social construction, but also the instability of categories used to interpret sex, gender, and sexuality, including such categories as male and female, heterosexual and homosexual, and so forth.[32]

Thus queer theory is as much involved in the critical deconstruction of heterosexuality as it is in questions about homosexuality.[33] It usually refuses to separate the analysis of sexuality from the analysis of gender, and increasingly studies both sexuality and gender in relation to such matters as race and class as well.[34]

In alliance with queer theory, gender criticism extends its critical lens from the "gender" half of the sex/gender distinction to the "sex" half of that distinction. Although the sex/gender distinction facilitates recognition of cross-cultural variations in gender roles and gendered meanings, such a distinction also allows the division between male and female biological sexes to remain uninterrogated. While many scholars use the sex/gender distinction to undermine the naturalization of social gender roles and cultural gender notions, more radical critics suggest that binary distinctions between biological sexes in fact function to naturalize social systems of heterosexuality. Monique Wittig, for example, argues that "the categories 'man' and 'woman' . . . are political categories and not natural givens."[35] Such categories lead us to grant social and ontological significance to, or "mark" bodies in terms of, exactly those parts of the body that are most useful for sexual reproduction (as opposed to other parts of the body that might be "marked" socially in order to organize categories of human beings in other ways). Binary categories of biological sex therefore function to secure the imperatives of heterosexual intercourse and sexual reproduction. In Wittig's words, "the category of sex is the political category that founds society as heterosexual."[36]

Writing partly under the influence of Wittig, Judith Butler has asked whether binary notions of biological sex are not themselves "the effect of the apparatus of cultural construction designated by *gender*."[37] Attempting to provide an account of gender that does not understand it simply as the social organization and cultural interpretation of natural sex differences, Butler has developed a "performative" theory of gender with widespread influence in feminism, lesbian and gay studies, and queer theory. This approach to gender suggests that the illusory stability of both sex and gender results from repeated and ritualized practices that, over time, and under the influence of heterosexual imperatives, create the impression of binary biological sexes and core gender identities. Such practices do not express stable truths of sex and gender. Rather, for Butler, sex and gender are themselves effects of the "*stylized repetition of acts*":

> The effect of gender is produced through the stylization of the body and, hence, must be understood as the mundane way in which bodily gestures, movements, and styles of various kinds constitute the

illusion of an abiding gendered self. This formulation moves the conception of gender off the ground of a substantial model of identity to one that requires a conception of gender as a constituted *social temporality*. Significantly, if gender is instituted through acts which are internally discontinuous, then the *appearance of substance* is precisely that, a constructed identity, a performative accomplishment which the mundane social audience, including the actors themselves, come to believe and to perform in the mode of belief.[38]

As Butler subsequently makes clear, "performative" here is not to be identified exactly with "performance."[39] The background for Butler's notion of gender performativity rather lies in the theory of linguistic speech acts, according to which performatives are speech acts that do not so much describe objects as bring into existence the things of which they speak. Thus, for example, the proper words spoken by the proper persons in a wedding ceremony do not describe a marriage, but rather accomplish it.[40] Just as such speech acts presuppose and "cite" prior sociolinguistic conventions and norms, so also the "citation" of gender norms (whether linguistically or through the embodied reenactment of such norms) presupposes and to some degree extends the norms in question.[41] Thus, gender performativity is not the unconstrained production of a free performing subject, but rather a matter of "iterations" or repetitive acts of gender that are partly constrained by gender conventions. Yet such conventions change through time, and vary across cultures and contexts. Moreover, just as performative speech acts can "misfire"[42] (when, for example, the required context and conditions for a certain type of speech act are not met), so also the reiteration or "citation" of gender norms frequently produces occasions in which sex, gender, sexual desire, and sexual practice are not, according to the dominant norms, aligned consistently. That is to say, "male" and "female" actors and speakers may act or speak in ways that stand in tension with, or contradict, the norms of "manhood" and "womanhood" to which, in a given context, "males" and "females" are supposed to conform. As Butler observes, gender "is an assignment which is never quite carried out according to expectation, whose addressee never quite inhabits the ideal s/he is compelled to approximate."[43] Such moments are for Butler potentially important, since they both expose the contingency of norms of sex and gender and offer possible openings for the destabilization and transformation of such norms.

What is the relevance of this philosophical argument for biblical interpretation? When they refer to or presuppose social assumptions about sex, gender, sexual practice, and kinship, both biblical texts and interpretations of them "cite" norms of sex and gender. As a result of such citations, these norms are continually (re)installed as norms; and they come to seem quite solid and substantial. Yet there are differences, gaps, moments of confusion, and multiple possibilities for meaning among these citations, not only as between biblical texts but also as between texts and their interpretations. In certain texts, for example, biblical characters, to borrow Butler's phrasing, fail to "inhabit the ideal" they are "compelled to approximate." By highlighting such ambiguities, tensions, and failures, gender critics call attention to the contingency of supposed biblical contributions to sex/gender systems, suggesting that recognition of this contingency may well provide openings for the destabilization and transformation of those systems.[44]

Thus, gender criticism asks questions such as the following about any biblical text: What norms or conventions of gender seem to be presupposed by this text? How might attention to the interdisciplinary study of gender allow readers of the Bible to tease out such presuppositions? How are assumptions about gender used in the structure of a particular plot, or manipulated for purposes of characterization? How is gender symbolism related to other types of symbolism used in the text? How does the manipulation of gender assumptions in a text relate to other textual dynamics, including not only literary but also theological and ideological dynamics? Which characters embody cultural gender norms successfully, and which characters fall short of such norms or embody them in unexpected ways? Might a character's success or failure at embodying gender norms result from a strategy to cast that character in a particular light, whether positive or negative? Is the text itself always successful at manipulating gender assumptions? Do biblical texts, like persons, sometimes fail to "cite" gender conventions in expected ways or according to dominant norms? How does our attention to these and other questions contribute to our understanding of both gender and the Bible?

GENDER CRITICISM AND JUDGES: THE "UN-MANNING" OF ABIMELECH

In order to examine further the possible relevance of gender criticism for biblical interpretation, let us consider its use in the interpretation of a specific text: the story of Abimelech in Judges 9. We have already noted how the language of manhood is used by two enemies in Judges 8:21 to draw a contrast between the greater manliness of Gideon and the lesser manliness of his son. Although the son involved in that incident is Gideon's eldest son, Jether, the doubts raised about the manhood of Gideon's son in chapter 8 may well cause the reader to view with suspicion all or any one of Gideon's sons, including Abimelech.

When Abimelech is first mentioned in the text, moreover, matters of gender and kinship already play a role. The narrator distinguishes Abimelech from the other sons of Gideon when, after noting Gideon's seventy sons and many women in Judges 8:30, he states in 8:31 that Gideon's "concubine who was in Shechem also bore him a son, and he named him Abimelech." The word normally translated as "concubine" in this verse is the Hebrew term *pilegesh*, applied in the Hebrew Bible to a class of women who are in some sort of sexual relationship to male characters. The precise nature of that relationship, however, is difficult to specify. Although most commentators understand a *pilegesh* more or less along the lines of Soggin, who in his commentary on Judges refers to a *pilegesh* as "a legitimate wife, but of second rank,"[45] a great deal of ink has been spilled in recent years over the proper translation and understanding of this term; and in spite of the attention given to it, much uncertainty remains.[46]

For gender criticism, the fact that such uncertainties exist is itself potentially important. After all, the difficulties modern readers have in understanding the meaning and social function of a *pilegesh* derive not only from the fact that we have limited evidence to help us decide the matter, but also from the lack of fit that exists between the system of sex, gender, and kinship found in the Bible and that presupposed by later interpreters. By calling attention to this lack of fit, gender criticism contributes to the historicizing or denaturalizing approach to sex, gender, and kinship that was implicit already in the formulation of a sex/gender distinction but has been carried much further in queer theory. Instead of moving hastily to resolve ambiguities such as those surrounding the term *pilegesh*, gender criticism may choose instead to highlight the historical contingency of systems of sex, gender, and kinship that produce such ambiguities in the first place.

At the same time, enough evidence exists about the biblical use of the word *pilegesh* to allow us to move forward with an interpretation of the likely function of that word's appearance in the story of Abimelech. The specification that Abimelech's mother is a *pilegesh* functions in the story not simply as information about that mother, but rather to draw a distinction between Abimelech and the other sons of Gideon, whose mothers are referred to as *nashim*, "women" or possibly "wives."[47] This distinction between Abimelech and his brothers may well be related to a distinction found in Genesis 25:6, where Abraham gives gifts to the children of his *pilagshim* but sends those children away from Isaac, his heir. The fact that a child's mother is a *pilegesh* appears to result, in some cases at least, in secondary status for that child, in comparison with other children of the same father; and such secondary status may well be assumed for Abimelech in comparison with his brothers in the story line of Judges. The distinction between Abimelech and his brothers that is made with reference to Abimelech's mother therefore prepares the reader for the conflict between Abimelech and those brothers that soon follows. In addition, by specifying that Abimelech's mother is from Shechem, the text provides a rationale for Abimelech to use when attempting to persuade the lords of Shechem to cast their lot with Abimelech rather than with his brothers. The narrative is thus structured around matters of sex, gender, and kinship from the start of Abimelech's story; and a female character, the mother of Abimelech, by virtue of her status as *pilegesh* mediates or determines relations between the story's male characters.[48]

Abimelech's name literally means "my father is king." Although the "father" referred to in this name may have been understood in ancient Israel as God, the reader can hardly fail to see a certain irony in Abimelech's name, in the context of the narrative of Judges.[49] For in that narrative, the Israelites desire to make Abimelech's father, Gideon, and Gideon's sons and grandsons rule over them (though Gideon refuses; Judg 8:22-23); and Abimelech, in particular, wishes to and does rule over Shechem (9:1-6).[50] In order to rule, Abimelech, with financial backing from the Shechemites, kills all but one of his seventy brothers. The legitimacy of the selection of Abimelech as ruler in Shechem is then called into question by a parable and speech spoken by Abimelech's surviving brother, Jotham.

Shortly thereafter, God sends an "evil spirit" to stir up trouble between Abimelech and the lords of Shechem as consequence for the killing of Abimelech's brothers (9:23-24). Although the reference to an "evil spirit" from God may strike some readers as strange, similar references appear in 1 Samuel (16:14; 18:10). In those texts, too, God sends an "evil spirit" in a situation involving divine displeasure with the current ruler, specifically on that ruler—Saul—whose legitimacy as ruler has been undermined by God's selection of David.

This intertextual link between Judges and 1 Samuel may well interest the gender critic. Susan Ackerman has argued, in a discussion much informed by contemporary theories of gender and sexuality, that the legitimization of the House of David in place of the House of Saul is accomplished in 1 Samuel, in part, through a kind of "feminization" of Saul's son (and David's potential rival for the throne), Jonathan. This feminization, which in the ancient world would also signify social submission, is, on

Ackerman's reading, accomplished in 1 Samuel both by the use of homoerotic language to describe Jonathan's love for David and through structural textual parallels between the role of Jonathan and the roles of David's
wives, including Jonathan's sister(s).[51]

Because references to the rare "evil spirit" from God already hint at parallels between the story of the House of Saul (represented especially by
Saul and his son Jonathan) in 1 Samuel and the story of the House of
Gideon (represented especially by Gideon and his son Abimelech) in
Judges, Ackerman's analysis might lead the gender critic to ask whether
other parallels exist between the two narratives that involve feminization
of male characters. Is Abimelech, like Jonathan, feminized? Although, as
we have seen, questions are raised about the manliness of Gideon's son
even while Gideon is still alive, the homoerotic language that Ackerman
notes in the story of Jonathan is absent from the story of Abimelech. However, an explicit reference to gender dynamics that represents a fear, on
Abimelech's part, of being remembered as somehow unmanly occurs at
the end of his story. After a woman throws an "upper millstone" from the
tower of Thebez and crushes his skull, Abimelech orders his armor-bearer,
"Draw your sword and kill me, so people will not say about me, 'A woman
killed him'" (9:54). Abimelech's request seems to be an example of what
T. M. Lemos has called male "shame" over "defeat at the hands of a
woman" in the Bible and other ancient texts. As Lemos recognizes, in a
context where male status is closely related to military abilities, such a
defeat "calls . . . masculinity into question" for the man who is defeated.[52]

Although she does not mention the story of Abimelech, Lemos does
note, as an example of gender-based shame that is linked to "defeat at the
hands of a woman," another story from Judges: that involving Barak, who
in chapter 4 fails to receive glory for the defeat of Sisera when Sisera is
killed by a woman, Jael. That story offers an intriguing point of comparison with Abimelech's death, not only by referring to Barak's loss of military glory, but also in its representation of the slaying of Sisera. Indeed,
the fact that the narrated deaths of Abimelech and Sisera are both structured in Judges around a shared "ideologeme of shame and gender" has
been underscored by Mieke Bal.[53] It is important to note, moreover, not
only that both Abimelech and Sisera are warriors killed by women, but
also that, for both soldiers, death comes from above. Judges 4:21 tells in
graphic detail how Jael thrusts her weapon into the head of the sleeping
general, so that it "went down into the ground." In Judges 9, the weapon
used against Abimelech is thrown by a woman from a tower. In order to
reflect on possible connotations of these parallel downward and deadly
movements, the gender critic may recall Bourdieu's point that the oppo-

sition between male and female gains its symbolic power partly through insertion into a series of "homologous oppositions," including those between subject and object, and up and down. Bourdieu relates the significance of the opposition between up and down, "on top or underneath," to male erection and sexual intercourse.[54] Such intercourse is, throughout the ancient world and in many cultures still, understood as the conjunction of a dominant subject (which, moving on top, penetrates its object) and a subordinate object (which is penetrated from above). While the former position is normatively associated with men, the latter position is normatively reserved either for women or for subordinate males who become feminized. It is not only the case, then, that Abimelech and Sisera are both shamed by being killed by women. The shame associated with their deaths seems to be intensified when the text makes both men objects of female subjects who come at them from the male position up above, or on top. That is to say, Abimelech and Sisera are slain by women who are each, in turn, represented in symbolic phallic positions.

This point may even be underscored by the women's choice of weapons. As Gale Yee notes, Jael's tent peg appears to function as "the ravaging phallus" in the "un-manning" of Sisera in Judges 4 and 5.[55] The millstone used as a weapon by the woman in chapter 9, however, has drawn much less attention. When scholars do refer to it, they seldom inquire about its possible gendered connotations, restricting their reflections on gender to such matters as the fact that "one woman" (which is what we find literally in the text at 9:53) might be unable to throw a millstone by herself. Thus Boling concludes on this basis that the story must be "hyperbole."[56] But such a conclusion, which uses naive realism as its reference point, may miss entirely the symbolism of gender and sexuality that structures the story and motivates the choice of weapon for the woman of Thebez; for, according to Bourdieu, a millstone symbolizes in some Mediterranean cultures sexual intercourse by virtue of "its moving upper part and its immobile lower part."[57] Like Jael with her tent peg, then, the woman at Thebez uses a weapon that can symbolize a "ravaging phallus" in order to "un-man" a male opponent. Thus the "un-manning" of Abimelech, like that of Sisera, is accomplished in multiple ways by the gender symbolism used in Judges.

Abimelech, of course, wishes to avoid the fate of being remembered for dying in a way that would be seen as shameful by most ancient men (and no doubt some modern ones as well). For this reason, he asks his armorbearer to slay him instead. However, his attempt to avoid an ignominious fate is futile; for the only biblical reference to him outside of the book of Judges occurs in 2 Samuel 11:21, where he is remembered precisely for being killed when a woman drops a millstone on him from a wall, but where no mention of his armor-bearer is made at all.

With this reference to the memory of Abimelech recounted in 2 Samuel 11:2, however, we return to the possibility that links exist between Abimelech's story and the books of Samuel. Several scholars have argued that the final form of the book of Judges is put together in such a way as to promote the interests of Judah and, in particular, Judah's Davidic dynasty.[58] Scholars who read the book in such a fashion emphasize that this agenda is accomplished in part through a polemic against Saul, especially in the closing chapters of Judges (with its attention to Gibeah and Benjamin). As we have seen, however, Abimelech's story also contains intertextual links to the story of Saul much earlier in the book of Judges. Saul, like Abimelech, suffers consequences of an "evil spirit" from God. Moreover, Saul, like Abimelech, actually asks to be killed by his armor-bearer to avoid dying under shameful circumstances (1 Sam 31:4). Although the agent of death that Saul wishes to avoid is not a woman, Saul does refer explicitly to the "uncircumcised" nature of his opponents, the Philistines. As David Jobling has suggested, the frequent references to the Philistines as "uncircumcised" in Judges and 1 Samuel arguably occur in the context of a representation of those Philistines as in some sense "womanish."[59] Thus Saul, too, like Abimelech, is attempting to avoid being killed by an opponent who, from the Israelite point of view, rightly occupies a female or feminized role, but who threatens to feminize the Israelite warrior in turn by making him the object of phallic destruction. Gender criticism allows us to suggest, therefore, that the story of Abimelech's illegitimate rule and unmanly death may fit into the anti-Saulide polemic of Judges that other scholars note when dealing with other parts of the book. Inasmuch as Abimelech's story calls Saul's story to mind, Abimelech's un-manning may function as a parallel of sorts not only to Saul himself but also to the feminization of Jonathan pointed out by Ackerman and others.

This gender-mediated polemic is carried even further in the closing section of Judges. Though full consideration of the last three chapters of the book cannot be attempted here, it is important to note that several intertextual connections to Saul do appear in those chapters.[60] The tribe of Benjamin and the town of Gibeah, both associated closely with Saul, are represented quite negatively in Judges 19–21. Several other places that play important roles in the final chapters of Judges, such as Jabesh-gilead and Mizpah, are also important for the story of Saul. Moreover, the Levite's act of cutting the body of his *pilegesh* into twelve pieces, and using those pieces to call together the tribes of Israel (Judg 19:29–30), is a striking parallel to Saul's act of cutting oxen into pieces and using those pieces to muster troops in 1 Samuel 11:7.

If scholars are right to have concluded from such intertextual connections that a polemic against Saul is taking place in Judges 19–21, then it is unsurprising that motifs of male feminization, which Ackerman has noted in the story of Saul's son Jonathan and which we have seen already in the story of Abimelech, appear in these closing chapters of Judges as well; for in the opening scene of chapter 19, a *pilegesh* takes the step of leaving her husband to return to her father, thereby adopting the position of female sexual subject and so threatening to "un-man" the Levite who, within the framework of Israel's patriarchal kinship system, should rightly serve as subject in the male traffic in women. After that Levite attempts to reclaim his manhood by reclaiming his *pilegesh* from the woman's father (his partner in woman trafficking), he avoids stopping at Jerusalem, a city associated eventually with David and the Judahite monarchy, and stops instead at Gibeah, the town known as the home of Saul. There the men of Gibeah threaten to un-man the Levite in a more graphic fashion, through male same-sex rape. That is to say, they threaten to place that Levite in the position of object, which, in Israel as in many other cultures, is normatively reserved for women. Although the threatened rape of the Levite does not take place, the men of Gibeah do, as I have argued elsewhere, symbolically feminize him by raping his *pilegesh*.[61] Yet gender tables are turned on the Gibeahites and their Benjaminite kin when the Israelite tribes defeat them in battle. Because military "defeat is a feminine-associated event"[62] in ancient Israel as elsewhere in the ancient Near East, the extended attention to this defeat in chapter 20 of Judges serves to highlight the feminization of Saul's tribe. The insult is only compounded in chapter 21 when the surviving members of that tribe have to be assisted and instructed by others in the quintessentially manly role of securing women.

CONCLUSION

By implying through gendered representations that certain men and groups of men (Abimelech, Saul, Jonathan, Benjamin, Levites) are inadequate embodiments or practitioners of norms of manliness, narratives in the books of Judges and Samuel participate in a polemic that is only partially "hidden."[63] Although sections of Judges, including the story of Abimelech's father Gideon, express a negative opinion of monarchy as such, and not only of northern monarchy, in the context of the book as a whole this gender polemic may well reconfirm a preference for Judah and its Davidic dynasty by highlighting the unmanliness of Saul and his fore-runner in the north, Abimelech. Inasmuch as this polemic relies on the instabilities of manly performance, however, the strategy is a risky one for supporters of the Judahite dynasty, for Davidic kings, too, can act in ways that might lead one to ask whether any one of those kings is "good at being a man." As the recurrence of Abimelech's name and unmanly death in 2 Samuel 11 indicates, and as other stories about David, Absalom, Adoni-jah, and Solomon remind us, the dynamics of un-manning can be deployed against Davidic kings as easily as non-Davidic ones.[64] Indeed, because gender norms themselves are unstable, their citation in practice is never perfect or predictable, as Butler reminds us; and so the effects of such citation cannot ultimately be controlled. When the manhood of its kings and aspiring kings is represented so often at risk, the manhood of Israel itself would seem to be uncertain. Biblical iterations of gender begin to appear much more often as failed approximations to an ideal, to use Butler's language; and the Bible's contributions to stable norms of sex and gender seem much less clear.

Cultural assumptions about gender play important roles in the book of Judges, and in other parts of the Bible as well. They contribute not only to the book's literary techniques (such as characterization and plot develop-ment) but also to its political polemics, which have long intrigued even those scholars who show little interest in gender. Yet the gender notions presupposed and used by biblical literature do not function solely to reconfirm sharp distinctions between male and female. On the contrary: as we have seen with the story of Abimelech, along with other stories inside and outside Judges that are connected to it intertextually, the Bible exploits the fact that gaps exist between ideal gender norms (such as those used to define "manliness") and the actual persons and practices that are judged against such norms. By calling attention to and interpreting such gaps, gender criticism sheds light on biblical literature while illuminating the dynamics and instabilities of gender itself. It therefore contributes to our understanding both of the biblical world and of our own.

FURTHER READING

General

Bourdieu, Pierre. *Masculine Domination*. Trans. Richard Nice. Stanford, Calif.: Stanford University Press, 2001. An important analysis of the ways in which social gender assumptions and practices are naturalized.

Butler, Judith. *Bodies That Matter: On the Discursive Limits of "Sex."* New York and London: Routledge, 1993. A collection of complex but important essays by Butler that clarify and develop her views on sex, gender, performativity, and queer theory.

———. *Gender Trouble: Feminism and the Subversion of Identity.* 2d ed. New York and London: Routledge, 1999. The influential volume that introduced Butler's theory of gender performativity, with a new preface.

Gilmore, David, ed. *Honor and Shame and the Unity of the Mediterranean.* Washington, D.C.: American Anthropological Association, 1987. A collection of essays on an area of anthropological research that sheds useful light on biblical notions of honor, shame, gender, and sexuality.

Rubin, Gayle. "The Traffic in Women: Notes on the 'Political Economy' of Sex." In *Toward an Anthropology of Women.* Edited by Rayna Reiter, 157–210. New York: Monthly Review, 1975. A justly famous essay that has been influential for numerous studies in anthropology, feminist criticism, lesbian and gay studies, and gender criticism.

Sedgwick, Eve Kosofsky. "Gender Criticism." In *Redrawing the Boundaries: The Transformation of English and American Literary Studies.* Edited by Stephen Greenblatt and Giles Gunn. New York: Modern Language Association of America, 1992. A discussion of gender analysis that sheds light on Sedgwick's move, as a feminist critic, in the direction of lesbian and gay studies and queer theory.

Biblical

Ackerman, Susan. *When Heroes Love: The Ambiguity of Eros in the Stories of Gilgamesh and David.* New York: Columbia University Press, 2005. Reexamines the appearance of homoerotic language in the Gilgamesh epic and the books of Samuel in the light of recent theories of gender and sexuality, including queer theory.

Brenner, Athalya. *The Intercourse of Knowledge: On Gendering Desire and 'Sexuality' in the Hebrew Bible.* Leiden: Brill, 1997. A careful investigation of gender and sexual matters in a wide range of biblical texts.

Chapman, Cynthia R. *The Gendered Language of Warfare in the Israelite-Assyrian Encounter.* Winona Lake, Ind.: Eisenbrauns, 2004. Demonstrates and analyzes the role played by gender in biblical and ancient Near Eastern representations of warfare.

Stone, Ken. *Practicing Safer Text: Food, Sex and Bible in Queer Perspective.* London: T. & T. Clark, 2005. Examines the roles of food and sex in a number of biblical texts from the perspectives of queer theory, anthropology, and gender analysis.

———. *Sex, Honor and Power in the Deuteronomistic History*. Sheffield: Sheffield Academic Press, 1996. Uses anthropology and literary analysis to investigate biblical narratives in which gender and sexual practice play a role.

Tolbert, Mary Ann. "Gender." In *Handbook of Postmodern Biblical Interpretation*. Edited by A. K. M. Adam. St. Louis: Chalice, 2000. A convenient summary of contemporary theories of gender written by a biblical scholar.

Yee, Gale A. *Poor Banished Children of Eve: Woman as Evil in the Hebrew Bible*. Minneapolis: Fortress Press, 2003. Integrates gender criticism as part of ideological criticism to analyze a wide range of biblical texts.

10

CULTURAL CRITICISM

Viewing the Sacrifice of Jephthah's Daughter

DAVID M. GUNN

CULTURAL CRITICISM

Culture, as a saying goes, is what your butcher would have if he were your surgeon.[1]

This quotation neatly sums up a popular view about culture. But Hall's point is that culture is much more than a marker of social class (where a society may deem surgeons more "cultured" than butchers): rather, all members of a society share a culture or, more often, intersecting and competing cultures; and "popular" culture is as important a subject of study as "high" culture. Culture is a language or set of codes—spoken, written, acted, pictured, manufactured—through which people share values and beliefs, behave in certain approved ways, make and use artifacts in common. Culture lends people identity, helps them relate to each other, and provides the glue that sustains a society. Culture is transmitted through generations, by imitation and learning. So culture is not just about artistic productions or cultivated manners, but will likely involve notions of time and space, social roles and skills, property, sexuality, violence, conflict resolution, and the meaning of social symbols (flags and football, for example). Culture both produces and governs thought, feeling, and action, and is itself, over time, produced by these. How cultural change occurs is an important question in cultural studies.

What do cultural critics do? What methods define the discipline? Well, many would say that cultural criticism is precisely not a discipline. Rather it is an interdiscipline or a cross-discipline or a multidiscipline or, perhaps better, a set of activities that share a focal point, culture, while invoking a range of disciplines to provide theories of culture and methods by which to investigate it. So a reader of cultural studies will likely encounter some of the approaches discussed in this book—literary critical, feminist, sociological, and ideological, for example. Issues of race, ethnicity, national-ity, social class, gender, sexuality, and religious identity are among recurring topics of inquiry. Critics of culture also tend to be alert to economic systems—who controls the means of production?—and the cultural impact of technology. Cultural criticism may be a political activity, articulating the need for social change, or it may be less evaluative than analytic, exposing, without explicit advocacy, how culture shapes human thought and conduct.

Studies of the Bible in culture are not new. Scholars, often from other disciplines like English literature or art history, have written extensively about how dramatists, novelists, poets, visual artists, and musicians have used the Bible. Usually these have been studies of "high" culture, the artistic genres "cultivated" by the elite or well-to-do. Only in the latter half of the twentieth century did "popular" culture—films, pop songs, comic books, children's stories, for example—become a regular subject of academic inquiry. Until the 1990s, few biblical scholars joined these investigations. Now, a number of them are writing on the Bible in culture(s) of all kinds and drawing on cultural materials for courses, especially on film ("the Bible at the movies," so to speak) and the fine arts.[2]

Reception History

One approach to the question of how Bible and culture interact is to trace the interactions historically and comparatively, through time and location. Here cultural criticism merges with the history of interpretation. The latter traces the way professional interpreters and scholars produced interpretive methods for reading the Bible; for example, it shows how in the nineteenth and early twentieth centuries German historical criticism (especially "source" criticism) came to dominate in European and eventually British and American universities. Cultural criticism's interest in how the Bible is *used*—learned, thought about, assumed, depicted—shifts the focus to a broader cross-section of society. A study of the nineteenth and early twentieth centuries would show that for most people in Europe and America the many books on women in the Bible (increasingly affordable and often written by women), the abundance of illustrated Bible story books for children (largely absent in previous centuries), and the profusion of pictures and anecdotes about what life was like in the "Holy Land" past and present were much more relevant to their lives than German theories of biblical composition. These features of Bible usage track the changing status of women and major technological innovations in printing, publishing, and travel (e.g., the steamship). This kind of cultural criticism is sometimes called "reception history." It gives an account of how the Bible has been understood through the centuries without making scholars the central characters; and it explores how the Bible's use or impact relates to the social circumstances and culture of those who use it or are influenced by it.[3]

Clearly, the term "reception history" is a less than satisfactory one, because "reception" can suggest passivity and it is an axiom of cultural studies that texts and their readers or users are in a reciprocal relationship. Texts do not simply offer meaning to recipients; rather, readers or users actively ascribe meaning to texts, even if that meaning is determined or "received" through tradition or convention. In this respect, reception history as a form of cultural studies is closely linked to reader-response criticism in literary theory, the idea that for a text to have meaning it must have a reader. It is the reader or listener who "makes sense" of the written or spoken codes that constitute the text.

If reception history is about the use of the Bible, what is the use of reception history?[4] The cultural critic might reply that it helps us understand how cultures work in the lives of individuals and communities, how culture is connected to other aspects of social life such as economics and technology, and how much we simply accept or assume ideas, practices, and values that are cultural "givens." It also enlarges our understanding of specific cultures where the Bible has played a significant role, as in the United States. Perhaps most important, reception history demonstrates *empirically* that the meanings of biblical texts, like those of other cultural products, depend on who is using them, at what time, in what place, and for what reason. That understanding prompts the useful question: What circumstances, and what hidden cultural assumptions, govern our own use of the Bible? By examining our reactions to the ways others, in different times and places, have used the Bible, we may be led to challenge our own assumptions about the responsible use of religious texts today.

What difficulties face the critic examining the Bible's effects on culture and the effects of culture on the use of the Bible? A major one is about choice—what material to study. If the biblical text (the story of Jephthah and his daughter, say) has limits, the cultural data that could be brought into discussion are potentially endless. Yet the data selected will determine the picture of biblical use. Choosing certain cultures (British in the eighteenth century, say) or certain cultural practices or expressions (religious education or political sermons) over others privileges the chosen. Cultural differences (and so different uses of the Bible) are easy to overlook, such as those between social and economic classes, religious and ethnic communities, males and females. An important question to ask, then, is: *Whose* sources are being discussed?

Some choices are constrained by the evidence available. In Europe, for example, prior to printing's arrival in the fifteenth century, literacy was low, and so surviving from the medieval period are mostly the voices of the educated elite speaking to each other. In seventeenth-century England, however, improvements in typeface technology resulted in the publication of many religious-political tracts and sermons. We are better informed, therefore, on what many laypeople learned about Judges, if not always what they thought about what they were reading or hearing. It is the industrial revolution and the huge expansion of cheap publishing and production in the nineteenth century that give easy access to a wide spectrum of society. So accessibility influences selection.

In this present essay, the focus will be on visual culture, specifically printed Bible illustrations, drawing on materials readily available in libraries and private collections. We shall look in particular at some depictions of the sacrifice of Jephthah's daughter.

Bible Illustrations and Texts

While Bible illustrations share many features with paintings of biblical subjects, and are sometimes copies of them, they also differ in a crucial regard.[5] They are usually embedded in a text. Sometimes there are more pictures than there is text (in some children's Bible storybooks, for example), sometimes there is a balance between the two, but frequently, as with illustrated Bibles, the space accorded to the text far and away predominates. Indeed, we are accustomed to think of illustration generally as an aid to understanding text, and so subordinate to it. When the text is the Bible, deemed by many readers to be authoritative, that subordination seems all the more pronounced.

Yet we are also accustomed to saying, "A picture is worth a thousand words!" Or, as Miss E. J. Whately put it in the 1878 volume of *The Sunday at Home*: a good picture, executed properly according to the best available knowledge, was "far more likely to impress a looker-on than any description in words could do."[6] Such a picture might then enable all, and the young and unlearned especially, "to take clear and simple views of the sacred narrative."

Moreover, Western culture customarily treats visual images as more potent than written words: a newspaper account of men being decapitated in Baghdad may run into a storm of protest if it includes pictures of the incident. Likewise, a young woman may be sacrificed, "offered up," in the biblical text, but not shown having her throat cut. You may scoff at the idea of a potent, magical relation between a picture and what it represents, but how would you respond if asked to take a photograph of your mother and cut out the eyes?[7]

Here, then, are two important questions to consider: First, are viewers more affected by pictures than readers are by words? Second, do pictures communicate more directly and simply with viewers than words do with readers? Miss Whately thought the answer to both questions was in the affirmative. But was she right? And would the answers be true of all cultures at all times? There is not space to explore these questions further here, but we could begin by making the case that images do not necessarily convey meaning in a simple and direct fashion.

Some theorists argue that pictures are made up of conventional signs or codes, just like language, and that these are not innate but learned.[8] In other words, what pictures present, or represent, cannot simply be recognized by anyone who sees them. Rather, the viewer must decode the signs. One viewer may decode by simply drawing upon the meanings of the codes assumed from the viewer's own culture. A more sophisticated viewer may reflect upon the codes of both the culture that produced the picture and the viewer's own culture, and produce in turn a meaning— actually, an interpretation—that attempts to recognize that both picture and viewer are historically located, not timeless.

Not all theorists agree with this "semiotic" or "conventionalist" approach. Others ("perceptualists") argue that at least some depicted objects so resemble objects perceived in the real world that viewers just instinctively know what they are. We recognize a tree, a house, or a person in a picture without a decoding process. This seems to be the commonsense understanding and, in practice, when we talk about pictures we usually take for granted that some objects will be recognized by all. Thus we may recognize a square containing another small square in the top left quadrant, with an inverted V on top of the square, and a small square set into the inverted V with squiggles vertical to it. It is a house with a window, pitched roof, and smoking chimney. But would we recognize it as a habitable place if such buildings were unknown to our society? What if the "window" and "chimney" were missing? What if the inverted V did not overlap the sides of the box? How many visual clues or signs do we need to construe it as a "house"? And if chimneys disappeared from houses, would the cottage picture still be recognized as a house? (That is, does it have a life of its own as a sign?) Now let us put the word *home* underneath and ask the same questions. How do we recognize the image of a home? The simplest answer is that we are taught. Children in North America *learn* to associate the little smoking cottage with "home" even if their own homes look nothing like this.

The pictures we shall look at are much more complicated. We may recognize people, but they wear clothes unlike ours and are doing unusual
things. And in each case they have text associated with them that is also
more complicated than the labels "house" or "home." One picture is called
Jephthah's rash Vow, another *The Virgin Sacrificed*. To take the latter: "virgin" and "sacrifice" are words each with many connotations (start thinking of some!), but what happens when you put them together? If you were
to read the words without looking at the picture, what might you think
they meant? But then, after looking at the picture, would that visual image
modify your meaning(s)? And if you decided to investigate the biblical
text on the opposite page, would that control your meaning(s) further?
And would it make a difference if you followed through these steps but in
a different order? But what if you were an eighteenth-century reader/
viewer? Do you think you would come up with the same responses? To
take but two small elements: What did the word *virgin* signify to your
eighteenth-century reader, and what was his or her likely response to the
image of a young kneeling woman with her breasts bared? Would it have
made a difference if the viewer were a "him" or a "her"? And what if he
was rich and educated and she poor and little used to viewing fine copper
plate engravings in large Bibles? In short, do you think that Miss Whately
got it right?

In the discussion to follow we shall inquire into some, though not all,
of these questions. No doubt many others will occur to you, the
reader/viewer of this chapter.

Reading Narrative Pictures

Some steps we could take to explore our illustrations and open up some
of these questions are discussed by Perry Nodelman in his book *Words
about Pictures*.[9] His subject is the narrative art of children's picture books,
but his method applies well also to illustrated family Bibles and Bible histories.

For a start he urges us to consider separately the pictures and the texts
before considering the implications of their being complementary to each
other.[10] Although we may not always opt to follow this advice strictly (and
casual readers/viewers do not necessarily look at pictures this way), his
point is worth taking. We can usefully allow that the *picture* deserves its
own careful attention and refrain from too quickly determining its meaning by appeal to what we think the *text* means.

We could ask, moreover, What kind of book are we looking at, what
size and shape is it, and whom is it for? Does the shape constrain the

pictures? Most illustrated Bibles in the eighteenth and nineteenth centuries are taller than they are wide—just like humans—and so are their illustrations (unless printed sideways, as occasionally). The pictures, therefore, tend to present figures prominently and setting much less so. (Where the setting is striking, it is usually in a vertical dimension.) This design constraint lends importance to the poses of figures, their facial features, and the actions they perform. This last focus is congenial to biblical narrative, which usually privileges plot (and speech) over setting, though poses and expressions have to be inferred from action and speech because rarely does the biblical text describe them.

The illustrations we shall look at are engravings, mostly copper plates or steel plates (in use after about 1820). Because they are all printed in black ink, line, shape, light, and shade are important means of creating the picture. Use of heavy contrast, for example, can draw the viewer immediately to certain areas of the picture to the exclusion of others. Subtler shading leaves the eye to roam more freely, and to consider details more carefully.

The more we notice objects, the more "visual weight" they have.[11] Faces tend to have great visual weight because, as a rule, humans tend to pay special attention to faces and are highly attuned to determining facial expressions. Hidden faces create interpretive (decoding) problems for us. Gestures and poses—which may vary from culture to culture—are likewise important. Often such features take on conventional or symbolic meanings in particular artistic traditions. A head tilted with upturned eyes in eighteenth- or nineteenth-century European religious art likely indicates a person looking to, or beseeching, Heaven. Plants, animals, and inanimate objects also acquire conventional meanings—today, for example, red roses are associated with love. So a question we need to ask of our pictures is whether they show gestures or contain objects whose codes we would recognize if we were an appropriately acculturated viewer. Often, as in real life, a clue to the codes is found in the context, in the relations of visual objects to each other.

One way human figures relate to each other is through looking. Some theorists have argued that men in Western culture are conditioned to gaze at women ("the male gaze") in such a way as to render them "objects" of desire and that women are conditioned to regard their being gazed at as important to their identity as women. Looking at another person is understood to involve an asymmetrical exercise of power, in which case gazing at women is a way men, as subjects, sustain power over women, as objects. Film and art, it is argued, have typically been a vehicle for this male gaze. Critics of the theory say it disregards women's actual agency, including the ways they can exercise power over men through their bodies, denies a "female gaze," and censors erotic looking by both men and women. Nevertheless, for our purposes, the theory offers reason enough for us to take account of who is looking at whom in our pictures, and how we are disposing our own gaze as viewers.

Because our pictures illustrate narratives, we might also consider how they depict action and the passing of time.[12] Our pictures are frozen in time, but there may be various ways in which they suggest both immediate action and continuing events. People reach, point, and hold objects in midair to convey what comes next. In the sixteenth century it was common to include in the background miniature scenes depicting earlier and later episodes of the narrative. In eighteenth-century pictures it is common to find other visual components—figures or objects—that relate to the story's antecedents or to its continuation or culmination. In short, a well-designed picture can effectively convey a narrative.

Of course, the major way a biblical illustration takes on narrative meaning is precisely through its being located alongside the text that tells its story. And here we find ourselves back considering the complex relationship between pictures and words that we considered earlier.

The Book of Judges in Bible Illustration

In Britain during the eighteenth century, pictures were often found in large (folio) annotated "Family Bibles," with biblical text plus commentary, or in Bible "Histories" that retold and explained the Bible in the style of a narrative history. Small-format "Scripture Histories" expressly written for youth began to appear regularly from the end of the eighteenth century, often sold by subscription in parts that were later bound, and these publications increasingly included pictures, sometimes one plate to two pages of text, through the whole Bible. Such volumes were initially for educated, well-to-do families, but because of improved technology and a growing middle-class market (as a result of the industrial revolution in Britain and later the rapidly expanding North American economy) they became more and more affordable as the nineteenth century progressed.

In the eighteenth century, the topics chosen to illustrate Judges were similar to those appearing earlier in Bibles, Bible histories (including translations of the ancient author Josephus), and the suites of printed pictures that were popular in the seventeenth century. Not all the stories in Judges received equal attention. Most popular, and more or less compulsory in children's books, was Samson—wrestling with the lion, wielding a jawbone, carrying off Gaza's gates, or asleep in Delilah's lap having his hair cut. Gideon appears often, visited by the angel, testing the fleece, observing his men lapping (or not), and in a foray with trumpets and torches against the Midianites. The other two stories consistently chosen to illustrate were those of Jael and Jephthah's daughter. With Jael is always Sisera: either a tent peg protrudes from his head or he is about to be impaled. We meet the scene in a wide range of books, devotional and educational. Deborah, however, is rarely depicted. Jephthah's daughter regularly meets her father, and in the nineteenth century her lamenting with her companions also becomes popular. Her sacrifice, commonly depicted in the eighteenth century, becomes rarer in the next, though one earlier design enjoys a revival in mid-century Victorian Britain. The daughter, like Jael, appears also in children's books, though by the century's end she is seen less often and in the meeting scene, not the sacrifice.

Of other stories, Abimelech is regularly seen—by children and adults—about to be struck on the head or appealing to be finished off, and from time to time Ehud stabs Eglon. Adoni-bezek's mutilation is often depicted in eighteenth- and early-nineteenth-century Bibles, but rarely after that. The daughters of Shiloh, dancing and/or being carried off, likewise disappear. Apart from a particular picture popular in the nineteenth century, Achsah is little found. Micah is rare. The Levite's wife is also no favorite, though occasionally the Levite discovers her on the threshold. Her dismemberment is mostly avoided after the early eighteenth century.

It is noticeable that the sacrifice of Jephthah's daughter, like the mutilation of Adoni-bezek, was commonly illustrated in the eighteenth century but lost its place appeal in the following century. Why that happened is one of the questions a cultural critic might try to answer.

JEPHTHAH'S DAUGHTER

The Sacrifice: Dr. S. Smith's Family Bible, 1752

In Smith's *Family Bible* is a picture that appears in several English eighteenth-century family Bibles (plate 1).[13] A soldier is about to plunge a dagger into the daughter's bared breast. He looks too young to be her father. In the right foreground, some other maidens cluster sorrowfully at the burning altar, one placing upon it a garland of roses, another holding lilies, and yet another what might be a small jewelry box. Behind the daughter, to the left, a woman with tightly clasped hands looks away from

The Virgin Sacrificed

PLATE 1. *The Virgin Sacrificed.* In Dr. S. Smith's *Family Bible*, 1752.

the sacrifice towards her hooded neighbor. Further behind, soldiers stand in ranks, spears in hand, in the shadow of the castle walls.

The young woman and her executioner are bound to draw a viewer's eye rapidly: the two are closely knit and the space around them isolates them as a dramatic focus (plate 2). His right shoulder and arm make an ironic cradle for her head, and his right hand on her shoulder could be comforting if we did not see what was in his left hand. Her hands are obviously tied behind her back. The curved patches of light upon his breast mimic those on hers, except that his squared collar draws attention to his military jerkin or cuirass, while the cord falling from her shoulder leads to the robe rucked beneath her breasts and emphasizes that her body has been bared for the knife. His shadowed left leg matches the line of her thigh. He holds his head straight, she turns hers away from the instrument of death. His lips are tightly pursed while hers hang open, and while his eyes stare ahead (and not at his target) hers incline heavenwards.

The object that most fills the right foreground is a circular altar, aflame. Although small as altars go, its placement and strong lighting make it a prominent feature of the scene. It also forms a visual base for the group of maidens, no doubt the daughter's companions who had been with her in the hills, and the carved drapery that encircles the altar makes a strong visual link to the drapes of their clothes. Their heads are drawn together in a tight circle—they are, after all, companions—but their eyes look this way and that. One strongly averts her head while her friend behind her looks heavenwards, much as the daughter does. Another stares fixedly forward, like the executioner. But the fourth, who reaches out over the flames with the garland of roses, looks directly at the daughter. Her left hand points to her also, as does her friend's left hand (while also supporting the casket). The rose is a traditional symbol of love: so the garland symbolizes the marriage that will not take place, a prospect reduced to the ashes of sacrifice. From the roses our eyes rise to the lilies, one of which is almost framed by the stone arch of the castle behind. The picture's title, *The Virgin Sacrificed*, may help us decide that because the lily is a symbol of purity and is often associated with the Virgin Mary, these flowers are the sign under which the daughter meets her death, the sign of purity, the sign of the virgin. What, then, does the box signify? A tomb?

The altar, in some respects, anchors the whole picture. A line from the altar to the daughter and executioner takes us beyond them to the two figures behind. They are presented less distinctly in tones of grey, fitting perhaps for "background" figures, though the one visible face is sharply outlined, light separates the figures from the soldiers behind, and patches

PLATE 2. *The Virgin Sacrificed.* Detail.

of light in the robes, especially vertically, create a strong connection with the daughter and her slayer. Most striking is the gesture of the shrouded figure. It might be bringing cloth to wipe weeping eyes; it might be blocking sight of what is to happen; it might be a gesture of mourning. In any case, it hides the figure from the viewer. Who is this person that so avoids and grieves? Is it a faithful old nurse, perhaps? Or the mother who is missing from the text?

The soldiers form a broad shadowy band across the page merging into the shaded castle wall. Beyond in the sunlight is a pastoral scene of hills, trees, a distant hilltop building, and the sky with drifting cloud. Are these the hills to which the daughter and her companions retreated? Does this represent the peaceful life she is leaving? Yet the soldiers and fortress remind us of the war that lies behind the story; they make a barrier between the hills and the daughter; the war has fatally confined her. As if to reinforce the point, the executioner's head, by way of his hair, merges with the soldiers, linking them to him and the long dagger that is about to plunge.

The man who steadies the young woman for the death thrust does not seem to be her father. Conventionally, Jephthah is usually depicted as an older man, a general, often bearded and with distinguishing clothing such as a plumed helmet. Eighteenth-century readers of Judges 11 all knew this to be the story of Jephthah's "rash vow." Where he was when his daughter was put to death was a question many readers would have asked of the story and this scene. How could he have borne to see his daughter sacrificed? But then it was *his* vow for which she was paying the price, so how could he have *not* attended, even if it was not he who struck the blow? Where, then, is he? He has become conspicuous by his absence.

The female figures before and behind the daughter (assuming the hooded person to be a woman) have the curious effect of isolating the male figure with the weapon. Although the altar is a space normally reserved for men, here it has been made part of a circle of women. And the man has become a violent intruder into the women's space. Were women's circles separate from those of men in the ancient world of the story, and were they separate in the experience of the picture's eighteenth-century viewers? Might men and women view this scene differently, in part because their experience of social relationships is different? If so, what might the social differences be and how might these find themselves expressed in different responses to this picture of a violent male in a circle of women?

One possible response to this design, the single weapon-wielding man among the women, is for a viewer to connect this story to that of Jael and Sisera. Jael is popularly depicted, spike and mallet in hand, about to slay the enemy general. The space where death is delivered is her tent, women's space, as commentators noted. So in that story the man intrudes to meet his fate at the hand of a woman. In the present scene the man intrudes to slay a woman. And in each case a certain ritual is enacted, in one case a ritual of hospitality, in the other a ritual of sacrifice. What might these connections and contrasts mean for a reader's response to each story and how might they relate to the meaning of the book as a whole?

The prominence of the female figures may also prompt a viewer to recall that the daughter is said at the end to be annually lamented, precisely by women (Judg 11:39-40). Occasionally, such a scene is included separately in family Bibles and Bible histories with a picture of women in procession to the daughter's tomb, carrying flowers and other tributes to lay at her grave. In the present picture, we see the daughters already bringing their tributes, as they will do a year hence. Read this way, from left to right as it were, the picture moves us through time to the story's textual ending. The story ends not with sacrifice but commemoration.

The Virgin Sacrificed: The Daughter

The Virgin Sacrificed is what the picture is called. What do we know from the eighteenth century of written responses to this violent subject?

One response was to praise the daughter. She was a model of purity and obedience, of selfless devotion to father and country. Commentator Matthew Henry (1708) summed it up. The story "magnifies the law of the fifth commandment" ("Honour thy father and thy mother") by teaching

> that it well becomes Children, obediently and cheerfully to submit to their Parents in the Lord, and particularly to comply with their pious Resolutions for the Honour of God and the keeping up of Religion in their Families, though they be harsh and severe, as . . . Jephtha's Daughter here, who for the satisfying of her Father's Conscience, and for the Honour of God and her Countrey, yielded her self as one devoted.[14]

Writing for a youthful readership in 1783, pioneer educator Mrs. [Sarah] Trimmer confirms Henry's view. The young woman was possessed of "uncommon fortitude." Her death represented the voluntary sacrifice of a pious soul "in acknowledgment of God's mercy in preserving her father, and delivering her country."[15] In "Jephtha's Daughter" (1815), the popular Romantic poet Lord Byron has her tell her father that she will smile as she dies:

> Since thy triumph was bought by thy vow—
> Strike the bosom that's bared for thee now! . . .
> I have won the great battle for thee,
> And my Father and Country are free!

Likewise, "My God, my land, my father" are what move the daughter in the poem "A Dream of Fair Women" (1832) by the Victorian favorite, Alfred (later Lord) Tennyson. "How beautiful a thing it was to die / For God and my sire!" she exclaims, and is comforted by the thought that she subdued herself to her father's will, "Because the kiss he gave me, ere I fell, / Sweetens the spirit still." In the United States, decades later, the Rev. John Howard assures his young readers that her cheerful resignation deserves imitation because they should all "be ready to submit to the will of their parents."[16] The biblical historian, observes Harriet Beecher Stowe (1873), famous for her novel *Uncle Tom's Cabin*, "has set before us a high and lovely ideal of womanhood in the Judaean girl. There is but a sentence, yet what calmness, what high-mindedness, what unselfish patriotism, are in the words! 'My father, if thou has opened thy mouth to the Lord . . .'"[17]

The Virgin Sacrificed: The Father

If readers of the story responded with praise for the daughter, they just as commonly condemned her father—Jephthah was rash and ignorant of right religion. Matthew Henry again: "Most condemn Jephthah; he did ill to make so rash a vow, and worse to perform it. He could not be bound by his vow to that which God had forbidden by the letter of the sixth commandment: Thou shalt not kill. God had forbidden human sacrifices, so that it was . . . in effect a sacrifice to Moloch." Another often-quoted discussion (1725) begins, "No body can read Jephthah's Vow, and the Execution of it . . . without Horror and Amazement."[18] "It is a very affecting story," writes Mrs. Trimmer, "and cannot, I think, be read without painful emotions." She addresses her young reader directly: "I fancy, my dear, you are quite dissatisfied with Jephthah, and what to say in his excuse I know not, for indeed I find it has puzzled the learned." Perhaps in exile he had learned heathen practices and really did intend a human sacrifice. Hence "God taught him to understand the enormity of this horrid crime, by suffering him to be involved in such extreme distress."[19]

In the nineteenth century, and up to the present day, Jephthah has found few allies, though occasionally an effort is made. However rash the vow, writes the Rev. John Howard, "we cannot but admire the self-denial with which he accomplished it."[20] The daughter's virtue was obedience, the father's denial of self!

THE SACRIFICE

The Vow Performed: Dr. Samuel Newton's Complete Family Bible, *1771*

A further response was to reconsider the sacrifice. What exactly did it entail? Let us turn to an illustration of Judges 11:39 in a Bible annotated by the Rev. Dr. Samuel Newton (plate 3).[21] It is titled *Jephthah Performeth his Vow on his Daughter.* Below, in impeccable cursive, is the verse: "And it came to pass at the end of two months that she returned unto her father, who did with her according to his vow which he had vowed: and she knew no man."

Jephthah Performeth his Vow on his Daughter. Judges Ch.XI.39.

And it came to pass at the end of two months that she returned unto her father, who did with her according to his vow which he had vowed: and she knew no man.

PLATE 3. *Jephthah Performeth His Vow on His Daughter.* In Dr. Samuel Newton's *Complete Family Bible*, 1771. After a painting by Antonio Arrigoni.

The composition is simpler than in Smith's Bible. An altar is central.
Behind it rises a large fluted column and an archway through which are
visible sky, a hill, and trees. Before it, the daughter kneels, hands clasped
before her. She forms a distinct group with two women, their overlapping
figures forming a visual triangle that separates them from the men
(plate 4). Her attendants are swathed in clothes, whereas her outer robe is
open to the viewer and her white inner robe has fallen slightly off her
shoulder. Facing her is clearly the father, in military garb (Roman fashion
to match the classical architecture) with flowing cloak and plumed helmet. A young man peeps out behind him; his spear mingles with the column's lines. Whereas the women belong with the arch, the father and
bodyguard connect to the column. Both the father's hands gesture towards
the daughter: the extended fingers of one hand and the open palm of the
other. On the altar is a smoking vessel and some foliage (or lilies?). From
behind, a man leans forward; another looks over his shoulder. Presumably, the main figure is the officiating priest, wearing perhaps a prayer
shawl. His figure links altar and sky (the heavens?). On the altar step,
between father and daughter, are two small-mouth vases or urns, possibly funereal but perhaps alluding to the daughter's virginity.

What moment is captured? Are we looking at a last parting of father
and daughter before the sacrifice? Her posture is steady and she looks at
him resolutely. His posture is awkward, his head and upper body drawn
back behind his raised hand. And what is his gesture? Does it signal fear,
as if she had just met him returning from battle? Or is it one of blessing,
a final benediction on the dutiful daughter, only child, he is about to lose?
The priest looks directly at her and points to her. Perhaps he is inviting
her to confirm her assent. The two attending women draw their robes
modestly around them; indeed, the one crouching seems almost to be hid-
ing behind the daughter, peering timidly around her shoulder at the standing general. Her apprehension adds to our sense of the daughter's
composure.

But the picture is missing something. Why is there no implement of
death to be seen—no sword, dagger, or axe? Even Jephthah the soldier
wears no sword. For an illustration of a sacrifice, this is an unusual picture. This thought might give a viewer pause: Am I, as a twenty-first-
century viewer, missing something else? As it happens, a cultivated
eighteenth-century viewer could well have brought to this picture an
understanding of the vow and sacrifice that puts the picture in a different
light. (Is that sunlit arch an allusion to a rainbow?)

An educated upbringing in the eighteenth century likely included an
acquaintance with the writings of Isaac Watts, not only through singing

PLATE 4. *Jephthah Performeth His Vow.* Detail.

hymns such as "When I Survey the Wondrous Cross," but through learning the answers in his catechism. On Jephthah, Watts says:

> It is a Matter of Doubt and Controversy among the Learned, whether *Jephthah*, being a Soldier, in those Days of Ignorance, did not really offer his Daughter for a Sacrifice, *according to his Vow*, as the Scripture seems to express it; or whether he only restrained her from Marriage and bearing Children, which in those Days was accounted like a Sacrifice, and as a Sentence of Death passed on them.[22]

An adult reader of biblical commentaries on Judges would have certainly met this alternative ending, often the subject of a long disquisition and frequently favored. The cultivated viewer who had attended one of the performances of the oratorio *Jephtha* (first performed in 1751), by the popular composer George Frideric Handel, would probably not have been surprised by the oratorio's happy outcome.[23] Jephthah thinks he must sacrifice (put to death) his daughter Iphis, and she urges the fearful priests to execute her father's will and the call of Heaven. But at the last minute an angel intervenes to stay "the slaught'rous hand." The vow has been dreadfully misunderstood. The warrior vowed, "What, or whoe'er shall first salute mine eyes, / Shall be forever Thine, or fall a sacrifice." Parsed properly, the promise is to dedicate to God (alive) *or* to offer as a sacrifice (dead). Because human sacrifice is forbidden, the first option applies. So she must, as Matthew Henry earlier put it, take herself off to a nunnery.

The argument that Jephthah sent his daughter into seclusion derives from Jewish poet and scholar Abraham ben Meir Ibn Ezra in the twelfth century. It hinges on Hebrew grammar, taking the Hebrew connective (w^e) as disjunctive (*or*) instead of, more usually, conjunctive (*and*). Rather than requiring the firstcomer to be devoted to God *and* offered as a sacrifice (the usual reading), the vow stipulates *either* devoted to God (if a person) *or* offered as a burnt-offering (if an animal fit for sacrifice). The grammarian David Kimchi soon added two supports: the daughter bewails her virginity, not death (Judg 11:37); and upon return from the mountain, her subsequent seclusion is confirmed by the clause "she did not know a man" (Judg 11:39). The daughter's "survival" came into Christian interpretation in the fourteenth century through Nicholas of Lyra, an advocate of the "literal sense" of Scripture. He envisioned the daughter like a nun, secluded, praying, fasting, and performing pious works. To those who asked why, if she were still alive, the women went annually to lament the daughter, a standard answer was that the Hebrew word could also mean "talk with"—and this alternative translation appears in the margins of the 1611 King James Version.[24]

The interpretation appealed because it solved some problems. The vow was not so awful after all and, for Christians, the praise of Jephthah in Hebrews 11 was vindicated. In the eighteenth century when the Bible was under attack by the rationalists known as Deists—who in North America included several of the most influential "founding fathers"—this ending was additionally appealing. For example, Voltaire, famous throughout Europe, invoked the story of Jephthah sacrificing his daughter to attack the Old Testament and its god for barbarous morality and intolerance. Backed by the survival argument, orthodox Christians could retort that Voltaire failed to understand the text. Not so, replies Voltaire. The daughter's death, he says (in 1763), "is plain by the text."[25]

The argument over whether the daughter survived or not continued through the nineteenth century, consuming much space in commentaries and dictionaries. Then, towards the end of the century, the survival argument rapidly lost ground to assertions (like those of Voltaire earlier) that the meaning of the text was "plain," so that in recent decades it is mostly either not discussed at all or mentioned only to be dismissed. Instead, queries about the nature of the vow usually concern whether Jephthah intended a human or an animal sacrifice.

Returning to the illustration in Newton's Bible, however, we now have another way of viewing it. We understand better why this illustration sets the whole of verse 39 before the viewer, including the final phrase, "and she knew no man." In this alternative construal, the scene does indeed show Jephthah performing his vow on his daughter but this action does not involve her death. Rather, Jephthah is bidding her go into seclusion with his blessing. The priest who points to her across the smoking altar is sanctioning the action as the fulfillment of the vow. Behind the daughter, the heavily garbed women may be nuns, alluding to a life of pious seclusion. Perhaps they are here to fetch her. And perhaps the sunlit arch does indeed allude to the rainbow.

Pictures, Texts, and Contexts: Iphigenia

An educated eighteenth-century viewer (more likely a man than a woman) might also have seen something else in both these pictures. The classical style of clothing, artifacts, and architecture indicates the ancient world, with ancient Israel hardly differentiated from ancient Greece or Rome. In the nineteenth century that changed. Increased travel to Turkey, the Levant (modern Syria, Palestine, Israel), and Egypt brought to Europe and America pictures of a daily life that was thought to replicate life in the ancient Holy Land, and those pictures looked different from the classical world. (Excavations of ancient Assyria and Babylon reliefs added to the sense of difference.) But for the eighteenth-century viewer the setting of this scene spelled simply the ancient world. It was easy to associate the daughter before the altar with comparable scenes in classical literature.

The story of a virgin sacrificed haunts the ancient Greek tragedy *Agamemnon* by Aeschylus (458 B.C.E.). In order to appease the goddess Artemis (Diana), who was preventing the Greek fleet from sailing on an expedition against Troy, Agamemnon, the general commanding the Greeks, had offered his daughter Iphigenia as a sacrifice. The play enacts his return under the shadow of her death. In a later play, Euripides (*Iphigenia at Aulis*, 410 B.C.E.) explores the events leading up to the offering. Appalled at first, Iphigenia eventually agrees to the sacrifice for the sake of the Greek army and the honor of Greek women. At the last minute, however, Artemis substitutes a deer and takes Iphigenia to be her priestess at Taurus. The parallels have intrigued readers of the biblical story from earliest times.[26] Whereas today in Britain or the United States these plays are little known, in the eighteenth and nineteenth centuries reading such classical literature was considered essential for a superior education. Many whose families could afford one of these large illustrated Bibles would have been familiar with the Greek tales.

One effect of considering the picture of *The Virgin Sacrificed* with Agamemnon's story in mind is that we may decide to ask again where the young woman's *mother* might be. Is she the figure whose face is shielded behind the kneeling daughter? Why is she absent from the biblical text? In the play by Aeschylus, we learn that Iphigenia's mother, Clytemnestra, harbors deep resentment against her husband Agamemnon for his terrible deed, so much so that on his return from Troy she murders him. In the play by Euripides, Clytemnestra strongly remonstrates with her husband and desperately tries to enlist Achilles to help save her daughter. Certainly these depictions of Iphigenia's mother underlie the long narrative poem "Jephthah's Daughter" (1865) by Canadian Charles Heavysege, in which he gives Jephthah's daughter a mother who relentlessly denounces her "cruel" and "ruthless" husband for robbing her of her child, using the daughter "As altar-fuel, that might shed a flame / To light thy taper-glory in the field." The daughter, who at first eloquently protests, comes, like Euripides' Iphigenia, to own that "There *is* some signal bliss awaiting those / Who perish for their country," and finally speaks as Heavysege's contemporaries, Byron and Tennyson, would have her do: "Father, you shall not say I disobeyed." Yet the poem ends ambivalently. The mother's accusations against the father are not answered, her trust that Jehovah will repudiate the sacrifice appears ill placed, and no word at all is uttered in the deity's defense. The narrator, however, is not ambivalent about the daughter, "who bowed her to a parent's urgent need, / enduring irreparable wrong." And so she died, "Self-forgetful;—yet, immortal, lives, / Loved and remembered to the end of time."[27]

Moving the focus to the daughter, loved and remembered, does have the advantage of shifting attention from the roles of the father and the deity, long a source of puzzlement to the story's readers, especially to Christians believing that Hebrews 11 endorses Jephthah's relationship with God as "faithful." As we have just seen, the comparable classical texts about Iphigenia offer a voice of protest, against both father and deity, which readers of Judges can borrow to fill a gap in the biblical text. Why does the father so readily accept the daughter's acquiescence? In the classical texts, Clytemnestra's remonstrations elicit from Agamemnon anguish as well as his reasons for persevering with the sacrifice. Why does the deity not intervene? In Euripides' play, the goddess Artemis replaces the daughter with a sacrificial deer, just as in the story of Abraham and Isaac an angel substitutes an animal for the son.

Earlier we asked of the illustration in Smith's Bible, Where is Jephthah? He seemed to be absent. What did that say about his willingness to face the consequences of his actions? In the "survival" illustration in Newton's Bible he is very much present, though his twisted body suggested a person deeply conflicted. Because many who perused those volumes were also interested in the Iphigenia parallels, what might they have viewed in pictures of the ancient Greek sacrifice? Paintings of the scene were popular in the seventeenth and eighteenth centuries. How was Agamemnon depicted? The answer is that he was always present, but usually unable to look at his daughter by the altar. Indeed, a traditional rendering, widely followed, showed him covering his face with his cloak. The model was apparently a celebrated painting by Timanthes (c. 406 b.c.e.), mentioned by the Roman authors Cicero and Quintilian whose dissertations on rhetoric were a staple of the eighteenth-century educational curriculum. They claimed that covering the face was the only way the painter could express such emotional intensity as was felt by Agamemnon.[28] So here we have another possible way of "reading" the figure hidden by a cloak in Smith's Bible. It is the father, present after all but emotionally overcome, unable to look at the dreadful proceedings (plate 5).

Curiously, then, the classical parallels in text and image have the effect of filling the hidden figure with competing or, better perhaps, overlapping meanings. It is the mother. No, it is the father. What if it is both? Could they share grief? What emotions will a viewer allow the sacrificing father to have? And did it in the eighteenth century, and does it now, make a difference whether the viewer is male or female?

Finally, another question: What difference does it make that Euripides gives a voice to mother, father, and daughter, as the sacrifice looms, but the biblical narrator tells us only, in stony tones, that the daughter returned and the father "did with her according to his vow which he had vowed"? What do we expect of a story? What "gaps" can we pass over in silence? How is our reading and viewing of biblical text and illustration determined by what we habitually want from narrative texts and images and what we think they want from us?

PLATE 5. A fresco from first-century Herculaneum in Italy shows a hooded, face-covering figure. Is it Agamemnon (following Timanthes) or Clytemnestra? (The statuette is the goddess Artemis/Diana.) The "antiquities" of newly excavated Herculaneum created great interest in the later eighteenth century, as renditions like this (nineteenth-century) plate were published.

INTERSECTIONS: PICTURES AND TEXTS

We have seen how these illustrations can refer us to comparable texts outside the Bible, providing we have already been acculturated to those texts. The reference sets up what some would call "intertextuality"—whereby our reading of the one text is inescapably a reading of the other, when our responses to Judges 11 are permeated with our responses to *Agamemnon* or *Iphigenia at Aulis*. Often, however, we are unconscious of the intersections. We simply think we are reading the text at hand. Ferreting out the "intertexts" that intersect and influence our reading and viewing is an important job for the cultural critic.

Another kind of "intertextuality" that takes many cultural forms is the interplay of meanings set up by the immediate juxtaposition of words and images. In the case of the illustrations we have been looking at, this can happen in at least two important ways. First, there is the picture title, or the biblical verse, or the moralizing ditty that is incorporated into or directly attached to the illustration. Second, there is the main text or narrative that accompanies the illustration on the adjacent page or pages. Does the image determine the meaning of the text or the text the meaning of the image? An answer might depend on what are the cultural meanings or relative authority of "text" and "image" for a given reader or viewer. But, that issue aside, we might also consider whether text and image might subvert as well as determine meaning. So let us look at how our particular images intersect with their texts.

Incorporated onto the plate in Smith's Bible is a supertitle in businesslike capitals, *Judges, Chap. XI,* and a prominent and contrasting subtitle in fine cursive, *The Virgin Sacrificed.* We have discussed some of the ways the subtitle coheres with the picture. The annotation on the opposite page, however, is a different matter. It starts with an expression of horror at the sacrifice that we have already met: "No one without horror or amazement, can suppose Jephthah sacrificed his daughter for a burntoffering." It goes on, however, to clarify the writer's stance: "They, who believe Jephthah's daughter was actually sacrificed for a burnt-offering, must be stranger to the Old Testament notions [against human sacrifice] and to human nature." Smith's lengthy comment is actually extracted more or less verbatim from Laurence Howel's popular and frequently borrowed discussion of the vow, and it includes Howel's conclusion that the daughter was not sacrificed but secluded.[29] So *The Virgin Sacrificed*, a dagger plunged into her heart, was not after all sacrificed. What is a reader/viewer to do? Accept the text and discount the picture? Accept the picture and discount the text? Accept that text and picture subvert each other? Await, as in Handel's opera, a heavenly visitor to stay the slayer's hand? Fault the publisher for inserting in the text an inappropriate plate? Or perhaps go back to Judges and reread the text? Or ask, Why am I drawn to the one version rather than the other?

The "survival" illustration in Samuel Newton's Bible creates less conflict. We have noted how the supertitle speaks of Jephthah performing his vow and how the subtitle quotes the whole verse, including the final phrase, pertinent to survival arguments, "and she knew no man." In elaboration of the incident Newton says only (and neutrally) that "This passage has given occasion to a great controversy among commentators, whether Jephthah really offered his daughter for a burnt-offering, or consecrated her to the service of God." Yet, as we have seen, the illustration most readily lends itself to the latter alternative. In this case, then, the image (with its incorporated text) appears to tilt the balance. Did Newton approve of the picture? Does that matter to the meaning?

Plate 6. *Jephthah's Rash Vow.* In the Rev. E. Blomfield's *New Family Bible*, 1813.

The version of Newton's "survival" picture in the Rev. E. Blomfield's *Family Bible* (1813) has *Judges Chap. XI.* V.39 for a supertitle, and a subtitle in cursive, *Jephthah's rash Vow,* leaving the nature of the vow open (plate 6).[30] Blomfield draws the notes for his Bible from Matthew Henry (a century earlier) and he chooses carefully here. From Henry's extensive discussion he extracts the moral as Henry sees it, that "we must learn, not to think it strange, if the day of our triumphs in this world prove upon some account or other the day of our griefs, and therefore must always rejoice with trembling." Blomfield then cuts to Henry's final paragraph:

> Jephthah did ill to make so rash a vow, and worse to perform it. He could not be bound by his vow to that which God had forbidden. . . . And probably the reason why it is left dubious by the inspired penman, whether he sacrificed his daughter or no, was, that they who did afterwards offer their children, might take any encouragement from this instance. Concerning this, and some other such passages in the sacred history, which learned men are in the dark, divided, and in doubt about, we need not much amuse ourselves; what is necessary to our salvation, thanks be to God, is plain enough.

The key words are "dubious," "dark," "divided," and "in doubt." A reader might well gain the impression that Henry himself was "dubious" on the question of sacrifice or survival. But in fact Henry makes plain in his detailed discussion that the arguments for survival do not persuade him. Thus Blomfield's extract conveniently leaves plenty of space for a "survival" illustration. Henry's text lends support to a "view" of the vow's performance that Henry himself did not share!

THE DAUGHTER SACRIFICED: JOHN OPIE'S VERSION

A favorite picture for several generations is one version or another of a painting by Cornish artist and Royal Academy of Art member John Opie (1761–1807). In the Rev. Dr. Benjamin Kennicott's *Family Bible* (1793) it is titled *The Sacrafice* [sic] *of Jephthah's Daughter* (plate 7).[31] The daughter kneels, blindfolded, and bare-breasted; an aged priest grimly leans over, knife poised to plunge; a young acolyte crouches apprehensively, bowl at the ready. To one side stands a large intact pitcher. Behind are two figures, one, garlanded, sorrowfully pinioning the daughter's arms, the other,

THE SACRAFICE of JEPHTHAH'S DAUGHTER.

Judges Ch. XI. V. 39. 40.

PLATE 7. *The Sacrifice of Jephthah's Daughter.* In Dr. Benjamin Kennicott's *Universal Family Bible,* 1793.

hooded, turned away as if unable to look. Is the latter a woman? A smokey fire burns on the shadowy altar to one side; behind is a dark archway.

In the accompanying textual notes, Kennicott is adamant: "Jephthah's daughter was not sacrificed, but only devoted to perpetual virginity." He declares that it is "really astonishing that the general stream of commentators, should take it for granted, that Jephthah murdered his daughter!" He thinks it probable that the Greeks stole this story to concoct the "fable" of Iphigenia (i.e., Jephtigenia) and observes that Agamemnon in the end did not murder her.

What does this picture say to a viewer, and how does it relate to both Kennicott's notes and the biblical text? How is it different from Smith's illustration and do those differences matter? What cultural assumptions or practices underlie this picture—and the one that follows?

Half a century later, in Thomas Gaspey's *Family Devotions* (c. 1850), the scene has grown starker, yet set now within a delicately decorated frame (plate 8).[32] The background figures are gone, heightening the contrast with the young woman's white body, for the archway behind now leads into black darkness, as if into a tomb. Yet the priest's mouth is no longer so grimly set, the daughter might faintly smile, and the boy looks on almost eagerly.

To the present-day viewer who suspects that eroticism played a part in the appeal (to men?) of Opie's picture, a perusal of another Victorian favorite, "Jephthah's Daughter" by American editor and essayist Nathaniel Parker Willis, might suggest such latent sentiments were not rare:

. . . and the wind,
Just swaying her light robe, revealed a shape
Praxiteles might worship . . . .
Her lip was slightly parted, like the cleft
Of a pomegranate blossom; and her neck,
Just where the cheek was melting to its curve
With the unearthly beauty sometimes there,
Was shaded, as if light had fallen off,
Its surface was so polished. She was stilling
Her light, quick breath, to hear; and the white rose
Scarce moved upon her bosom, as it swelled,
Like nothing but a lovely wave of light,
To meet the arching of her queenly neck . . . .
Her countenance was radiant with love.
She looked like one to die for it . . . .[33]

PLATE 8. *Jephthah's Rash Vow.* In Thomas Gaspey's *Family Devotions*, c.1850.

Still, as we consider such nineteenth-century sentiment, we might note that Harriet Beecher Stowe chose this poem (along with Byron's) to accompany her comments on the daughter.[34]

A MODEL DAUGHTER?

Textual responses to the story of Jephthah's daughter remained constant for nearly two hundred years from the beginning of the eighteenth century to the closing decades of the nineteenth. But then, as noted, the survival argument lost ground, and, remarkably, a voice was raised disputing the notion that the daughter was an appropriate model for young women.

Admiration for her daughterly devotion was widely shared between men and women, and continued into the twentieth century. The daughter's behavior offers us a "glimpse of obedience as perfect as any the world has known," declared Florence Bone (c. 1915). She wondered whether the modern woman took her freedom for granted. In Jephthah's daughter she saw rather a woman "whose nature becomes fine and rare, whose work is achieved, in spite of terrible odds. . . . She had not thought of being daunted, and there was absolutely nothing in her character of the disposition to whine and pity herself. She was entirely brave."[35]

The American suffragist Elizabeth Cady Stanton, however, took a different view (1898). She is scathing in her criticism of Jephthah, as also of Abraham, "these loving fathers" who "thought to make themselves specially pleasing to the Lord by sacrificing their children to Him as burnt offerings." Her own context as a woman fighting for equal rights with men informs her evaluation of the daughter:

> The submission of Isaac and Jephthah's daughter to this violation of their most sacred rights is truly pathetic. But, like all oppressed classes, they were ignorant of the fact that they had any natural, inalienable rights. We have such a type of womanhood even in our day. If any man had asked Jephthah's daughter if she would not like to have the Jewish law on vows so amended that she might disallow her father's vow, and thus secure to herself the right of life, she would no doubt have said, "No; I have all the rights I want," just as a class of New York women said in 1895, when it was proposed to amend the constitution of the State in their favor.

She remarks that the daughter is given no name, a sign of being owned absolutely by her father, and she sharply contests the lauding of her "beautiful submission and self-sacrifice." "To me it is pitiful and painful. I would that this page of history were gilded with a dignified whole-souled rebellion." To drive home the point she offers a countertext, the manifesto of an independent and brave young woman who would sternly rebuke her father:

> I will not consent to such a sacrifice. Your vow must be disallowed. You may sacrifice your own life as you please, but you have no right over mine. . . . I consider that God has made me the arbiter of my own fate and all my possibilities. My first duty is to develop all the powers given to me and to make the most of myself and my own life. Self-development is a higher duty than self-sacrifice. I demand the immediate abolition of the Jewish law on vows. Not with my consent can you fulfill yours.[36]

CONCLUSIONS

In our exploration of these illustrations from times past we have found ourselves drawing on various methods presented earlier in this book, as well as finding our way with some new ones—reading printed pictures along with texts and locating their cultural context. Clearly, our attempt to characterize cultural contexts involves historical investigation but also sociological and ideological inquiry about class, education, and religion, for example. In our attention to formal aspects of the illustrations we have imitated a concern of both narrative criticism and structuralism. Our questions about the representation of women vis-à-vis men have a home in feminist inquiry. The tensions and unstable meanings produced by reading some of the pictures against their texts are characteristic of both structuralist and deconstructive analysis. Furthermore, our investigation of the Iphigenia story raises questions of "intertextuality" with which literary critics are familiar, and we have seen that another important interest of literary theory, how readers find and treat "gaps," lies at the heart of this story when considered through the lens of reception history.

This kind of cultural criticism may both refocus our attention on familiar questions regarding the biblical text—how to evaluate the vow, for example, and the daughter's response—and direct our attention to other questions. What might result, for example, if today we were to read the biblical story of Jephthah and his daughter alongside the Greek stories of Agamemnon and *his* daughter? What ancient cultural context might these stories share? What attitudes towards women? What understanding of divine power?

PLATE 9. (a) *The Punishment of Adoni-bezek,* in Pieter Mortier's "Great Bible," 1700. (b) *Judith and Holofernes.* In Dr. Samuel Newton's *Complete Family Bible,* 1771.

An advantage of reception history is that it shows how responses to biblical texts have been culturally conditioned. The evidence puts in question not only claims that the text has some "culture-free" meaning but also that a reader can acquire some definitive method of interpretation. It also helps us glimpse some of our own cultural conditioning. If today's reader is disturbed by Smith's picture of the young woman as a sacrificial victim, what exactly has changed since the picture was deemed edifying? And if it reveals changed feelings between the eighteenth century and now, does it not also suggest that the sensibilities of an ancient reader of the story might be different again?

Why *did* pictures of the daughter's sacrifice and Adoni-bezek's mutilation disappear, just as books with illustrations of Bible stories were becoming cheaper and reaching a wider readership? One reason could be that cultural attitudes towards public executions and punishment by mutilation changed. In England in the mid-seventeenth century ears were cut off for some offenses and branding for theft was practiced. Men convicted of treason were half-hanged, then disemboweled, castrated, quartered, and decapitated. By the early nineteenth century all these practices had been abolished. Arguments were leveled against public executions as not suitable for viewers, especially women and children, and the last public execution took place in England in 1868. A change in sensibility towards the bodily suffering of others had been taking place.[37]

In part this change was a response to the logical arguments against torture and judicial cruelty of eighteenth-century thinkers such as Cesare Beccaria and Voltaire, and in part it was a response to the Romantic movement's validation of feeling, emotion, and sensitivity. By the mid-nineteenth century it had become accepted practice in Britain among the middle and upper classes to feel and express feelings for those inflicted with pain and death by the state. This change in sensibility may be why, by the end of the nineteenth century, pictures freely reproduced in the previous century, such as the young man joining in the mutilation of Adoni-bezek (plate 9a),[38] or the crowd (with children) celebrating Judith's decapitation of Holofernes (plate 9b),[39] or the slaughter of Jephthah's daughter as John Opie saw it, ceased to be acceptable in the cultural practice of family viewing. And, more or less, that is how things still stand today.[40]

FURTHER READING

Adams, Laurie Schneider. *The Methodologies of Art.* New York: HarperCollins, 1996. Suited for students, it shows how art may have multiple levels of meaning.

Aichele, George, ed. *Culture, Entertainment and the Bible*. JSOT Supplement Series 309. Sheffield: Sheffield Academic Press, 2000. Highbrow, lowbrow, including Delilah in song.

Bach, Alice, ed. *Biblical Glamour and Hollywood Glitz. Semeia* 74. Atlanta: Scholars, 1996. Edited by a trendsetter in the field; includes Delilah and the Western.

Berger, Arthur Asa. *Cultural Criticism: A Primer of Key Concepts*. London: Sage, 1995. Very accessible: covers the subject from many perspectives with skill and humor.

Berger, John. *Ways of Seeing*. London: BBC and Penguin, 1972. Seeing comes before words.

Boer, Roland. *Knockin' on Heaven's Door: The Bible and Popular Culture*. Biblical Limits. London and New York: Routledge, 1999. Provocative.

Bohn, Babette. "Death, Dispassion, and the Female Hero: Artemisia Gentileschi's *Jael and Sisera*." In *The Artemisia Files*. Edited by Mieke Bal, 107–27. Chicago: University of Chicago Press, 2005. An art historian helps us see the baroque Bible.

Bottigheimer, Ruth B. *The Bible for Children from the Age of Gutenberg to the Present*. New Haven: Yale University Press, 1996. Already the classic book on the subject.

Clines, David J. A. *The Bible and the Modern World*. Sheffield: Sheffield Phoenix Press, 2005 (first published 1997). An engaging chapter on the Bible and "high" culture.

De Hamel, Christopher. *The Book: A History of the Bible*. London and New York: Phaidon Press, 2001. A well-told story of Bible production and use. Color illustrations in plenty.

Exum, J. Cheryl. *Plotted, Shot, and Painted: Cultural Representations of Biblical Women*. Gender, Culture, Theory 3. Sheffield: Sheffield Academic Press, 1996. One of the foremost critics; includes "Why, Why, Why, Delilah?"

———. "Lovis Corinth's *Blinded Samson*." In *Beyond the Biblical Horizon: The Bible and the Arts*. Edited by J. Cheryl Exum, 152–67. Leiden: Brill, 1999. On the mutual influence of Bible and art.

Exum, J. Cheryl, and Stephen D. Moore, eds. *Biblical Studies/Cultural Studies*. Gender, Culture, Theory 7. Sheffield: Sheffield Academic Press, 1998. With an excellent introduction on how cultural studies has developed.

Forshey, Gerald E. *American Religious and Biblical Spectaculars*. Westport, Conn. and London: Praeger, 1992. The sword-and-sandal movies in their cultural context.

Gunn, David M. *Judges*. Blackwell Bible Commentaries. Oxford: Blackwell Publishing, 2005. Traces professional and popular uses of stories and characters from late antiquity to the present.

Gutjahr, Paul C. *An American Bible: A History of the Good Book in the United States, 1777–1880*. Stanford: Stanford University Press, 1999. Touches numerous aspects of the Bible's cultural appropriation and economic exploitation.

Jeffrey, David Lyle. *A Dictionary of Biblical Tradition in English Literature*. Grand Rapids, Mich.: W. B. Eerdmans, 1992. Incomparable, a mine of information.

Langston, Scott. M. *Exodus Through the Centuries*. Blackwell Bible Commentaries. Oxford: Blackwell Publishing, 2006. Ranges widely; especially strong on American political and social history.

Long, Burke O. *Imagining the Holy Land: Maps, Models, and Fantasy Travels*. Bloomington and Indianapolis: Indiana University Press, 2003. A must-read on how the Bible seeps into the cultural imagination—"the real-imagined" Bible.

McDannell, Colleen. *Material Christianity: Religion and Popular Culture in America*. New Haven and London: Yale University Press, 1995. A fascinating survey of material culture.

Marcus, David. *Jephthah and His Vow*. Lubbock, Tex.: Texas Tech University Press, 1986. Traces interpretive history and makes a modern case for "survival."

Sawyer, John F. A., ed. *The Blackwell Companion to the Bible and Culture*. Oxford: Blackwell Publishing, 2006. Since ancient times, and across the globe. An invaluable resource.

Sherwood, Yvonne. *A Biblical Text and Its Afterlives: The Survival of Jonah in Western Culture*. Cambridge: Cambridge University Press, 2000. Elegantly written by a postmodern critic.

Sjöberg, Mikael. *Wrestling with Textual Violence: The Jephthah Narrative in Antiquity and Modernity*. Sheffield: Sheffield Phoenix Press, 2006. Five responses to the story, from Josephus, via Handel, to novelist Amos Oz.

Stocker, Margarita. *Judith: Sexual Warrior: Women and Power in Western Culture*. New Haven and London: Yale University Press, 1998. Shows Judith's many cultural uses from the Middle Ages to the present.

Taylor, Marion Ann, and Heather E. Weir. *Let Her Speak for Herself: Nineteenth-Century Women Writing on Women in Genesis*. Waco, Tex.: Baylor University Press, 2006. An annotated anthology. Includes Trimmer, Stowe, Cady Stanton, and many more.

GLOSSARY

Actantial model—a proposal for organizing the character roles in a narrative event under six categories. A *sender* initiates the action, in order to transfer an *object* to a *receiver.* The action is carried out by a *subject,* who is aided and/or opposed by *helpers* and *opponents.* The entity occupying one of these categories is called an **actant.**

Androcentric—male-centered.

B.C.E.—before the common era or before the Christian era; the equivalent of B.C., but expressed without being Christocentric.

Anticonquest ideology—the literary ideology that allows colonizers to claim foreign lands while asserting their virtue.

Bêt ʾāb—"house of the father"; the household, which was the smallest basic unit of social organization in ancient Israel.

Bilateral kinship—tracing one's descent through both one's mother's and one's father's relatives.

Binary opposition—a pair of concepts felt (within some human groups) to be opposed to each other, for example, male/female. Some structuralist theories hold that the human mind works by positing and mediating such oppositions.

Characters—people who participate in the events of a story, and are usually portrayed through their own actions or speeches, the speeches of other characters, or by the narrator's comments.

Chiasmus—a literary device that structures words, phrases, sections of a work, and so on by balancing them in an A B B' A' pattern. The artistic focus is usually on the center of the chiasmus, in this case, the B B'.

Contact zone—a term used in postcolonial criticism to describe the place where people of different geographic and historical backgrounds come into contact with each other. Usually a place of conflictual and inequitable relations.

Culture—a language or set of codes (spoken, written, acted, pictured, manufactured) through which people share values and beliefs, behave in certain approved ways, make and use artifacts in common. Transmitted by imitation and learning, culture lends people identity, helps them relate to each other, and provides the glue that sustains a society.

Deconstructive criticism—an act of reading that exposes the ways in which texts contradict themselves and accents the textual elements that traditional readings have overlooked or have intentionally ignored. A deconstructive reading is one that explores the complexity (even the conflictual nature) of a text's production of meaning, as opposed to a reading that reduces a text's meaning to a single or a dominant interpretation.

Deuteronomist(s)—the author(s) or editor(s) of the "Deuteronomic History (DH)," which, according to a hypothesis popular in biblical studies, forms a coherent and originally separate work.

Deuteronomistic History—the name given to the biblical books of Joshua, Judges, 1 and 2 Samuel, and 1 and 2 Kings. Often abbreviated as DH.

Diachronic—literally, "through time"; a form of study that considers changes in some phenomenon over the course of time (contrast *synchronic*).

Direct discourse—refers to occasions where the narrator reports the speeches of characters in the story.

Discourse—the various symbolic and linguistic systems and narratives used in human communication; for example, newspaper articles, academic textbooks and articles, films, songs, paintings, poetry, stories, and so on.

Endogamy—marriage within boundaries established by the individual's group.

Ethnocentrism—projecting one's own contemporary notions of the world onto other social systems without considering whether or not this is an appropriate view of reality.

Exogamy—marriage outside boundaries established by an individual's group.

Familial mode of production—a kinship or lineage-based *mode of production* whose members own the principal means of production and do not pay tribute or taxes to an external ruling elite.

Focalization—a term some narrative theorists use to refer to the perspective from which a narrative event is presented. An event may be focalized by the narrator or by a character.

Form criticism—a method of exegesis that examines the literary forms of biblical genres and their life settings in a believing community.

Gender—the cultural definition of behavior considered to be appropriate to the sexes in a given society at a given time. Whereas sex is a biological given, gender is culturally created. For example, only women can give birth; thus giving birth is a sex role. Both men and women are capable of raising children, but most societies assign this role to women; it is therefore a gender role.

Gender criticism—An approach to reading that analyzes the role of gender in society and cultural products while simultaneously problematizing, or showing the instability of, the categories and norms associated with gender (e.g., "man" and "woman," "masculine" and "feminine").

Hybridity—a term that expresses a complex process when two or more cultures interact; on the one hand, it expresses a fusion of disparate elements (linguistic, cultural, racial, etc.) that emerges when two or more cultures come in contact, and, on the other hand, it expresses negotiation and contestation between cultures.

Ideological criticism—a method of exegesis that incorporates both sociohistorical and literary approaches to investigate the production and (re)production of ideology in a text.

Ideology—a complex system of meaning that constructs a "reality" for people and helps them understand their place in the world as natural, inevitable, and necessary. It is not the "reality" itself.

Intertextuality—the notion that texts are interrelated through direct citation or allusion, subtle influence, or by the very fact that all texts, as products of language, form a boundless network. Intertextual reading is reading that attends to how textual connections participate in any one text's production of meaning.

Langue—French for "language"; used in structuralism (in contrast to *parole*) to refer to language as a system of relationships and, by extension, to the system of relationships underlying any cultural phenomenon.

Liminality—an in-between space in which *hybridity*—contestation and fusion of cultures—takes place.

Lineage—a descent group that is composed of a number of residential groups.

Linguistics—the science of language.

Material/materialist—refers to the production and distribution of economic goods and the social relationships of owners and workers.

Mediation—used in a special sense by structuralists to refer to an attempt (for example, in myth) to hold together the two incompatible sides of a *binary opposition.*

Mode of production—the complete operation of social relations (family organization, status, class, gender, etc.) and the forces (technological, political, juridical, etc.) of a society's material production. Ancient Israel had three dominant modes of production at different historical times: familial, tributary, and slave.

Narrated discourse—refers to occasions where the narrator speaks and relates aspects of the story.

Narrative criticism—a literary method of analysis that focuses on plot, character, setting, point of view, and compositional techniques such as repetition and the use of narrated discourse or direct discourse.

Narratology—the theory of narrative.

Narrator—the person who tells the story; usually a third-person, omniscient narrator in biblical narratives.

Neolocal residence—the practice of newlyweds taking up a new place of residence separate from both sets of parents after marriage.

Orientalism—a system of thought and scholarship that constructed the rest of the world from the perspective of the West as the Other, the conquerable, and the inferior.

Parole—French for "word"; used in structuralism (in contrast to *langue*) to refer to the individual linguistic utterance, and, by extension, to any individual cultural production.

Patriarchy/patriarchal—refers to both a social system and an ideology in which women are subordinated to men and younger men to older men.

Patrilineal descent—descent traced from fathers to sons.

Pilegesh—secondary wife.

Plot—the sequences of events related in terms of their causes and consequences.

Point of view—the perspective from which the story or portions of the story is told. Usually the vantage point of the third-person, omniscient narrator, but often the more limited viewpoint of a particular character.

Polycoity—a form of marriage in which a man takes women who are of lower status than his primary wife as his secondary wives.

Polygyny—a form of marriage in which a man may have more than one wife at a time, but in which the wives are of equal status to one another.

Postcolonial criticism—an exegetical strategy that focuses on colonialism and its continuing effects on the present world and modern biblical scholarship and brings questions and concerns that rise from the experience of the marginalized to the interpretive process.

Queer theory—Growing out of lesbian and gay studies and feminist theory, queer theory analyzes critically the various categories and frameworks that we use to talk about gender and sexuality (e.g., "man" and "woman," "heterosexual" and "homosexual") and uses marginal phenomena associated with gender and sexuality to question norms of sex and gender.

Reception history—the study of the Bible's use, influence, and impact through the centuries. As a cultural inquiry, it treats popular as well as professional use, and finds its sources in a variety of media (visual and textual), times, and social locations.

Redaction criticism—a method of biblical exegesis that analyzes the final written stages of a text by various editors. Many scholars currently accept the theory of a Josianic and/or an exilic Deuteronomistic redactor for the final editing of the book of Judges.

Repetition—multiple use of words or phrases, motifs or themes, or a sequence of actions for the purpose of indicating narrative structure, identifying key themes, or emphasizing central ideas.

Semantics—the study of meaning, particularly as a branch of *linguistics.*

Semiotics—the study of signs and signification. The object of study may be the ways that the natural world signifies things to humans, or the ways that humans signify things to each other.

Semiotic square—a visual representation of the system of logical relations generated by a *binary opposition.* If the terms of the opposition are A and B, the square relates A, B, their contradictory terms non-A and non-B, and more complex combinations.

Serial monogamy—a form of marriage in which an individual may have only one spouse at a time.

Setting—the locales where the narrative events take place.

Social-scientific criticism—an approach that emphasizes collective, or group, organization rather than individual perspective.

Structuralism—a philosophical view according to which the mind apprehends reality as sets of relationships among items rather than as individual items. Also, methods of study in the human or social sciences based on this assumption.

Structure—in narrative criticism, refers to the organization of events into an ordered and coherent story.

Subaltern—a term, meaning "of lower or inferior rank," used to express the marginalized people in general.

Synchronic—literally, "at the same time"; a form of study that considers some phenomenon as a set of relationships existing at a given moment in time (contrast *diachronic*).

Tradition criticism—a method of biblical exegesis that studies the transmission and development of the oral and written stages of tradition before the final editing of the text.

Tributary mode of production—a *mode of production* characterized by a stratified, hierarchically ordered society where a king or ruling elite demands tributes or taxes from the lower classes. In a native tributary mode of production, the ruling elite are indigenous to the land. In a foreign tributary mode of production, the land is administered by foreign colonizers or conquerors.

NOTES

PREFACE

1. See Fernando F. Segovia, ed., *They Were All Together in One Place? Toward Minority Biblical Criticism* (Semeia Studies: Atlanta: Society of Biblical Literature, forthcoming 2008, and Daniel Patte, ed., *Global Bible Commentary*, (Nashville: Abingdon, 2004).

1. INTRODUCTION

1. Cf. 9:22; 10:2-3; 12:7, 9, 11, 14; 15:20; 16:31.

2. Judges 4–5; 9:53-54. See also Gale A. Yee, "By the Hand of a Woman: The Metaphor of the Woman Warrior in Judges 4," *Semeia* 61 (1993): 109–114.

3. See Mieke Bal, *Death and Dissymmetry: The Politics of Coherence in the Book of Judges* (Chicago: University of Chicago Press, 1988), for the most extensive treatment of the countercoherence of Judges.

4. See the entries under Barton, Hayes and Holladay, and McKenzie and Haynes in the bibliography at the end of this essay for a more complete discussion of these historical-critical methods.

5. Source criticism, the determination of the different sources of the Pentateuch, was called literary criticism in earlier scholarly circles. This older understanding of literary criticism should be differentiated from the literary criticism discussed later in this chapter. For an example of literary criticism in its earlier, historical-critical sense, see Norman Habel, *Literary Criticism of the Old Testament* (Guides to Biblical Scholarship; Philadelphia: Fortress Press, 1971).

6. Tradents are groups that circulate and hand down ancient traditions. They could be family groups; lineages; disciples, scribes; priestly, juridical, or wisdom schools; and so forth.

7. According to Judges 18, the tribe of Dan will migrate and settle in a region north of the Sea of Galilee.

8. Robert G. Boling, *Judges: A New Translation with Introduction and Commentary* (Anchor Bible 6A; Garden City, N.Y.: Doubleday, 1975), 31.

9. The technical term for the life setting(s) of a particular form is *Sitz(e) im Leben*.

10. Martin Noth, *The Deuteronomic History*, 2d ed. (JSOTSup 15; Sheffield: JSOT, 2001). A translation of *Überlieferungsgeschichtliche Studien* (Tübingen: Max Niemeyer Verlag, 1957, 2d ed.), 1–110. The first edition appeared as *Schriften der Königsberg Gelebreten-Gesellschaft. Geisteswissenschaftliche Klasse* 18 (1943): 43–266.

11. Noth, *Deuteronomistic History*, 42–53.

12. Frank Moore Cross, *Canaanite Myth and Hebrew Epic: Essays in the History of the Religion of Israel* (Cambridge: Harvard University Press, 1973), 274–89. See also Richard Elliott Friedman, *The Exile and Biblical Narrative: The Formation of the Deuteronomistic and Priestly Works* (Chico, Calif.: Scholars Press, 1981), and Richard D. Nelson, *The Double Redaction of the Deuteronomistic History* (Sheffield: JSOT, 1981).

13. Robert G. Boling, "Judges, Book of," *Anchor Bible Dictionary* 3:115–16; idem, "In Those Days There Was No King in Israel," in *A Light unto My Path*, ed. H. M. Bream, R. D. Heim, and C. A. Moore (Philadelphia: Temple University Press, 1974), 33–48; idem, *Judges: A New Translation*, 29–38.

14. Daniel I. Block, *Judges, Ruth* (New American Commentary, vol. 6; Nashville: Broadman & Holman Publishers, 1999), 49–50, 66–67.

15. Social-scientific criticism will be discussed at length in chapter 3. For a recent commentary adopting a social-scientific reading of Judges, see Victor H. Matthews, *Judges and Ruth* (New Cambridge Bible Commentary; Cambridge: Cambridge University Press, 2004).

16. J. P. U. Lilley, "A Literary Appreciation of the Book of Judges," *Tyndale Bulletin* 18 (1967): 93–94.

17. Ibid., 98–99.

18. Ibid., "101.

19. D. W. Gooding, "The Composition of the Book of Judges," in *Eretz-Israel, Archeological Historical and Geographical Studies, vol. 16: Harry M. Orlinsky Volume* (Jerusalem: Israel Exploration Society, 1982), 70–79.

20. Alexander Globe, "Enemies Round About: Disintegrative Structure in the Book of Judges," in *Mappings of the Biblical Terrain*, ed. V. Tollers and J. Maier, (Lewisburg, Pa.: Bucknell University Press, 1990), 233–51.

21. A chiasmus is a literary device that structures words, phrases, sections of a work, and so forth by balancing them in an A B B' A' pattern. The artistic focus is on the center of the chiasmus; in this case, the B B'.

22. A complete survey of all literary-critical studies of the book of Judges is beyond the scope of this chapter. For a good start, see J. Cheryl Exum, "The Centre Cannot Hold: Thematic and Textual Instabilities in Judges," *Catholic Biblical Quarterly* 52 (1990): 410–31, especially the footnotes on the relevant literature.

23. David M. Gunn, "Joshua and Judges," in *The Literary Guide to the Bible*, ed. Robert Alter and Frank Kermode, (Cambridge: Harvard University Press, 1987) 102–21.

24. Barry G. Webb, *The Book of the Judges: An Integrated Reading* (JSOTSup 46; Sheffield: JSOT, 1987).

25. Lillian R. Klein, *The Triumph of Irony in the Book of Judges* (JSOTSup 68; Sheffield: Almond, 1988).

26. Robert H. O'Connell, *The Rhetoric of the Book of Judges* (VTSup 63. Leiden: Brill, 1996). So also the conclusion of Marc Zvi Brettler, *The Book of Judges* (Old Testament Readings; New York: Routledge, 2002).

27. For an analysis of the problems in author-, text-, or reader-centered approaches, see Gale A. Yee, "The Author/Text/Reader and Power: Suggestions for a Critical Framework in Biblical Studies," in *Reading from This Place: Social Location and Biblical Interpretation*, ed. Fernando F. Segovia and Mary Ann Tolbert (Minneapolis: Fortress Press, 1995), 109–18.

28. Robert Warrior, "Canaanites, Cowboys, and Indians," *Union Seminary Quarterly Review* 59, no. 1–2 (2005): 1–8 [first published in *Christianity and Crisis* 49 (1989): 261–65]. Idem, "Response to Special Issue on Religion and Narratives of Conquest." *Union Seminary Quarterly Review* 59, no. 1–2 (2005): 125–30. See also the other essays in this special *USQR* volume.

29. Koala Jones-Warsaw, "Toward a Womanist Hermeneutic: A Reading of Judges 19–21," in *A Feminist Companion to Judges*, ed. Athalya Brenner (Sheffield: Sheffield Academic Press, 1993), 172–86.

30. Yani Yoo, "*Han*-Laden Women: Korean 'Comfort Women' and Women in Judges 19–21," *Semeia* 78 (1997): 37–46.

31. Patrick S. Cheng, "Multiplicity and Judges 19: Constructing a Queer Asian Pacific American Biblical Hermeneutic." *Semeia* 90/91 (2002): 119–33.

32. Valerie Cooper, "Some Place to Cry: Jephthah's Daughter and the Double Dilemma of Black Women in America," in *Pregnant Passion: Gender, Sex, and Violence in the Bible*, ed. Cheryl A. Kirk-Duggan (Semeia Studies; Atlanta: Society of Biblical Literature, 2003), 181–91.

2. NARRATIVE CRITICISM

1. *New Yorker* (September 20, 1993): 106.

2. For other assessments, see Mark Allen Powell, *What Is Narrative Criticism?* (Minneapolis: Fortress Press, 1990), 85–98, and Tremper Longman III, *Literary Approaches to Biblical Interpretation* (Grand Rapids: Zondervan, 1987), 47–62.

3. See Umberto Eco, *The Limits of Interpretation* (Bloomington: Indiana University Press, 1990), and Stefan Collini, *Interpretation and Overinterpretation: Umberto Eco* (Cambridge: Cambridge University Press, 1992).

4. Robert Scholes and Robert Kellogg, *The Nature of Narrative* (London: Oxford University Press, 1966), 240.

5. Literary critics often further distinguish between the narrator, the implied author, and the real author. In biblical narrative these usually merge into one figure, which I shall identify as the narrator. For a discussion of the three figures as they relate to biblical narrative, see Elizabeth Struthers Malbon, "Narrative Criticism: How Does a Story Mean?" in *Mark and Method: New Approaches to Biblical*

Studies, ed. Janice Capel Anderson and Stephen D. Moore (Minneapolis: Fortress Press, 1992), 27–28.

6. Some scholars disagree. See, for example, David M. Gunn and Danna Nolan Fewell, *Narrative in the Hebrew Bible* (London: Oxford University Press, 1993), 53–56.

7. The terminology is Phyllis Trible's. For examples, see *God and the Rhetoric of Sexuality* (Philadelphia: Fortress Press, 1978), and *Texts of Terror* (Philadelphia: Fortress Press, 1984). For a seminal discussion of this topic, see Robert Alter, "Between Narration and Dialogue," in *The Art of Biblical Narrative* (New York: Basic Books, 1981), 63–87.

8. Unless otherwise noted, all translations are from the NRSV.

9. Mieke Bal, *Death and Dissymmetry: The Politics of Coherence in the Book of Judges* (Chicago: University of Chicago Press, 1988), 26.

10. Achsah's assertiveness is also recognized in the literary analyses of Barry Webb in *The Book of Judges* (Sheffield: Sheffield Academic Press, 1987), 87, and Lillian Klein in *The Triumph of Irony in the Book of Judges* (Sheffield: Sheffield Academic Press, 1988), 26.

11. My translation, following the RSV.

12. Achsah's request is not without precedent. See the request of the daughters of Zelophehad in Numbers 27:1-11; 36:1-13 and Joshua 16:3-6.

13. Adapted from Webb, *The Book of Judges,* 81, 123, 181.

14. See ibid., *The Book of Judges,* 124–25.

15. Webb regards the Abimelech episode as a structural and thematic sequel to the Gideon episode. For a discussion, see ibid., 154–59, and also Stone's analysis in this volume.

16. See Scholes and Kellogg, "Plot in Narrative," in *The Nature of Narrative,* 207–39.

17. Adapted from Robert Alter's discussion in *The Art of Biblical Narrative,* 95–96.

18. For a more extensive discussion of setting, see Powell, "Settings," in *What Is Narrative Criticism?* 69–75.

19. See Scholes and Kellogg's discussion "Point of View" in *The Nature of Narrative,* 240–82.

20. Cited in Scholes and Kellogg, *The Nature of Narrative,* 160.

21. Adapted from Alter, *The Art of Biblical Narrative,* 117.

22. For an appropriation of my understanding of God in Judges, see J. Clinton McCann, *Judges* (Louisville: Westminster John Knox, 2002), 100–101.

3. SOCIAL-SCIENTIFIC CRITICISM

1. For a full introduction to the issues, see Robert R. Wilson, *Sociological Approaches to the Old Testament,* (Guides to Biblical Scholarship series; Philadelphia: Fortress Press, 1984).

2. Norman K. Gottwald, *The Hebrew Bible: A Socio-Literary Introduction* (Philadelphia: Fortress Press, 1985), 26.

3. Martin Noth, *Das System der zwölf Stämme Israels* (Stuttgart: W. Kohlhammer, 1930); idem, *The History of Israel* (New York: Harper & Brothers, 1958), 85–108.

4. The data that form the basis of this critique may be conveniently found in John H. Hayes and J. Maxwell Miller, eds., *Israelite and Judaean History* (Philadelphia: Westminster, 1977), 299–308.

5. Gottwald, *The Hebrew Bible,* 284–88; idem, *The Tribes of Yahweh: A Sociology of the Religion of Liberated Israel,* 1250–1050 B.C.E. (Maryknoll, N.Y.: Orbis Books, 1979), 293–621.

6. One notes that all of these labels categorize marriage from the male point of view. The expectation is for one husband to have one or more wives. When a woman is married to more than one husband, the marriage is labeled polyandry. The biblical texts typically consider the absence of progeny to be the fault of the wife; sterility of men is not addressed in the Hebrew Bible. The lack of data regarding male sterility may be attributed either to incorrect understanding of the process of reproduction or to male pride regarding the fathering of a child.

7. Jack Goody, "Polygyny, Economy and the Role of Women," in *The Character of Kinship,* ed. Jack Goody (Cambridge: Cambridge University Press, 1973), 180.

8. A fuller discussion of these issues may be found in Naomi Steinberg, *Kinship and Marriage in Genesis: A Household Economics Perspective* (Minneapolis: Fortress Press, 1993), 5–30.

9. Gottwald, *The Tribes of Yahweh,* 292.

10. Ibid., *The Tribes of Yahweh,* 338–41.

11. Norman K. Gottwald, "Social Class as an Analytic and Hermeneutical Category in Biblical Studies," *Journal of Biblical Literature* 112 (1993): 3–22.

12. "Ibid., 5, where Gottwald cites Gerhard Lenski, *Power and Privilege: A Theory of Social Stratification* (Chapel Hill and London: University of North Carolina Press, 1984), title of chap. 1.

13. In Judges 9:18, Jotham refers to Abimelech's mother as an *'āmâ* rather than as a *pilegesh.* The former word refers to a woman of secondary status, which describes Jotham's perspective—he is, after all, a son of Gideon by his primary wife.

14. Gale A. Yee, in "By the Hand of a Woman: The Metaphor of the Woman Warrior in Judges 4," *Semeia* 61 (1993): 111–12, argues that the lack of distinction between the domestic and public spheres in premonarchical Israel meant that war was not strictly considered men's work. The connection between the military and the domestic worlds is illustrated by the fact that Abimelech's murderer uses a millstone, that is, a domestic item, to kill him. Yee concludes that women's involvement in military actions was acceptable, though not normative, at this time in Israel.

15. Mieke Bal argues that the anthropological interest of the stories in Judges lies in the understanding of "house" at this time in Israelite history. She under-

stands the violence against women in Judges to relate to a change from living with the bride's father to living with the groom's father. In the context of Judges, which Bal believes to convey information earlier than that provided in the narratives of Genesis, *pilegesh* refers to a particular type of wife, that is, one who lives with her father instead of with the groom's father rather than to a concubine or secondary wife, as it does in Genesis. Bal believes that the conflict in Judges 9 lies between Gideon's seventy sons, who live with their father's family, and Abimelech, who lives with his mother's kin. In Judges 8:31 Abimelech's mother is labeled a *pilegesh;* the term does not actually appear in Judges 9. For a full discussion of her position on these issues as well as an analysis of the texts in Judges describing violence against women, see Mieke Bal, *Death and Dissymmetry: The Politics of Coherence in the book of Judges* (Chicago: University of Chicago Press, 1988).

16. Scholars note that before the time of the monarchy, "Israel" was a term that referred to individuals of marginalized sociopolitical status, whereas after the inception of the monarchy, that is, in the tenth century, the term refers to citizenship in a particular geographic area; See Robert G. Boling, *The Early Biblical Community in Transjordan* (Social World of Biblical Antiquity series; Sheffield: Almond, 1988), 57.

17. Bal, *Death and Dissymmetry,* 89.

18. J. Alberto Soggin, *Judges* (Old Testament Library series (Philadelphia: Westminster, 1979), 169–70.

19. Ibid., 185.

20. Wilson, *Sociological Approaches to the Old Testament,* 42.

21. Soggin, *Judges,* 173–79.

22. It is possible that the kinship link between Gideon and Abimelech is an editing device used by the Deuteronomist to connect what were originally separate stories.

4. FEMINIST CRITICISM

1. Gerda Lerner, *The Creation of Patriarchy* (New York: Oxford University Press, 1986), 6.

2. Lerner, *Creation of Patriarchy,* 4–5.

3. S. D. Goiten, "Women as Creators of Biblical Genres," *Prooftexts* 8 (1988): 1–33; Athalya Brenner and Fokkelien van Dijk-Hemmes, *On Gendering Texts: Female and Male Voices in the Hebrew Bible* (Leiden: Brill, 1993).

4. The question of legitimacy in interpretation could be considered androcentric. As Jonathan Culler notes, in the literary criticism of a patriarchal culture one might expect to find "that there would be a great concern about which meanings were legitimate and which illegitimate (since the paternal author's role in the generation of meanings can only be inferred); and that criticism would expend great efforts to develop principles for, on the one hand, determining which meanings were truly the author's own progeny, and on the other hand, controlling inter-

course with texts so as to prevent the proliferation of illegitimate interpretations" (Jonathan Culler, *On Deconstruction: Theory and Criticism after Structuralism* [London: Routledge & Kegan Paul, 1982], 61).

5. See chapter 9 on gender criticism in this volume.

6. Carol Meyers, *Discovering Eve: Ancient Israelite Women in Context* (New York: Oxford University Press, 1988); eadem, "Guilds and Gatherings: Women's Groups in Ancient Israel," in *Realia Dei: Essays in Archaeology and Biblical Interpretation in Honor of Edward F. Campbell, Jr. at His Retirement*, ed. Prescott H. Williams and Theodore Hiebert (Atlanta: Scholars Press, 1999), 154–84; see also Carol Meyers, "Where the Girls Are: Archaeology and Women's Lives in Ancient Israel," in *Between Text and Artifact: Integrating Archaeology in Biblical Studies Teaching*, ed. Milton C. Moreland (Atlanta: Society of Biblical Literature, 2003), 31–51.

7. Jo Ann Hackett, "In the Days of Jael: Reclaiming the History of Women in Ancient Israel," in *Immaculate and Powerful: The Female in Sacred Image and Social Reality*, ed. Clarissa W. Atkinson, Constance H. Buchanan, and Margaret R. Miles (Boston: Beacon, 1985), 15–38; eadem, "1 and 2 Samuel," in *The Women's Bible Commentary*, ed. Carol A. Newsom and Sharon H. Ringe (Louisville: Westminster John Knox, 1992), 85–95.

8. Naomi Steinberg, *Kinship and Marriage in Genesis: A Household Economics Perspective* (Minneapolis: Fortress Press, 1993).

9. Phyllis Bird, "The Place of Women in the Israelite Cultus" and "Israelite Religion and the Faith of Israel's Daughters: Reflections on Gender and Religious Definition," in *Missing Persons and Mistaken Identities: Women and Gender in Ancient Israel* (Minneapolis: Fortress Press, 1997), 81–102 and 103–20 respectively; Carol Meyers, "From Household to House of Yahweh: Women's Religious Culture in Ancient Israel," in *International Organization for the Study of the Old Testament Congress Volume, Basel 2001*, ed. A. Lemaire (Vetus Testamentum Supplements 92; Leiden: Brill, 2002), 277–303; see also Susan Ackerman, *Warrior, Dancer, Seductress, Queen: Women in Judges and Biblical Israel* (New York: Doubleday, 1998).

10. See, for example, Mieke Bal, *Death and Dissymmetry: The Politics of Coherence in the Book of Judges* (Chicago: University of Chicago Press, 1988); Alice Bach, *Women, Seduction, and Betrayal in Biblical Narrative* (Cambridge: Cambridge University Press, 1997).

11. For an example from Judges, see Claudia V. Camp, "Riddlers, Tricksters and Strange Women in the Samson Story," in *Wise, Strange and Holy: The Strange Woman and the Making of the Bible* (Sheffield: Sheffield Academic Press, 2000), 94–143; see also Yvonne Sherwood, *The Prostitute and the Prophet: Hosea's Marriage in Literary-Theoretical Perspective* (Sheffield: Sheffield Academic Press, 1996).

12. See, for example, J. Cheryl Exum, "Prophetic Pornography," in *Plotted, Shot, and Painted: Cultural Representations of Biblical Women* (Sheffield: Sheffield Academic Press, 1996), 101–28.

13. See, for example, Valerie C. Cooper, "Some Place to Cry: Jephthah's Daughter and the Double Dilemma of Black Women in America," in *Pregnant Passion:*

Gender, Sex, and Violence in the Bible, ed. Cheryl A. Kirk-Duggan (Semeia Studies 44; Atlanta: Society of Biblical Literature, 2003), 181–91, and the essays in *Feminist Interpretation of the Bible and the Hermeneutics of Liberation*, ed. Silvia Schroer and Sophia Bietenhard (Sheffield: Sheffield Academic Press, 2003).

14. See Judith E. McKinlay, *Reframing Her: Biblical Women in Postcolonial Focus* (Sheffield: Sheffield Phoenix Press, 2004), and the articles in *Her Master's Tools? Feminist and Postcolonial Engagements of Historical-Critical Discourse*, ed. Caroline Vander Stichele and Todd Penner (Atlanta: Society of Biblical Literature, 2005).

15. Compare Meir Sternberg's comment in *The Poetics of Biblical Narrative: Ideological Literature and the Drama of Reading* (Bloomington: Indiana University Press, 1985), 274: "Of the two leaders, it is he who plays the woman; and having been summoned to do a man's job, he refuses to act unless the woman who delegated it to him comes along to give him moral courage." The same ideology is found in the story of Abimelech, who dies dishonorably because he is felled by a woman's hand (Judg 9:54).

16. Mieke Bal, *Murder and Difference: Gender, Genre, and Scholarship on Sisera's Death* (Bloomington: Indiana University Press, 1988), 134; similarly, Robert Alter, *The Art of Biblical Poetry* (New York: Basic Books, 1985), 49; Danna Nolan Fewell and David M. Gunn, "Controlling Perspectives: Women, Men, and the Authority of Violence in Judges 4 and 5," *Journal of the American Academy of Religion* 58 (1990): 394.

17. Fewell and Gunn, "Controlling Perspectives," 403; for their argument, see pp. 393–94 and n. 11.

18. The obscurity of Judges 5:30 limits our ability to interpret it precisely. If translated "for the necks of the spoiler," then the victorious men get the finery and the women. It is a moot point, however, since the women on the winner's side will share the booty.

19. Fewell and Gunn, "Controlling Perspectives," 408.

20. Bal, *Death and Dissymmetry*, 43.

21. This kind of narrative judgment occurs elsewhere within the individual stories in Judges; for example, Gideon (8:27), Abimelech (9:56-57). Compare 2 Samuel 11:27.

22. I see this as the narrator's way of displacing the blame from God onto the woman. Jephthah's vow was, after all, made under ambiguous circumstances (is he not under the influence of the spirit of the Lord when he makes it?) and in ignorance of its outcome. For fuller discussion of this problematic aspect of the story, see J. Cheryl Exum, *Tragedy and Biblical Narrative: Arrows of the Almighty* (Cambridge: Cambridge University Press, 1992), 45–69.

23. The story assumes the inviolability of Jephthah's vow, whereas Leviticus 27:1-8 stipulates monetary payment by which a person vowed to God could be released.

24. This is Bal's argument (see *Death and Dissymmetry*, chaps. 2, 4, and 5). See also Peggy L. Day, "From the Child Is Born the Woman: The Story of Jephthah's

Daughter," in *Gender and Difference in Ancient Israel,* ed. Peggy L. Day (Minneapolis: Fortress Press, 1989), 58–74.

25. As Lerner (*Creation of Patriarchy,* 242) points out, when women "are confined by patriarchal restraint or segregation into separateness (which always has subordination as its purpose), they transform this restraint into complementarity and redefine it."

26. Midrash Rabbah to Numbers 10:5 identifies her with the Hazzelelponi of 1 Chronicles 4:3.

27. See Esther Fuchs, "The Biblical Mother: The Annunciation and Temptation Type-Scenes," in *Sexual Politics in the Biblical Narrative: Reading the Hebrew Bible as a Woman* (Sheffield: Sheffield Academic Press, 2000), 44–90.

28. Robert G. Boling, *Judges* (Anchor Bible 6A; Garden City, N.Y.: Doubleday, 1975), 274; Yair Zakovitch, "The Woman's Rights in the Biblical Law of Divorce," *Jewish Law Annual* 4 (1981): 39; Bal, *Death and Dissymmetry,* 88.

29. This is true in Hebrew as well as English; see Phyllis Bird, "'To Play the Harlot': An Inquiry into an Old Testament Metaphor," in *Missing Persons and Mistaken Identities,* 219–36; see also Bal, *Death and Dissymmetry,* 86; and Andrea Dworkin, *Pornography: Men Possessing Women* (New York: Plume, 1981), 203–9.

30. I borrow this notion from Elaine Showalter, *Sexual Anarchy: Gender and Culture at the Fin de Siècle* (New York: Penguin, 1990), 110.

31. Dworkin, *Pornography,* 51–53.

5. STRUCTURALIST CRITICISM

1. Peter Caws, *Structuralism: The Art of the Intelligible* (Atlantic Highlands, N.J.: Humanities International, 1988), 1.

2. According to Caws, we seek intelligibility in "the matching of structured systems," which "is experienced by us as primordially meaningful" (ibid., 112). Our minds simply do not develop in a way that lets us experience things in isolation; it is only as systems of relationships that we are capable of coming to terms with what we experience; hence, "structure is fundamental to intelligibility, not merely one aspect of it" (ibid., 114).

3. Even "word" is a simplification—a linguist would speak of word-elements, or "morphemes," such as the "-ation" at the end of a class of English nouns.

4. For the following, see Ferdinand de Saussure, *Course in General Linguistics,* ed. Charles Bally, et al.; trans. Wade Baskin (New York: McGraw-Hill, 1959).

5. The French terms are usually retained in English discussion, but another pair of terms, "performance" and "competence," have virtually the same meanings.

6. Vladimir Propp, *Morphology of the Folktale,* 2d ed., trans. Laurence Scott (Austin: University of Texas Press, 1968). For what follows, see pp. 19–65.

7. The hero may be female, but in that case she is a "victim" rather than a "seeker" hero (ibid., 36). I am discussing in this paragraph the message of the seeker hero type of tale.

8. The material that does *not* fit the pattern consists of Judges 3:31, 8:33—10:5, and 12:8-15.

9. Robert Culley, *Themes and Variations: A Study of Action in Biblical Narratives* (Atlanta: Scholars Press, 1992). For Culley's own comment on the relationship of his work to Propp, see p. 11.

10. Ibid., 47–76.

11. Ibid., 97–109.

12. See Claude Lévi-Strauss, *The Elementary Structures of Kinship,* rev. ed., trans. James Harle Bell, John Richard von Sturmer, and Rodney Needham (Boston: Beacon, 1969).

13. This does not mean that his other work has been neglected in biblical studies. See, for example, Mara E. Donaldson, "Kinship Theory in the Patriarchal Narratives," *Journal of the American Academy of Religion* 49 (1981): 77–87; Mary Douglas, *Purity and Danger: An Analysis of Concepts of Pollution and Taboo* (London: Routledge & Kegan Paul, 1966); Terry J. Prewitt, *The Elusive Covenant: A Structural-Semiotic Reading of Genesis* (Bloomington: Indiana University Press, 1990).

14. Claude Lévi-Strauss, "Structure and Form: Reflections on a Work by Vladimir Propp," in *Structural Anthropology II,* trans. Monique Layton (London: Allen Lane, 1977), 115–45.

15. Ibid., 118–19; cf. 129–38. See Propp, *Morphology of the Folktale,* 19–20.

16. Analysis into binary (two-term) oppositions is fundamental to Lévi-Strauss and to all structuralism in the Saussurean tradition.

17. Claude Lévi-Strauss, *The Raw and the Cooked,* trans. John Weightman and Doreen Weightman (New York: Harper & Row, 1970); idem, *From Honey to Ashes,* trans. John Weightman and Doreen Weightman (New York: Harper & Row, 1973); idem, *The Origin of Table Manners,* trans. John Weightman and Doreen Weightman (New York: Harper & Row, 1978); idem, *The Naked Man,* trans. John Weightman and Doreen Weightman (New York: Harper & Row, 1981). These four volumes constitute *Introduction to a Science of Mythology,* but are always known by their individual titles. The best brief statement of Lévi-Strauss's approach is his essay "The Structural Study of Myth," in *Structural Anthropology,* trans. Claire Jacobson and Brooke Grundfest Schoepf (New York: Basic Books, 1963), 206–31.

18. In what follows, I summarize the diagram on p. 133 of *The Raw and the Cooked,* and the discussion that precedes it.

19. Edmund Leach, "Anthropological Approaches to the Study of the Bible during the Twentieth Century," in Edmund Leach and D. Alan Aycock, *Structuralist Interpretations of Biblical Myth* (Cambridge: Cambridge University Press, 1983), 7–32 (I deal here with pp. 26–28). In addition to Leach's essays in this book, see also Edmund Leach, *Genesis as Myth and Other Essays* (London: Jonathan Cape, 1969), which contains the most successful of his biblical essays, "The Legitimacy of Solomon."

20. Many scholars believe that this traditional translation of the Hebrew *pilegesh* is unsatisfactory, and that "secondary wife" or "matrilocal wife" would be better. See, for example, Mieke Bal, *Death and Dissymmetry: The Politics of Coherence in the Book of Judges* (Chicago: University of Chicago Press, 1988), 80–86.

21. Leach, "Anthropological Approaches," 28.

22. Ibid., 29.

23. A. J. Greimas, *Structural Semantics: An Attempt at a Method* (Lincoln: University of Nebraska Press, 1983), 207.

24. Roland Barthes, "Wrestling with the Angel: Textual Analysis of Genesis 32:23-33," in *The Semiotic Challenge*, trans. Richard Howard (New York: Hill and Wang, 1988), 246–60.

25. Ibid., 257.

26. David Jobling, *The Sense of Biblical Narrative: Structural Analyses in the Hebrew Bible*, vol. 2 (Sheffield: JSOT, 1986), 24–26.

27. The mature system is summarized in the entry "Narrative Schema," in A. J. Greimas and J. Courtés, *Semiotics and Language: An Analytical Dictionary*, trans. Larry Crist et al. (Bloomington: Indiana University Press, 1982) 203–6.

28. A. J. Greimas, *On Meaning: Selected Writings in Semiotic Theory*, trans. Paul J. Perron and Frank H. Collins (Minneapolis: University of Minnesota Press, 1987), 49. Arrows are often included at the ends of some of the lines in the diagram. This is done inconsistently, and I shall omit them.

29. Lévi-Strauss, *Structural Anthropology*, 224–25.

30. Greimas, *On Meaning*, 49–53.

31. Ibid., 168–70. My discussion expands considerably on Greimas.

32. Daniel Patte, *Structural Exegesis for New Testament Critics* (Minneapolis: Fortress Press, 1990). Students of the Jewish Bible need not worry about the title; the method is adaptable. This book does not make clear how the model is based on the semiotic square; readers wishing to understand the theory more deeply should consult Patte's *The Religious Dimensions of Biblical Texts* (Atlanta: Scholars Press, 1990).

33. See Richard Harland, *Superstructuralism: The Philosophy of Structuralism and Post-Structuralism* (New York: Methuen, 1987), 77–91 (on Greimas and others in his tradition), 52–64, 167–69 (on Roland Barthes and Julia Kristeva), 101–20, 155–66 (on Michel Foucault). See also The Bible and Culture Collective, *The Postmodern Bible* (New Haven: Yale University Press, 1995), especially chap. 2, "Structuralist and Narratological Criticism," 70–118.

34. See Christine Brooke-Rose, "Whatever Happened to Narratology?" *Poetics Today* 11 (1990): 287–89.

35. Ibid., 285–86.

36. Harland, *Superstructuralism*, 59–64.

37. Caws, *Structuralism*, 153.

38. Similar considerations should lay to rest any claim that structuralism, in its basic philosophical position, is ahistorical; ibid., 256–57.

39. Ibid., 237–41.

40. Ibid., 214; cf. 159–64.

41. See chapter 7 of this volume, and also David Jobling and Tina Pippin, eds., *Ideological Criticism of Biblical Texts* (*Semeia* 59; Atlanta: Scholars Press, 1992).

42. Fredric Jameson, foreword to Greimas, *On Meaning*, vi–xxii.

43. Ibid., xv. Greimas and his group are aware of this—see especially Patte's use of the terms "positive" and "negative" for the A and B points of the square (e.g., *Religious Dimensions,* 94–95).

44. Jameson, foreword to Greimas, *On Meaning,* xvi.

45. For a use, inspired by Jameson, of the semiotic square on a biblical text (Psalms) see Roland Boer, *Marxist Criticism of the Bible* (London and New York: T & T Clark International, 2003) 192–203.

46. Gérard Genette, *Narrative Discourse: An Essay in Method,* trans. Jane E. Lewin (Ithaca, N.Y.: Cornell University Press, 1980). Bal rarely uses the word structuralism, preferring critical narratology. For an account of her relationship to structuralism, see Mieke Bal, *On Story-Telling: Essays in Narratology,* ed. David Jobling (Sonoma, Calif.: Polebridge, 1991), 1–24.

47. For a tabular summary of the model, see Bal, *Death and Dissymmetry,* 248–49, and *On Story-Telling,* 166–67. The theoretical discussion of the model in *On Story-Telling* (159–68) is superior to that in *Death and Dissymmetry* (32–39). In her treatment of Judges texts, Bal does not always show *how* she is using the model, but she always *is* using it.

48. Judges 19:23b-24; my translation based on Bal's argumentation, *Death and Dissymmetry,* 122.

49. Mieke Bal, *Murder and Differences: Gender, Genre, and Scholarship on Sisera's Death,* trans. Matthew Gumpert (Bloomington: Indiana University Press, 1988). I am here summarizing Bal's discussion of the two semiotic squares on pp. 41 and 44.

50. The geographic reference here is different from the other two stories, and rather obscure: "the waters as far as Beth-barah, and also the Jordan," instead of "the fords of the Jordan." I suspect that "the Jordan" has been tacked on as a result of the very process whereby the separate stories have developed into a set of structurally related stories.

51. For example, see Lévi-Strauss, *Structural Anthropology,* 224–27. For a much more elaborate example of the creation of a "middle semantics" to mediate between extremes, see my treatment of Genesis 2–3 (Jobling, in *The Sense of Biblical Narrative,* vol. 2, 27–39).

52. My essay "The Jordan a Boundary" in *The Sense of Biblical Narrative,* vol. 2 (88–134), from which the foregoing analysis is taken (125–27), contains verification of this suggestion from elsewhere in the Bible.

53. There are other indications of this problematic. The Ehud story seems to equate "Israelites" with Ephraimites (Judg 3:27). In both the Gideon and the Jephthah stories, the Ephraimites turn quarrelsome when they cross the Jordan (7:25; 12:1)—perhaps merely doing so makes them ill at ease. The Jephthah story even posits a linguistic difference between the groups east and west of the river (12:5-6). It also suggests that Israelites living east of Jordan are "fugitives" from their proper place. This may explain the curious double use of "fugitives of Ephraim"; in 12:4 it refers to the Gileadites, but in 12:5 to the Ephraimites themselves. Perhaps by the very act of crossing the Jordan, the Ephraimites have made themselves "fugitives."

54. Claude Lévi-Strauss, *The Savage Mind* (Chicago: University of Chicago Press, 1966), 16–33.

55. Jameson, foreword to Greimas, *On Meaning,* viii.

6. DECONSTRUCTIVE CRITICISM

1. I would like to thank the following friends who have helped me formulate and sharpen this essay: my student Jione Havea, who has been especially helpful to the exegetical enterprise; my colleague Jouette Bassler and my editor Gale Yee, who have devoted their attention to the chapter's accessibility; my reliable resource on theory, Gary Phillips, who has served as a gentle but diligent educator on the subject of deconstruction. I strongly encourage readers to turn to Phillips's own work (cited in the notes and in Further Reading) to fill the theoretical gaps that I inevitably leave in this cursory treatment. The following discussion focuses almost exclusively on deconstruction as a way of thinking about language and texts. This, of course, is merely a part of a broader philosophical discourse that has profound social and cultural ramifications (some of which will be discussed in this essay). The notion of undecidability is the linguistic application of a larger understanding that questions anyone's ability to capture completely the nature of reality in any one theoretical description. Just as the world is more than any one can possibly comprehend, so, too, a text is elusive to comprehensive interpretation. For a more detailed treatment, see Gary Phillips, "Exegesis as Critical Praxis: Reclaiming History and Text from a Postmodern Perspective," *Semeia* 51 (1990): 7–49; and idem, "The Ethics of Reading Deconstructively, or Speaking Face-to-Face: The Samaritan Woman Meets Derrida at the Well," in *The New Literary Criticism and the New Testament,* ed. Elizabeth Struthers Malbon and Edgar McKnight, (Sheffield: Sheffield Academic Press, 1994), 283–325.

2. Other critics commonly associated with deconstruction are Roland Barthes, Jacques Lacan, Michel Foucault, and members of the "Yale School"—J. Hillis Miller, Geoffrey Hartman, and Harold Bloom.

3. Historical critics tend to ignore the challenge of deconstruction, treating it as if it had nothing to do with their enterprises. Literary critics tend to be divided: some ignore it; others either make an effort to deal with it (see Further Reading) or eschew it outright (see Robert Alter and Frank Kermode's "General Introduction" in *The Literary Guide to the Bible* [Cambridge: Harvard University Press, 1987] and the more recent writings of Alter).

4. The metaphor, taken from songwriter Paul Simon's lyric "The nearer your destination, the more you're slip-sliding away," seems particularly appropriate in this context because it implies (by analogy) the contribution of the reader and the reading process to the slipperiness of textual meaning.

Unfortunately, the metaphor of slipperiness has a negative connotation in a culture that values such notions as steadiness, certainty, stability, and consistency.

I would like to suggest that slipperiness is a positive image, which, unlike the conceptual repertoire of "steadfastness," represents the "beyondness" of our comprehension, the challenge to reach past authorized limits, the radical freedom of the world to be more than we can name.

5. Barbara Johnson uses excerpts from Rousseau's *Confessions* to illustrate this notion of the divided self and its analogy to textuality: "Rousseau's opening statement about himself is precisely an affirmation of difference: 'I am unlike anyone I have ever met; I will even venture to say that I am like no one in the whole world. I may be no better, but at least I am different.' (Penguin edition 1954, p. 17). Now, this can be read as an unequivocal assertion of uniqueness, of difference between Rousseau and the whole rest of the world. This is the boast on which the book is based. But in what does the uniqueness of this self consist? It is not long before we find out: 'There are times when I am so unlike myself that I might be taken for someone else of an entirely opposite character' (p. 126). 'In me are united two almost irreconcilable characteristics, though in what way I cannot imagine' (p. 112). In other words, this story of the self's difference from others inevitably becomes the story of its own unbridgeable difference from itself. Difference is not engendered in the space between identities; it is what makes all totalization of the identity of a self or the meaning of a text impossible" ("The Critical Difference: BarthesS/BalZac," in *The Critical Difference: Essays in the Contemporary Rhetoric of Reading* [Baltimore: Johns Hopkins University Press, 1980], 3–12; repr. in *Contemporary Literary Criticism: Modernism through Post-Structuralism,* ed. Robert Con Davis [New York and London: Longman, 1986], 439–46, 440–41).

6. David Gunn and I both have used the following image with great success with our students and have incorporated a version of it into the introduction of Danna Nolan Fewell and David M. Gunn, *Gender, Power, and Promise: The Subject of the Bible's First Story* (Nashville: Abingdon, 1993), 9.

7. Christopher Norris, *Deconstruction: Theory and Practice* (London and New York: Routledge, 1982; repr. 1991), 19.

8. Ibid., 46.

9. We are trained to be precise in our (scholarly) writing, to eschew irony and wordplay and humor. We are taught that the pursuit of knowledge and truth is serious business, and we constrain our writing to reflect that seriousness. Deconstructionists, on the other hand, following Derrida's lead, often employ wordplays in resistance to Western scholarly genres in order to accentuate excess of meaning.

10. As Timothy Beal writes, "In every text there are traces of that which has been excluded or repressed (Derrida has called them erasure marks), or even of that which is altogether absent. Indeed, a text's boundaries of meaning are always established through exclusion, repression, and marginalization. But traces remain. When attended to, these traces open beyond the narrow confines of the particular text and into relation with other texts. Traces lead readers to stray into the margins and off the page" ("Glossary," in *Reading between Texts: Intertextuality and the Hebrew Bible,* ed. Danna Nolan Fewell [Louisville: Westminster John Knox, 1992], 24).

11. Deconstruction is not a method per se. Method, of any stripe, strives toward systemization, universality, generalization. Method is not designed to appreciate the uniqueness of individual texts and consequently is not equipped to account for what is Other in a text. See Jacques Derrida, *Limited Inc.*, ed. Gerald Graff; trans. Samuel Weber and Jeffrey Mehlman (Evanston, Ill.: Northwestern University Press, 1988), and the helpful discussion in Phillips, "Ethics of Reading."

12. Jacques Derrida, *Dissemination,* trans. Barbara Johnson (Chicago: University of Chicago Press, 1981).

13. Derrida, *Limited Inc.*, 141.

14. Jacques Derrida, "Letter to a Japanese Friend," in *Derrida and Différance,* ed. David Wood and Robert Bernasconi (Evanston, Ill.: Northwestern University Press, 1988).

15. Barbara Johnson, "Teaching Deconstructively," in *Writing and Reading Differently: Deconstruction and the Teaching of Composition and Literature,* ed. G. Douglas Atkins and Michael L. Johnson (Lawrence: University of Kansas Press, 1985), 141. Italics mine.

16. David Jobling, "Writing the Wrongs of the World: The Deconstruction of the Biblical Text in the Context of Liberation Theologies," *Semeia* 51 (1990): 102.

17. Jacques Derrida, "The Conflict of Faculties," in *Languages of Knowledge and of Inquiry,* ed. Michael Riffaterr (New York: Columbia University Press, 1982). Cited in Jonathan Culler, *On Deconstruction: Theory and Criticism after Structuralism* (Ithaca, N.Y.: Cornell University Press, 1982), 156.

18. See Beal's quotation in note 10.

19. See Jobling, "Writing the Wrongs of the World."

20. Brenda K. Marshall, *Teaching the Postmodern: Fiction and Theory* (New York and London: Routledge, 1992), 3.

21. Jobling, "Writing the Wrongs of the World," 100.

22. Indeed, this is often the tactic used in scholarly debate. Some scholars seem to think that, in order to elevate their own theories, they are obliged to "dump on" (to put it gently) the theories of others. Of course, the "covering over" takes place in other ways, too, for example, through censorship in academic publication. For years, the works of literary critics in biblical studies were not accepted in standard biblical studies journals. Even today, editors and editorial referees are not always above academic politics when it comes to making selections for publication.

23. The work on individual stories is far too extensive to be listed here. Some of the more intentionally deconstructive work on the cycle/book-as-whole include David M. Gunn, "Joshua and Judges," in *The Literary Guide to the Bible,* ed. Robert Alter and Frank Kermode (Cambridge: Harvard University Press; London: Collins, 1987), 102–21; Gabriel Josipovici, "The Rhythm Falters: The Book of Judges," in *The Book of God: A Response to the Bible* (New Haven and London: Yale University Press, 1988), 108–31; J. Cheryl Exum, "The Centre Cannot Hold: Thematic and Textual Instabilities in Judges," *Catholic Biblical Quarterly* 52 (1990): 410–31; Danna Nolan Fewell, "Judges," in *The Women's Bible Commentary,* ed. Carol A. Newsom and Sharon H. Ringe, expanded ed. (Louisville: Westminster/John Knox, 1998), 73–83.

24. Mieke Bal, *Death and Dissymmetry: The Politics of Coherence in the Book of Judges* (Chicago: University of Chicago Press, 1988).

25. Barbara Johnson outlines these sites as well as what she calls fictional self-interpretation, that is, when texts "appear to comment upon themselves, to solve the enigmas they set up." One might interpret these comments as "allegories of reading" (Johnson, "Teaching Deconstructively").

Although this concept is less helpful for the following analysis of Judges 1:11-15, it can be illustrated in the broader text of Judges. For example, the narratorial comment that "in those days there was no king in Israel; every man did what was right in his own eyes" might be seen as an allegory about interpretation; that is, every reader reads what he or she thinks the text ought to say. Or, to be gender-specific (as the text is), men have the authority to read any way they want to, the implication being that women have no such freedom; that is, they read the way men tell them to and they are often the victims of men's readings.

26. Robert G. Boling, *Judges: A New Translation with Introduction and Commentary* (New York: Doubleday, 1975), 51, actually prints verses 14–15 in poetic verse. In order to lay the translations side by side, however, I have printed this material as prose. The question of whether these verses are prose or poetry can also affect the meaning of the passage. It not only raises the question of whether we are dealing with literal or more figurative language, but it also questions which words are actually to be included in the text itself. For example, it seems to encourage Boling to follow the LXX in including the phrase "her heart's desire"; he argues that the postulated Hebrew original, *kělibbah,* plays upon the name Caleb. Once "heart" is incorporated into the passage, Boling then notes that the heart was the seat of the mind and will (57). This observation could then, in turn, a/effect one's understanding of the character of Achsah as someone whose mind is made up and who is firmly stating her will.

27. H. Freedman's translation, "Joshua: Introduction and Commentary," in *Joshua and Judges,* ed. A. Cohen (London: Soncino, 1959), 89.

28. Indeed, the notion has been known to spawn sharp resistance. Notice, for example, the discomfort in H. Wheeler Robinson's explanation: "No inference can be drawn from such an etymology as to the literary life of Canaan. It is quite likely that some (unknown) Canaanite word, resembling *sepher* in sound, has been reproduced in a form familiar to Hebrew ears" (*Joshua* [Century Bible]; quoted by Freedman, 89).

29. In light of Derrida's argument that writing precedes speech, the actions of the Israelites are shown to be doubly arrogant. They not only think they can erase a city's history and identity by renaming it, their action suggests that their speech (which is present and immediate) should take priority over Canaanite writing (which represents what is past and absent). Ironically, Israelite speech (and victory) must be captured in writing in order to be remembered and is thus vulnerable to the same procedures of erasure.

30. I am indebted to Jione Havea for suggesting the wording "stuff," which has, of course, its own provocative "traces" in current American usage.

31. "A sign," writes Umberto Eco, "is everything which can be taken as significantly substituting for something else" (*A Theory of Semiotics* [Bloomington: Indiana University Press, 1976], 7).

32. Of course, even the method of "erasure" can be debated. The mission is to "strike" (*nkh*) and "capture" (*lkd*) the city. Is the strike a fatal or a nonfatal blow? Is the capture total destruction or is it a peaceful capture, like David's capture of Jerusalem? The rhetoric of the conquest would lead one to conclude total devastation (cf. Boling's translation), but the text is never explicit.

33. Unlike the story of the Levite's wife in Judges 19–21, where bodies become the most deafening signs. On this story, see Gale A. Yee, "Ideological Criticism: Judges 17–21 and the Dismembered Body," chapter 7 in this volume.

34. John Gray, *Joshua, Judges, Ruth*, New Century Bible Commentary (Grand Rapids: Eerdmans and Basingstoke, Eng.: Marshall, Morgan & Scott, 1986), 137.

35. Chris Weedon defines subjectivity as "the conscious and unconscious thoughts and emotions of the individual, her sense of herself and her ways of understanding her relation to the world," *Feminist Practice and Poststructuralism Theory* (Oxford and New York: Basil Blackwell, 1987), 32.

36. Alberto Soggin, *Joshua* (Old Testament Library series; Philadelphia: Westminster, 1972), and *Judges* (Old Testament Library series; Philadelphia: Westminster, 1981).

37. See Bal, *Death and Dissymmetry*, 275, n. 27.

38. Paul G. Mosca, "Who Seduced Whom? A Note on Joshua 15:18//Judges 1:14," *Catholic Biblical Quarterly* 46 (1984): 18–22.

39. Even Mieke Bal, so critical of ideological biases in others and despite the fact that she wants to underscore Achsah's subjectivity, argues (against the Hebrew text) that Othniel is the subject of the seduction in order to support her theory that the text is really about the conflict between virilocal versus patrilocal residence. See Bal, *Death and Dissymmetry*, 155–56.

40. Compare Martin Noth, *Das Buch Josua* (Tübingen: Mohr [Siebeck], 1953), 86; and Soggin, *Joshua*, 166.

41. Mosca, "Who Seduced Whom?" 21.

42. Danna Nolan Fewell and David M. Gunn, "Controlling Perspectives: Women, Men, and the Authority of Violence in Judges 4 and 5," *Journal of the American Academy of Religion* 56 (1990): 389–411, see 394, particularly n. 14.

43. Bal, *Death and Dissymmetry*, 151–55.

44. Some of the problems with Bal's reading are (1) the positing of metathesis from a foreign root; (2) the absence of the object "her hands" in the text in Judges 1:14//Joshua 15:18; and (3) the oddity in Judges 4:21 of a tent peg striking (if she takes the peg, as is traditionally assumed, to be the subject) without a clearly defined agent.

45. Although Genesis 24:64 also deconstructs itself with the use of the verb *npl*, usually translated "fall." Does Rebekah "fall" in the sense of "quickly dismount" or does she quite literally and unintentionally "fall" from her camel upon seeing Isaac?

46. Compare Judah Slotki, "Judges: Introduction and Commentary," in *Joshua and Judges*, ed. A. Cohen (London: Soncino, 1959), 160.

47. See n. 26.

48. See Marc Brettler, "The Book of Judges: Literature as Politics," *Journal of Biblical Literature* 108 (1989): 395–418, who argues that this section of the text was edited to reflect a pro-Judean bias.

49. Historians have long recognized the discrepancy. See, for example, the comments of Gray, *Joshua, Judges, Ruth,* 234, 237, and A. Graeme Auld, *Joshua, Judges, and Ruth* (Philadelphia: Westminster, 1984), 92.

50. My thanks to Jione Havea for reminding me of this intertextual connection. This connection is more often explored in discussions of the exile: the expulsion of the couple from Eden is a precursor to Israel's eventual expulsion from the land of promise.

51. See Robert C. Culley and Robert B. Robinson, eds., *Textual Determinacy, Part One, Semeia* 62 (1993), particularly Daniel Patte, "Textual Constraints, Ordinary Readings, and Critical Exegesis: An Androcritical Perspective," 59–79.

7. IDEOLOGICAL CRITICISM

1. Norman K. Gottwald, *The Hebrew Bible: A Socio-Literary Introduction* (Philadelphia: Fortress Press, 1981; 2003 with CD-ROM). Gottwald maintains that his socio-literary approach is "in deliberate continuity with older historical-critical scholarship" (xxvii), but it integrates the newer literary and social-scientific approaches that have taken biblical studies in new directions.

2. This unit has now reached "Section" status at annual meetings of the Society of Biblical Literature with six-year renewable terms.

3. The term "material" refers to the production and distribution of economic goods and the social relationships of owners and workers.

4. Ideology is a code people produce that helps them make sense of a confusing world; it is like a template keyed to a specific computer program, put over the computer keys to give the keyboard a specific pattern of meaning. The literary text "encodes" a particular ideological "worldview." It then transfers this constructed system of values and perceptions into its rhetoric. In many ways this code feature is similar to allegory.

5. For an introduction, see James H. Kavanagh, "Ideology," in *Critical Terms for Literary Study,* 2d ed., ed. Frank Lentricchia and Thomas McLaughlin (Chicago: University of Chicago Press, 1995), 306–20.

6. Louis Althusser, "Ideology and Ideological State Apparatuses (Notes towards an Investigation)," in *Lenin and Philosophy and Other Essays*, trans. Ben Brewster (New York and London: Monthly Review, 1971), 162.

7. In Euro-American society, for example, those who wield the most social, economic, and political power are usually white males, and those who possess the least are women of color.

8. Fredric Jameson, *Political Unconscious: Narrative as a Socially Symbolic Act* (Ithaca, N.Y.: Cornell University Press, 1981), 53–54.

9. On this analogy between dramatic and textual production, see Terry Eagleton, *Criticism and Ideology: A Study in Marxist Literary Theory,* new ed. (London: Verso, 2006), 64–69.

10. In addition to investigating the text's production and reproduction of ideology, ideological criticism can also study how the text is received or read in the *consumption* of that ideology. However, because of constraints on length, this essay focuses primarily on the twin tasks of extrinsic and intrinsic analysis of a text. For the cultural reception of the text, see chapter 10 of this volume on cultural criticism.

11. For discussion, see Norman K. Gottwald, "Sociology (Ancient Israel)," *The Anchor Bible Dictionary,* 6:82–87. What Gottwald describes as a "communitarian" mode of production I refer to as a "familial" mode, along with David Jobling in "Feminism and 'Mode of Production,'" in *The Bible and the Politics of Exegesis,* ed. David Jobling, Peggy L. Day, and Gerald T. Sheppard (Cleveland: Pilgrim, 1991), 241–43.

12. These questions roughly follow Eagleton's "categories for a materialist criticism" (*Criticism and Ideology,* 44–63): (1) general mode of production; (2) literary mode of production; (3) general ideology; (4) authorial ideology; (5) aesthetic ideology; and (6) text.

13. Pierre Macherey, *A Theory of Literary Production: With a New Introduction by Terry Eagleton and a New Afterword by the Author,* trans. by Geoffrey Wall (London: Routledge and Kegan Paul, 1978; repr. London and New York: Routledge Classics, 2006), 95; italics his.

14. Susan Ackerman, in "What if Judges Had Been Written by a Philistine?" *Biblical Interpretation* 8 (2000): 33–41, speculates on a conspicuous absence in Judges, namely, the perspective of the Philistines, Israel's hated enemies that compelled the formation of the monarchy.

15. For a review, see Barry G. Webb, *The Book of the Judges: An Integrated Reading* (JSOTSup 46; Sheffield: JSOT, 1987), 19–40.

16. Carol Meyers, *Discovering Eve: Ancient Israelite Women in Context* (New York: Oxford University Press, 1988), 122–88.

17. In a *native* tributary mode of production, the king and his ruling elite are indigenous to the land. In a *foreign* tributary mode of production, the land is administered by foreign colonizers or conquerors.

18. Norman K. Gottwald, "Social Class as an Analytic and Hermeneutical Category in Biblical Studies," *Journal of Biblical Literature* 112 (1993): 3–9.

19. For a discussion of agrarian societies and their class hierarchies, see Gerhard Lenski, *Power and Privilege: A Theory of Social Stratification.* (New York: McGraw-Hill, 1966; Repr. Chapel Hill: University of North Carolina Press, 1984), 189–296.

20. Compare Joshua 13–21.

21. For example, Naomi Steinberg, "The Deuteronomic Law Code and the Politics of State Centralization," in *The Bible and the Politics of Exegesis,* ed.

David Jobling, Peggy L. Day, and Gerald T. Sheppard (Cleveland: Pilgrim, 1991), 161–70.

22. Meyers, *Discovering Eve,* 189–96. The effects of state formation on the position of women has been analyzed extensively by feminist anthropologists and historians. See, for example, Sherry B. Ortner, "The Virgin and the State," *Feminist Studies* 4 (1978): 10–33; Ruby Rohrlich, "State Formation in Sumer and the Subjugation of Women," *Feminist Studies* 6 (1980): 76–102; Barbara S. Lesko, "Women of Ancient Egypt and Western Asia," in *Becoming Visible: Women in European History,* 3d ed., ed. Renate Bridenthal, Susan Mosher Stuard, and Merry E. Wiesner (Boston: Houghton Mifflin, 1998), 14–45.

23. Richard D. Nelson, *The Double Redaction of the Deuteronomistic History* (Sheffield: JSOT, 1981), 121–23.

24. For the argument that Josiah's reform has more socioeconomic than religious intent, see W. Eugene Claburn, "The Fiscal Basis of Josiah's Reforms," *Journal of Biblical Literature* 92 (1973): 11–22 and, more recently, Shigeyuki Nakanose, *Josiah's Passover: Sociology and the Liberating Bible* (Maryknoll, N.Y. Orbis, 1993).

25. Nakanose, *Josiah's Passover,* 50.

26. Claburn, "Fiscal Basis of Josiah's Reforms," 17–21; Nakanose, *Josiah's Passover,* 59–60, 62–65.

27. Nakanose, *Josiah's Passover,* 104–12.

28. Mieke Bal, *Death and Dissymmetry: The Politics of Coherence in the Book of Judges* (Chicago: University of Chicago Press, 1988), 9–16.

29. A literal translation of the Hebrew.

30. Literary studies have highlighted the breakdown of the Deuteronomist's theological framework as well as the redactional unity between Judges 17–21 and the beginning of the book: D. W. Gooding, "The Composition of the Book of Judges," in *Eretz-Israel, Archeological Historical and Geographical Studies, Vol. 16, Harry M. Orlinsky Volume* (Jerusalem: Israel Exploration Society, 1982), 70–79; David M. Gunn, "Joshua and Judges," in *The Literary Guide to the Bible* (Cambridge: Harvard University Press, 1987), 102–21; Alexander Globe, "'Enemies Round About': Disintegrative Structure in the Book of Judges," in *Mappings of the Biblical Terrain,* ed. V. Tollers and J. Maier (Lewisburg, Pa.: Bucknell University Press, 1990), 233–51; and J. Cheryl Exum, "The Centre Cannot Hold: Thematic and Textual Instabilities in Judges," *Catholic Biblical Quarterly* 52 (1990): 410–31.

31. An ephod is a type of priestly garment worn over the breast. A teraphim is a cultic image of a household god.

32. Judges 17:3, 4; 18:14, 17-18, 20, 30-31.

33. According to Judges 13–16, the tribe of Dan was settled around the southern coast near Philistine territory. Although scholars presume that the Danites had to abandon their homeland because of Philistine incursions, the text is ambiguous on the matter, in keeping with the lack of clarity throughout these chapters.

34. Judges 18:25: literally, "men of bitter spirit"; translated "hot-tempered fellows" in the NRSV.

35. Yairah Amit, "Hidden Polemic in the Conquest of Dan: Judges 17–18," *Vetus Testamentum* 40 (1990): 4–20.

36. The violent story of the rape and dismemberment of the Levite's wife in Judges 19 has been a topic for a number of feminist biblical scholars. See chapter 4 on feminist criticism by Exum in this volume; also, J. Cheryl Exum, "Raped by the Pen," in *Fragmented Women: Feminist (Sub)versions of Biblical Narratives* (JSOTSup 163; Sheffield: JSOT, 1993), esp. 176–94; Susan Ackerman, *Warrior, Dancer, Seductress, Queen: Women in Judges and Biblical Israel* (New York: Doubleday, 1998), 235–40; and the essays by Ilse Müllner and Alice Bach in Athalya Brenner, ed., *Judges: A Feminist Companion to the Bible (Second Series)* (Sheffield: Sheffield Academic Press, 1999).

37. See the discussion of secondary wives in chapter 3 by Naomi Steinberg in this volume.

38. See, for example, the treatment of Hagar in Genesis 16–21.

39. Danna Nolan Fewell and David M. Gunn raise two other narrative possibilities regarding the Levite's inaction: his wounded pride holds him back, or, following Koala Jones-Warsaw, the concubine's secondary status does not rate an immediate response (*Gender, Power, and Promise: The Subject of the Bible's First Story* [Nashville: Abingdon, 1993], 133).

40. The Hebrew word used is *zanah*, usually mistranslated into English as "to play the harlot or whore, to prostitute oneself." See the discussion in Phyllis Bird, "'To Play the Harlot': An Inquiry into an Old Testament Metaphor," in *Gender and Difference in Ancient Israel*, ed. Peggy L. Day (Minneapolis: Fortress Press, 1989), 75–94.

41. Lila Abu-Lughod, "The Romance of Resistance: Tracing Transformations of Power through Bedouin Women," in *Beyond the Second Sex: New Directions in the Anthropology of Gender*, ed. Peggy Reeves Sanday and Ruth Gallagher Goodenough (Philadelphia: University of Pennsylvania Press, 1990), 311–37.

42. Compare Exum's reading in this volume on this same point. The Septuagintal rendering of the Hebrew *zanah* in this text as "to become angry" particularly corroborates the thesis that the woman's departure was an exercise of power. On women's quarrels, see Naomi Steinberg, *Kinship and Marriage in Genesis: A Household Economics Perspective* (Minneapolis: Fortress , 1993), 103–6.

43. Thus Ken Stone, "Gender and Homosexuality in Judges 19: Subject-Honor, Object-Shame?" *JSOT* 67 (1995): 87–107. See also chapter 9 on gender criticism in this volume.

44. Phyllis Trible, "An Unnamed Woman: The Extravagance of Violence," in *Texts of Terror: Literary Feminist Readings of Biblical Narratives* (Philadelphia: Fortress Press, 1984), 68.

45. Julian Pitt-Rivers, "The Law of Hospitality," in *The Fate of Shechem, or the Politics of Sex: Essays in the Anthropology of the Mediterranean* (Cambridge: Cambridge University Press, 1977), 101–2; Michael Herzfeld, "'As in Your Own House': Hospitality, Ethnography, and the Stereotype of Mediterranean Society," in *Honor and Shame and the Unity of the Mediterranean*, ed. David D. Gilmore (Washington, D.C.: American Anthropological Association, 1987), 77.

46. Michael Carden questions Stone's description (see n. 43) of the residents' intentions as homosexual rape, preferring to call it male–male rape ("Homopho-

bia and Rape in Sodom and Gibeah: A Response to Ken Stone," *JSOT* 82 [1999]: 83–96).

47. The parallel story in Genesis 19:4-5 describes "men of the city" and does not add the qualifier, "perverse lot," lit., "sons of Belial" (Judg 19:22).

48. Compare Genesis 19:7, where the words "Ravish them" do not appear.

49. Compare Genesis 22:10, where Abraham takes "the" knife (*hamma'akelet*), that is, a knife set aside for cultic purposes, in order to slay his son Isaac for a sacrificial offering.

50. Fewell and Gunn, *Gender, Power, and Promise*, 134.

51. Trible, "An Unnamed Woman," 79.

52. Susan Niditch, "The 'Sodomite' Theme in Judges 19–20: Family, Community, and Social Disintegration," *Catholic Biblical Quarterly* 44 (1982): 371–73; Alice Keefe, "Rapes of Women/Wars of Men," *Semeia* 61 (1993): 85–86.

8. POSTCOLONIAL CRITICISM

1. The terms "West" and "Rest" like other terms—"First World" and "Third World" or "Two-Thirds World," "Developed" and "Underdeveloped," "Northern Hemisphere" and "Southern Hemisphere"—are artificial, ideological, and certainly inadequate to describe and divide vast numbers of diverse and heterogeneous people living in the world into two categories. However, it is necessary to use such a dichotomy to acknowledge the existence of unequal relations between two groups of people. Such use of an artificial division is analogous to how race continues to matter and is used in the United States. Some wish to refrain from using the term "race" because it is an ideological construct; therefore, so the argument goes, fighting against racism perpetuates the illusion rather than eliminating it. But the problem is that racism has had a long and devastating effect in the United States. By ignoring its historical and structural legacies that are interwoven into the very fabric of American society, we are in danger of not adequately addressing these effects and legacies and allowing inequitable socioeconomic conditions between different "races" to remain intact.

2. Colonialism was the political policy implemented by the West, primarily by Europe, for nearly five hundred years to dominate non-Western people and their territory in order to extract their resources for the benefit of the West. In recent years, various forms of cultural exploitation that accompanied the expansion of Europe are being studied, in addition to political and economic effects.

3. It does not have to be this way. Postcolonial theorists must be careful not to limit postcolonialism to the theoretical arena of Western academia. It began from "below," from the experience of the people struggling to acquire their power, dignity, and voice. Postcolonial criticism needs to begin with the context rather than with the text or theory.

4. Franz Fanon's *The Wretched of the Earth* (New York: Grove, 1966) and Albert Memmi's *The Colonizer and the Colonized* (Boston: Beacon, 1965) were influential texts that eloquently articulated anticolonial sentiments.

5. Edward Said, *Orientalism* (New York: Random House, 1978).

6. The role of biblical scholars is elaborated especially on pages 130–49 in *Orientalism*. In fact, Said states that "by and large, until the mid-eighteenth century Orientalists were Biblical scholars, students of the Semitic languages, Islamic specialists, or, because the Jesuits had opened up the new study of China, Sinologists" (*Orientalism*, 51).

7. Among their works, Homi K. Bhabha's *The Location of Culture* (London: Routledge, 1994) and Gayatri Chakravorty Spivak's article "Can the Subaltern Speak?" in *Colonial Discourse and Post-colonial Theory*, ed. Patrick Williams and Laura Chrisman (New York: Columbia University Press, 1994), 66–111, are considered most influential.

8. "Hybridity" is a term that describes the creation of a new or "third" culture/identity when two or more cultures come into contact with one another. It assumes that culture is not static—there is no pure, permanent, or national culture—but is always in the process of change through interaction between different peoples. Bhabha uses the term to stress the interdependence and mutual construction of identity/culture in colonizer/colonized relations.

9. The works of R. S. Sugirtharajah, Kwok Pui-lan, and Fernando Segovia in the early 1990s were instrumental in introducing and disseminating postcolonial criticism to biblical studies: Sugirtharajah edited *Voices from the Margin: Interpreting the Bible in the Third World*, 3d ed. (Maryknoll, N.Y.: Orbis, 2006; 1st ed. 1991; 2d ed. 1995); Fernando Segovia coedited with Mary Ann Tolbert *Reading from This Place*, Vol. 1 (Minneapolis: Fortress Press, 1995); and Kwok Pui-lan published *Discovering the Bible in the Non-Biblical World* (Maryknoll, N.Y.: Orbis, 1995). In addition to these books, other key works in introducing postcolonialism to biblical studies include Laura E. Donaldson, ed., *Postcolonialism and Scripture Reading* (*Semeia* 75; Atlanta: Society of Biblical Literature, 1996), and Keith Whitelam, *The Invention of Ancient Israel: The Silencing of Palestinian History* (London: Routledge, 1996).

10. I want to make clear that reading from the West's perspective is not limited to Westerners only. Non-Western scholars read through the eyes of the West, many with greater enthusiasm and commitment than Western scholars.

11. Kwok, in *Discovering the Bible in the Non-Biblical World*, goes further and suggests that postcolonial interpreters should not use historical criticism as the primary method in interpreting the Bible.

12. Kwok, Pui-lan, *Postcolonial Imagination & Feminist Theology* (Louisville: Westminster John Knox, 2005), 63.

13. This is not to deny that there are those who think that the Rest greatly benefited at the expense of the West when the West brought its civilization to non-Western people. In fact, one can argue that non-Western people should be thankful for what they have received from the West. But is there a need to make a case that the suffering of the colonized was far greater than whatever benefit they might have received from the colonizer? Is there a need to make a case that the benefit to the West was greater than the sacrifice the West made in its effort to "civilize" the Rest?

14. Fernando Segovia talks about three levels of "texts" a reader must engage in: (1) the level of the biblical texts, which were written in the context of varying imperial/colonial formations; (2) the level of "modern texts," namely, the analysis of readings and interpretations of the Bible in modern, Western biblical scholarship, whose establishment and development parallel Western imperialism; and (3) the level of the "flesh-and-blood" readers of the Bible from around the world. See "Interpreting beyond Borders: Postcolonial Studies and Diasporic Studies in Biblical Criticism," in Fernando Segovia, ed., *Interpreting beyond Borders,* 11–34, (Sheffield: Sheffield Academic Press, 2000).

15. Martin Noth, *The Deuteronomistic History* (Sheffield: JSOT, 1981). See the introduction by Gale Yee in this volume.

16. Whitelam argues in *The Invention of Ancient Israel* that biblical scholars saw Israel as a nation-state representing "the ultimate in political evolution, the European nation state, and the pinnacle of civilization which surpasses and replaces that which is primitive and incapable of transformation" (56).

17. David M. Gunn, *Judges* (Blackwell Bible Commentaries; Oxford: Blackwell, 2005), 46.

18. Robert Boling, *Judges: A New Translation with Introduction and Commentary* (Anchor Bible 6A; Garden City, N.Y.: Doubleday, 1975), 15.

19. Mieke Bal, *Death and Dissymmetry: The Politics of Coherence in the Book of Judges* (Chicago: University of Chicago Press, 1988), 5.

20. Regina M. Schwartz, *The Curse of Cain: The Violent Legacy of Monotheism* (Chicago: University of Chicago Press, 1997), 120–42.

21. Ibid., 123.

22. J. Clinton McCann, *Judges* (Interpretation Bible Commentary; Louisville: John Knox, 2002), 17.

23. Ibid., 18.

24. Ibid., 19.

25. Schwartz, *The Curse of Cain,* 5.

26. Kwok, *Postcolonial Imagination & Feminist Theology,* 82.

27. Sam Keen, *Faces of the Enemy: Reflections of the Hostile Imagination* (San Francisco: Harper & Row, 1986).

28. The book of Judges can be divided into two parts according to two formulaic sayings: Part I, chapters 2–16, has the saying "evil in the sight of the Lord" (2:11, 3:7, 3:12, 4:1, 6:1, 10:6, 13:1), and the saying "in those days there was no king in Israel" (17:6, 18:1, 19:1, 21:25) connects Part II, chapters 17–21. In the first part, the narrative tries to forge a coherent identity of Israel by constructing the Other negatively, "Who we are not." In Part II, the narrative struggles to formulate the identity of Israel by looking internally, "Who belongs to Israel?"

29. The same word is used to refer to the Israelites in Judges 2:20 but is translated as "people" in the NRSV.

30. Schwartz, in *The Curse of Cain,* comments: "According to kinship thinking, Israel's identity is shored up by nature itself, by blood and by seed, by genealogy, by brother and sister, father and mother, cousins and cross-cousins" (78).

However, "After long and tortuous debates about the significance and forms of kinship systems, anthropologists are now telling us that there is virtually no such thing as kinship. There are *ideologies* of blood relations, *constructs* of brothers and sisters, but comparative cultural studies have shown us how diversely such notions are understood. There are no real blood relations" (ibid.).

31. There is, however, one instance when the narrator allows the Other to speak from its own perspective: "Our God has given Samson our enemy (*ʾoyev*) into our hand" (16:23) and "Our god has given us our enemy (*ʾoyev*) into our hand, the ravager of our country, who has killed many of us" (16:24).

32. Musa W. Dube, *Postcolonial Feminist Interpretation of the Bible* (St. Louis: Chalice, 2000), 60.

33. Ibid., 66.

34. Ibid.

35. As one commentator remarks on Jephthah's speech: "Even though he is logical, deeply emotional and articulate, in the end Jephthah demonstrates his great factual ignorance. . . . Jephthah has used the common logic of the day to be convincing in his disputation. However, the Ammonite king is likely surprised to be told that his god is Chemosh (who was the god of the Moabites). . . . This is an error, and it hardly impresses the Ammonite king!" (K. Lawson Younger, *Judges and Ruth* [Grand Rapids: Zondervan, 2002], 256–57).

36. The well-known account of how David conquered Jerusalem, inhabited by the Jebusites, and turned it into his city (2 Sam 5:6-10), further complicates the matter.

37. In the anticonquest ideology in colonial discourse, Dube states that the identity of the colonizer is critical because "those who have the right to travel to, enter, possess, and control distant and inhabited lands must be shown to be exceptionally different and well-deserving above their victims" (*Postcolonial Feminist Interpretation*, 66)

9. GENDER CRITICISM

1. Eve Kosofsky Sedgwick, "Gender Criticism," in *Redrawing the Boundaries: The Transformation of English and American Literary Studies*, ed. Stephen Greenblatt and Giles Gunn (New York: Modern Language Association of America, 1992), 271.

2. Ibid., 273, emphasis in original.

3. See Judith Halberstam, *Female Masculinity* (Durham, N.C., and London: Duke University Press, 1998); Suzanne J. Kessler, *Lessons from the Intersexed* (New Brunswick, N.J.: Rutgers University Press, 1998); Anne Fausto-Sterling, *Sexing the Body: Gender Politics and the Construction of Sexuality* (New York: Basic, 2000).

4. Numerous other languages do not distinguish between sex and gender in the same way that English does. On the complexities that this linguistic fact pro-

duces for the study of gender, see Donna Haraway, "'Gender' for a Marxist Dictionary: The Sexual Politics of a Word," in *Simians, Cyborgs, and Women: The Reinvention of Nature* (New York and London: Routledge, 1991), 127–48.

5. See Robert J. Stoller, *Sex and Gender: On the Development of Masculinity and Femininity* (New York: Science House, 1968).

6. See, for example, J. Cheryl Exum's chapter in this volume.

7. Joan Wallach Scott, "Gender: A Useful Category of Historical Analysis," in *Gender and the Politics of History* (New York: Columbia University Press, 1988), 32.

8. Teresa de Lauretis, *Technologies of Gender: Essays on Theory, Film, and Fiction* (Bloomington and Indianapolis: Indiana University Press, 1987), 5.

9. Gayle Rubin, "The Traffic in Women: Notes on the 'Political Economy' of Sex," in *Toward an Anthropology of Women*, ed. Rayna Reiter (New York: Monthly Review, 1975), 159.

10. Ibid., 165.

11. See Claude Lévi-Strauss, *The Elementary Structures of Kinship*, trans. James Bell, John Richard von Sturmer, and Rodney Needham (Boston: Beacon, 1969).

12. Rubin, "Traffic in Women," 174.

13. Except where otherwise noted, translations are taken from the NRSV.

14. See Athalya Brenner, *The Intercourse of Knowledge: On Gendering Desire and 'Sexuality' in the Hebrew Bible* (Leiden: Brill, 1997), 90–131.

15. Regina Schwartz, "Adultery in the House of David: The Metanarrative of Biblical Scholarship and the Narratives of the Bible," *Semeia* 54 (1991): 47. See also idem, *The Curse of Cain: The Violent Legacy of Monotheism* (London and Chicago: University of Chicago Press, 1997), 137.

16. Pierre Bourdieu, *Masculine Domination*, trans. Richard Nice (Stanford, Calif.: Stanford University Press, 2001), 7ff.

17. Ibid., 42–49. Cf. Rubin, "Traffic in Women," 174–77.

18. See Sedgwick's deployment of this point for purposes of literary analysis in *Between Men: English Literature and Male Homosocial Desire* (New York: Columbia University Press, 1985).

19. For further discussion along these lines, see Ken Stone, *Sex, Honor and Power in the Deuteronomistic History* (Sheffield: Sheffield Academic Press, 1996); idem, *Practicing Safer Texts: Food, Sex and Bible in Queer Perspective* (London: T & T Clark, 2005), esp. 68–89.

20. Naomi Schor, "Feminist and Gender Studies," in *Introduction to Scholarship in Modern Languages and Literatures*, 2d ed., ed. Joseph Gibaldi (New York: Modern Language Association of America, 1992), 271. For similar observations in biblical scholarship, see Alice Bach, "Reading Allowed: Feminist Biblical Criticism Approaching the Millennium," *Currents in Research: Biblical Studies* 1 (1993): 192–93; Yvonne Sherwood, *The Prostitute and the Prophet: Hosea's Marriage in Literary-Theoretical Perspective* (Sheffield: Sheffield Academic Press, 1996), 302.

21. See, however, Howard Eilberg-Schwartz, *God's Phallus: And Other Problems for Men and Monotheism* (Boston: Beacon, 1994); David J. A. Clines, *Interested Parties: The Ideology of Writers and Readers of the Hebrew Bible* (Sheffield:

Sheffield Academic Press, 1995), 212–43; Jan Tarlin, "Utopia and Pornography in Ezekiel: Violence, Hope, and the Shattered Male Subject," in *Reading Bibles, Writing Bodies: Identity and the Book*, ed. Timothy K. Beal and David M. Gunn (New York: Routledge, 1997); Stone, *Practicing Safer Texts*, 111–28.

22. Gideon's son is called a *naᶜar*, which the NRSV translates here as "boy" but which might be understood better in this instance as "youth" or "young man."

23. Tammi J. Schneider, *Judges* (Collegeville, Minn.: Liturgical Press, 2000), 126.

24. David D. Gilmore, *Manhood in the Making: Cultural Concepts of Masculinity* (New Haven: Yale University Press, 1990).

25. Ibid., 30–55. Cf. David D. Gilmore, ed., *Honor and Shame and the Unity of the Mediterranean* (Washington, D.C.: American Anthropological Association, 1987); Carol Delaney, *The Seed and the Soil: Gender and Cosmology in Turkish Village Society* (Berkeley: University of California Press, 1991); J. G. Peristiany and Julian Pitt-Rivers, eds., *Honor and Grace in Anthropology* (Cambridge and New York: Cambridge University Press, 1992).

26. Michael Herzfeld, *The Poetics of Manhood: Contest and Identity in a Cretan Mountain Village* (Princeton: Princeton University Press, 1985), 16, emphasis in original.

27. See Stone, *Sex, Honor and Power*; Gale A. Yee, "Hosea," in *Women's Bible Commentary: Expanded Edition with Apocrypha*, ed. Carol A. Newsom and Sharon H. Ringe (Louisville: Westminster John Knox, 1998); idem, *Poor Banished Children of Eve: Woman as Evil in the Hebrew Bible* (Minneapolis: Fortress Press, 2003); Mieke Bal, *Murder and Difference: Gender, Genre, and Scholarship on Sisera's Death*, trans. Matthew Gumpert (Bloomington: Indiana University Press, 1988), 115–24. The possibility that the anthropology of the Mediterranean world had relevance for the interpretation of ancient texts, including both Homer and the Hebrew Bible, was already suggested by one of the anthropologists most responsible for developing that anthropological subfield: Julian Pitt-Rivers, *The Fate of Shechem or the Politics of Sex: Essays in the Anthropology of the Mediterranean* (Cambridge and New York: Cambridge University Press, 1977).

28. On this point, see Cynthia R. Chapman, *The Gendered Language of Warfare in the Israelite-Assyrian Encounter* (Winona Lake, Ind.: Eisenbrauns, 2004).

29. Harry A. Hoffner, Jr., "Symbols for Masculinity and Femininity: Their Use in Ancient Near Eastern Sympathetic Magic Rituals," *JBL* 85 (1966): 328–29.

30. Ibid., p. 327. Cf. Chapman, *Gendered Language of Warfare*.

31. See Eve Kosofsky Sedgwick, *Epistemology of the Closet* (Berkeley: University of California Press, 1990); idem, *Tendencies* (Durham, N.C.: Duke University Press, 1993); Gayle Rubin, "Thinking Sex: Notes for a Radical Theory of the Politics of Sexuality," in *Pleasure and Danger: Exploring Female Sexuality*, ed. Carole S. Vance (London: Routledge and Kegan Paul, 1984); Gayle Rubin with Judith Butler, "Sexual Traffic: An Interview," in *More Gender Trouble: Feminism Meets Queer Theory, Differences* 6:2–3 (summer–fall 1994): 62–99.

32. See Ken Stone, "Queer Commentary and Biblical Interpretation: An Introduction," in *Queer Commentary and the Hebrew Bible*, ed. Ken Stone (Sheffield

and Cleveland: Sheffield Academic Press/Pilgrim, 2001), 11–34; Laurel C. Schneider, "Queer Theory," in *Handbook of Postmodern Biblical Interpretation*, ed. A. K. M. Adam (St. Louis: Chalice, 2000), 206–12.

33. See, for example, Jonathan Ned Katz, *The Invention of Heterosexuality* (New York: Dutton, 1995).

34. See Judith Butler, "Against Proper Objects," in *More Gender Trouble: Feminism Meets Queer Theory, Differences* 6:2–3 (summer–fall 1994): 1–26.

35. Monique Wittig, *The Straight Mind: And Other Essays* (Boston: Beacon, 1992), 14.

36. Ibid., 5.

37. Judith Butler, *Gender Trouble: Feminism and the Subversion of Identity*, 2d ed. (New York and London: Routledge, 1999), 11; emphasis in original. See also Butler's "Variations on Sex and Gender: Beauvoir, Wittig, Foucault," in *Feminism as Critique: On the Politics of Gender*, ed. Seyla Benhabib and Drucilla Cornell (Minneapolis: University of Minnesota Press, 1987), 128–42.

38. Butler, *Gender Trouble*, 179, emphasis in original.

39. See especially Judith Butler, *Bodies That Matter: On the Discursive Limits of "Sex"* (New York and London: Routledge, 1993). Cf. idem, *Excitable Speech: A Politics of the Performative* (New York and London: Routledge, 1997), and *Undoing Gender* (New York and London: Routledge, 2004).

40. See J. L. Austin, *How to Do Things with Words*, 2d ed., ed. J. O. Urmson and Marina Sbisà (Cambridge: Harvard University Press, 1975).

41. Butler here is influenced by the critical reading of speech-act theory in Jacques Derrida, *Limited Inc.*, ed. Gerald Graff (Evanston: Northwestern University Press, 1988). On the passage of the "performative" from Austin's speech-act theory, via Derrida, to Butler and queer theory, see Jonathan Culler, "Philosophy and Literature: The Fortunes of the Performative," *Poetics Today* 21:3 (fall 2000): 503–19.

42. Austin, *How to Do Things with Words*, 16ff.

43. Butler, *Bodies That Matter*, 231.

44. See Stone, "The Garden of Eden and the Heterosexual Contract," in *Bodily Citations: Religion and Judith Butler*, ed. Ellen T. Armour and Susan M. St. Ville (New York: Columbia University Press, 2006), 48–70; idem, *Practicing Safer Texts*, 111–28.

45. J. Alberto Soggin, *Judges: A Commentary*, trans. John Bowden (Philadelphia: Westminster, 1981), 159.

46. See, for example, Schneider, *Judges*, 128–30, who finally (and in my view wisely) decides simply to leave the term in transliteration.

47. Discussions of gender, kinship, and the Bible too often ignore the fact that no separate word for "wife" exists in biblical Hebrew. Rather, the word for "woman" is translated as "wife" when, in the opinion of translators, the context justifies such a translation. Jon Berquist is one of the few biblical scholars who—rightly, in my view—takes this lack of correspondence between biblical and contemporary vocabularies seriously as a possible indication that the "social institution" of marriage "is not the same in ancient Israel as it is in the modern

Western world." See Jon L. Berquist, *Controlling Corporality: The Body and the Household in Ancient Israel* (New Brunswick, N.J.: Rutgers University Press, 2002), 60–61. Such recognition is clearly important for queer readings of the Bible, as I point out in *Practicing Safer Texts*, 82ff.

48. For further discussion of the kinship dimensions of the story of Abimelech, see Steinberg's chapter in this volume.

49. See discussions of Abimelech's name in Robert G. Boling, *Judges* (New York: Doubleday, 1975), 162–63; Soggin, *Judges*, 166–67.

50. The irony here is more thematic than linguistic, as the verb used in these instances is *mashal* rather than *malak* (the latter of which is directly related to Abimelech's name).

51. Susan Ackerman, *When Heroes Love: The Ambiguity of Eros in the Stories of Gilgamesh and David* (New York: Columbia University Press, 2005), 165–231, esp. 218–31. On the use of homoerotic language in the story of Jonathan, see now also Saul M. Olyan, "'Surpassing the Love of Women': Another Look at 2 Samuel 1:26 and the Relationship of David and Jonathan," in *Authorizing Marriage? Canon, Tradition, and Critique in the Blessing of Same-Sex Unions*, ed. Mark D. Jordan (Princeton: Princeton University Press, 2006), 7–16.

52. T. M. Lemos, "Shame and Mutilation of Enemies in the Hebrew Bible," *JBL* 125 (summer 2006): 234.

53. Mieke Bal, *Death and Dissymmetry: The Politics of Coherence in the Book of Judges* (Chicago: University of Chicago Press, 1988), 217–18.

54. Bourdieu, *Masculine Domination*, 7–22.

55. Gale A. Yee, "By the Hand of a Woman: The Metaphor of the Woman Warrior in Judges 4," in *Women, War, and Metaphor: Language and Society in the Study of the Hebrew Bible*, ed. Claudia V. Camp and Carole R. Fontaine, *Semeia* 61 (1993), 116. See also Susan Niditch, "Eroticism and Death in the Tale of Jael," in *Gender and Difference in Ancient Israel*, ed. Peggy L. Day (Minneapolis: Fortress Press, 1989); Danna Nolan Fewell and David M. Gunn, "Controlling Perspectives: Women, Men, and the Authority of Violence in Judges 4 and 5," *JAAR* 58/3 (1990): 393–94; and Exum's chapter in this volume.

56. Boling, *Judges*, 182. For an interpretation of the gendered significance of the millstone that is different from my own, see Bal, *Death and Dissymmetry*, 220–21.

57. Bourdieu, *Masculine Domination*, 18.

58. See, for example, Marc Zvi Brettler, *The Book of Judges* (New York and London: Routledge, 2002), esp. 109–16; idem, "The Book of Judges: Literature as Politics," *JBL* 108:3 (1989). 395–418; Schneider, *Judges*.

59. David Jobling, *1 Samuel* (Collegeville, Minn.: Liturgical Press, 1998), 214–17, 230–31, with the word *womanish* applied to Philistines on p. 216.

60. In addition to the works by Brettler and Schneider, see on this point Yairah Amit, *Hidden Polemics in Biblical Narrative*, trans. Jonathan Chapman (Leiden: Brill, 2000), 178–84.

61. Ken Stone, "Gender and Homosexuality in Judges 19: Subject-Honor, Object-Shame?" *JSOT* 67 (1995): 87–107; idem, *Sex, Honor and Power*, 69–84.

62. Chapman, *Gendered Language of Warfare*, 167.
63. Cf. Amit, *Hidden Polemics*.
64. Cf. Stone, *Sex, Honor and Power*.

10. CULTURAL CRITICISM

1. From David Hall's introduction to Steven L. Kaplan, ed., *Understanding Popular Culture: Europe from the Middle Ages to the Nineteenth Century* (Berlin, New York, Amsterdam: Mouton Publishers, 1984), 16.
2. Examples are listed under Further Reading.
3. For recent "reception history" of Judges and other biblical texts, see Further Reading.
4. See further Mary Chilton Callaway, "What's the Use of Reception History" (2004), at www.bbibcomm.net [January 2007].
5. Raphael's frescoes for the Vatican loggia are among the most frequently copied. See Bernice F. Davidson, *Raphael's Bible: A Study of the Vatican Logge* (University Park: Pennsylvania State University Press, 1985).
6. E. J. Whately, "Use and Abuse of Pictures on Sacred Subjects," in *The Sunday at Home: A Family Magazine for Sabbath Reading* (London: Religious Tract Society, 1878), 346–50.
7. See W. J. T. Mitchell, *What Do Pictures Want? The Lives and Loves of Images* (Chicago & London: Chicago University Press, 2005), 6–11.
8. See James Heffernan, *Cultivating Picturacy: Visual Art and Verbal Interventions* (Waco, Tex.: Baylor University Press, 2006), 1–38.
9. Perry Nodelman, *Words about Pictures: The Narrative Art of Children's Picture Books* (Athens, Ga., and London: University of Georgia Press, 1988).
10. Following French literary theorist Roland Barthes, *The Responsibility of Forms* (New York: Hill and Wang, 1985), 4.
11. Nodelman, *Words about Pictures*, 101.
12. Ibid., 158–61.
13. Dr. S. Smith, *The Compleat History of the Old and New Testament, or, a Family Bible* (London, 1752).
14. Matthew Henry, *An Exposition of the Historical Books of the Old Testament* (London, 1708). He notes that some compare this sacrifice to that of Christ: "he was of unspotted Purity and Innocency, as she a chaste Virgin: He was *devoted* to death by his Father, and so made a *Curse* . . . for us; he submitted himself, as she did, to his Father's Will, *not as I will, but as thou wilt.*"
15. Mrs. [Sarah] Trimmer, *Sacred History Selected from the Scriptures, with Annotations and Reflections, Suited to the Comprehension of Young Minds* (London, 1783), 2:325–26; this work went through many editions over the following decades.
16. John Howard, *Scripture History for the Young* (New York: Virtue & Yorston, c. 1865), I:132.

17. Harriet Beecher Stowe, *Woman in Sacred History* (New York: J. B. Fort, 1873), 125–26.

18. Henry, *Exposition* (1708); Laurence Howel, *A Compleat History of the Holy Bible* (London: 1725), 323–24.

19. Trimmer, *Sacred History*, 326–27.

20. Howard, *Scripture History*, 132.

21. Dr. Samuel Newton, *The Complete Family Bible* (London: 1771).

22. Isaac Watts, *A Short View of the Whole Scripture History*, 9th ed. (London, 1769), 87.

23. Libretto at http://opera.stanford.edu/iu/libretti/jephtha.htm [January 2007].

24. See John L. Thompson, *Writing the Wrongs: Women of the Old Testament among Biblical Commentators from Philo through the Reformation* (Oxford: Oxford University Press, 2001), 111–54; Anna Linton, "Sacrificed or Spared? The Fate of Jephthah's Daughter in Early Modern Theological and Literary Texts," *German Life and Letters* 57:3 (2004): 237–55.

25. Cf. Voltaire, *A Treatise on Toleration . . .* , trans. Rev. David Williams (London: 1779), 75–76.

26. For a cross-cultural study, see Peggy L. Day, "From the Child is Born the Woman: The Story of Jephthah's Daughter," in *Gender and Difference in Ancient Israel*, ed. Peggy L. Day (Minneapolis: Fortress Press, 1989), 58–74.

27. In Charles Heavyseger, *Jephthah's Daughter* (Montreal: Dawson Bros., 1865), 33–34, 44–45, 53, 73–74.

28. See Cicero, *Ad Marcum Brutum Orator*, 74; Quintilian, *Institutio Oratoria*, ii, 13. The long-lived work of art criticism by fifteenth-century humanist Leon Battista Alberti, *De Pictura* (*On Painting*), which also drew attention to the device of the cloaked figure, was still being read in English in the mid-eighteenth century. Carle van Loo's painting of 1757, with Agamemnon's face turned away but visible, influenced a change away from the hidden face. See Heffernan, *Cultivating Picturacy*, 74–75; H. Fullenwider, "'The Sacrifice of Iphigenia' in French and German Art Criticism, 1755–1757," *Zeitschrift fur Kunstgeschichte* 52 (1989): 539–49.

29. Smith, *Compleat History*, 323–25.

30. Rev. E. Blomfield, *A New Family Bible* (Bungay: Brightly & Childs, 1813).

31. Dr. Benjamin Kennicott, *The Universal Family Bible* (Dublin, 1793). On account of its "fame" as a work of art (though "after some hesitation"), John Kitto includes a woodcut of Opie's picture in his popular *Pictorial Bible* (London: Charles Knight, 1836) while contending that the depiction exhibits "grievous historical improprieties." No such offering "could be made at God's altar, or by the high-priest, or by any regular and faithful member of the priesthood" (I:638–39).

32. Thomas Gaspey, *Family Devotions*, vol. 2 (London & Glasgow: J. & F. Tallis, c. 1850), opposite p. 527.

33. Nathaniel Parker Willis, "Jephthah's Daughter," in *Sacred Poems* (New York: Clark, Austin & Smith, 1860), 57–62; first published 1827; cf. Songs 4:1-7, 6:4-9.

34. Stowe, *Women in Sacred History*, 127–29.

35. Florence Bone, *The Girls of the Bible* (London: Pilgrim, c. 1915), 52–57.

36. Elizabeth Cady Standon, *The Woman's Bible*, Part II (New York: European Publishing Co., 1898), 24–26.

37. See Pieter Spierenburg, *The Spectacle of Suffering* (Cambridge: Cambridge University Press, 1984).

38. In Pieter Mortier's "Great Bible," *Historie des Ouden en Nieuwen Testaments* (Amsterdam, 1700).

39. In Newton's Bible (1771); similarly in Smith's Bible (1752).

40. A striking exception is in Barry Moser's *Pennroyal Caxton Bible* (London: Viking, 1999), 228.

INDEX OF TOPICS
AND NAMES